Teachers in Action

Tasks for in-service language teacher
education and development

Peter James

WITHDRAWN
FROM LIBRARY

KT-224-562

CAMBRIDGE
UNIVERSITY PRESS

PUBLISHED BY THE PRESS SYNDICATE OF THE UNIVERSITY OF CAMBRIDGE
The Pitt Building, Trumpington Street, Cambridge, United Kingdom

CAMBRIDGE UNIVERSITY PRESS
The Edinburgh Building, Cambridge CB2 2RU, UK
40 West 20th Street, New York, NY 10011–4211, USA
10 Stamford Road, Oakleigh, VIC 3166, Australia
Ruiz de Alarcón, 28014 Madrid, Spain
Dock House, The Waterfront, Cape Town 8001, South Africa

http://www.cambridge.org

© Cambridge University Press 2001

This book is in copyright. It is normally necessary for written permission for copying to be obtained *in advance* from a publisher. Because *Teachers in Action* contains resource material, those pages which carry the wording '© Cambridge University Press 2001' may be photocopied. The normal requirement is waived here and it is not necessary to write to Cambridge University Press for permission.

First published 2001
Reprinted 2001

Printed in the United Kingdom at the University Press, Cambridge

Typeset in Sabon 10/12pt

A catalogue record for this book is available from the British Library

Library of Congress Cataloguing-in-Publication data

James, Peter, 1954–
   Teachers in action: tasks for in-service language teacher education and development/Peter James.
      p. cm. -- (Cambridge teacher training and development)
      Includes bibliographical references and index.
      ISBN 0-521-59313-1 -- ISBN 0-521-59689-0 (pbk.)
      1. English language--Study and teaching--Foreign speakers. 2. Language and languages--Study and teaching (Primary)--Great Britain. 3. Language and languages--Study and teaching (Secondary)--Great Britain. 4. English language--Study and teaching--Great Britain. 5. Language teachers--In-service training. 6. English teachers--In-service training. 7. Language teachers -- Training of. 8. English teachers--Training of. 9. Second language acquisition. I. Title. II. Series.

PE1128.A2 J34 2001
428'.0071--dc21   2001025089

ISBN 0 521 59313 1 hardback
ISBN 0 521 59689 0 paperback

For my parents.

I would like to dedicate this book to the memory of John McDowell.

Contents

Thanks   x

Acknowledgements   xi

Introduction   1
Who this book is for   1
General aims of *Teachers in Action*   2
Effective in-service teacher education: background issues   2
Specific aims of *Teachers in Action*   10
How this book is organised   13
Investigating   14
The tasks   19
The worksheets   22
General suggestions   25
Further reading   27

1 Exploring teachers' knowledge   28
Introduction   28
1.1 Getting to know each other: What do we expect from the
    training programme?   29
1.2 How do I learn? How can we learn together?   32
1.3 Investigating: an overview   33
1.4 'It's quite obvious the gardener's a teacher': exploring
    teachers' metaphors   35
1.5 Mapping the whole: developing conceptual frameworks for
    educating, teaching and learning   38
1.6 Why teach English? Reflecting on the goals of educating,
    teaching and learning in the language classroom   40
1.7 Are we speaking the same language? Understanding general
    terms related to educating, teaching and learning   43
1.8 Reflecting on the nature of change in education: What helps
    us to change?   45
1.9 Innovation in our schools: How can we help to promote it?   47

2 Identifying topics to investigate   50
Introduction   50
2.1 Examining critical incidents   52
2.2 Effective educating, teaching and learning in the language
    classroom (1): What are our priorities?   54
2.3 Effective educating, teaching and learning in the language
    classroom (2): What are *my* priorities?   57
2.4 Our current professional practice: strengths, weaknesses,
    opportunities and benefits   59
2.5 My best lesson / teaching idea   60
2.6 General reading survey: a class library, bibliography and open
    forum   63
2.7 Keeping a classroom diary   67
2.8 Our experience of the training programme: discussion based on
    diaries   70
2.9 'We can do it!' Self-esteem, us and our learners   72

3 Exploring a topic   75
Introduction   75
3.1 Why, why, why? Examining our assumptions and beliefs
    about a topic   76
3.2 What do we understand by the topic 'x'? (What? Why?
    Who? etc.)   79
3.3 What do we already do in school or class regarding the
    topic 'x'? (Find someone who…)   82
3.4 Do we agree that…?   83
3.5 Writing about a topic: organising, developing and clarifying
    my ideas   85
3.6 Workshop: experiencing teaching ideas as learners   89
3.7 Understanding key terms related to a topic   91
3.8 Targeted reading: key extracts   94
3.9 Debate: understanding the wider implications of a topic   97

4 Investigating in class   100
Introduction   100
4.1 The benefits of investigating in class: teachers' perspectives   101
4.2 Which data collection method?   102
4.3 Our learners in action: using photographs of learners   105
4.4 Consulting our learners (1): using a simple questionnaire   110
4.5 Consulting our learners (2): What did you learn today?   113
4.6 Talking about real people: writing a learner profile   116
4.7 Informal interview with a learner   119
4.8 Experimenting in class   122

5 Evaluating learning 125

Introduction 125

5.1 Has this task helped me/us to learn? 127

5.2 Which learning strategies are helping us? 128

5.3 What I/we most like about our training programme is... 130

5.4 Making sense: reviewing and finding connections 133

5.5 Applying our learning: looking back and looking ahead 135

5.6 Teacher portfolios 138

5.7 Sharing our learning (1): giving informal presentations 140

5.8 Sharing our learning (2): joining forces in the wider educational community 144

6 Resources for the trainer 148

Introduction 148

List of resources for the trainer 149

Sections 6.1–6.39 151

Worksheets 223

List of worksheets 223

Worksheets 1–52 225

Bibliography 289

Index 293

Thanks

I wish to thank all my colleagues and all the teachers who I have worked with and who have contributed knowingly or otherwise to this book. Where possible and appropriate, I have mentioned names explicitly, but I apologise to any whose names I have unintentionally omitted. I am especially grateful to Beate, for her help and patience, Marga, for helping me to understand teachers' realities better, Françoise, for her insights, Anne Lennon, for her contributions to Tasks 2.1 and 5.2, and to Jon Roberts and Sarah Phillips, for commenting on an early draft. I am also indebted to the staff at Cambridge University Press, including Jane Clifford, Alison Sharpe, Frances Amrani and Julia Harding, and, last but not least, to the Series Editors, Marion Williams and Tony Wright, for their initial and sustained encouragement, as well as their patience and valuable advice throughout the gestation period of this book.

Acknowledgements

The authors and publishers are grateful to the following for permission to reproduce copyright material. It has not been possible to identify the sources of all the material used and in such cases the publishers would welcome information from copyright owners.

Critical Incidents in Teaching by D. Tripp, Routledge, 1993 on pp. 52 and 76–7; 'Encouraged to tell tales' by Carol Ward, *Times Educational Supplement* 15/11/96 © Times Supplements Limited on p. 61; *Process Writing* by R. V. White and V. Arndt, reprinted by permission of Pearson Education Limited © Longman Group Ltd. on p. 86; *How Languages are Learned (Second Edition)* by Patsy M. Lightbown and Nina Spada, Oxford University Press © Patsy M. Lightbown and Nina Spada, 1999 on pp. 92–3; *Teachers Education Factors Relating to Programme Design* by Parrott, M., Modern English Publications in association with the British Council, 1991 on pp. 153–4; *A Teacher's Guide to Classroom Research* by D. Hopkins, Open University Press, 1985 on pp. 155–6, 202, 248–9 and 274; *Effective in-service training: a learning resource pack* by Cline et al, University College London, 1990 on p. 161; *Method: Approach, Design and Procedure* by J. C. Richards and T. Rogers, 1982. In TESOL Quarterly, 16(2). Copyright © 1982 by Teachers of English to Speakers of Other Languages, Inc.: Diagram 6.10.2 on p. 165 used with permission; *Training Foreign Language Teachers: A Reflective Approach* by M. J. Wallace, Cambridge University Press, 1991: Diagram 6.10.3 on p. 165; *The Cubic Curriculum* by E. C. Wragg, Routledge, 1997: 6.11.1 on p. 166; *The School Curriculum: A Brief Guide*, DfEE, 1995. Crown copyright is reproduced with the permission of Her Majesty's Stationery Office; 6.11.2 on pp. 167–9; *Core Curriculum, Foreign Languages, Primary and Secondary Education*, Ministry of Science and Education, Madrid, 1995 Task 1.6 on p. 169–70 and Worksheet 10 on p. 236; 'Estudiantes compremetidos en un proyecto de igualdad' by M. Gutierrez in *Comunidad Escolar* 20/03/96: 6.14.2 on pp. 172–4; 'In her element' by Reva Klein and Victoria Neumark, *Times Educational Supplement* 03/01/96 © Reva Klein and Victoria Neumark on pp. 180–1; 'It's time we stood up for teacher' by Tim Kahn, *The Observer* 28/11/93 © *The Observer* on pp. 188–9; 'Strategies to help you fight stress' by Anne Cockburn, *Times Educational Supplement* 09/02/96 on pp. 190–1 © Times Supplements Limited; A. Pollard, with A. Filer, cited in *Reflective Teaching in the Primary School* A. Pollard and S. Tann. 1993: 6.32.1 on p. 204; 'Effective presentations' by J. Sallabank (p. 219) and I. Brussaards (p. 220), *IATEFL Newsletter*, Issue 128 (August 1995) reprinted by permission of IATEFL on pp. 210–220; *The ELT Curriculum* by R. V. White, Blackwell, 1988: Worksheet 16 on p. 243; Designing Questionnaires by M.B. Youngman in *Conducting small-scale Investigations in Educational Management* by Bell *et al* Paul Chapman Publishing in association with The Open University 1984: Worksheet 36 on p. 258–9.

Photograph on p. 61: ©Jacky Chapman; Photograph of schoolchildren using computers on p. 105: © Julie Houck/CORBIS; Photograph of girls on a field trip to Milan Castle on p. 105: © Ted Spiegel/CORBIS; Photograph of children seated in a circle for music on p. 106: © Bob Rowan; Progressive Image/CORBIS; Photograph of children in Chinese school on p. 106: © Keren Su/CORBIS; Photograph on p. 180: © Christopher Jones; Cartoon on p. 189: © Brian Bagnall; Illustration on p. 191: © Peter Kent.

Introduction

The idea to write *Teachers in Action* came about as a result of my own experience as a teacher trainer working with non-native-speaker teachers in various contexts. Although the tasks and materials that I have developed for this training work and for use in this book represent a very personal approach to in-service teacher education and development, I hope that they will also offer trainers in different contexts an accessible bank of ideas to employ in their work with teachers.

Who this book is for

Teachers in Action is intended for use by both experienced and inexperienced trainers working in the in-service education and development of primary and secondary foreign language teachers, especially teachers of English. Typically, these teachers will be attending a training, or re-training, programme in their own country, including programmes lasting a period of months, or a series of seminars throughout the teaching year. The teachers will also conform to some of the following characteristics in that they:

- are currently teaching
- are non-native speakers of English
- possibly have limited English
- possibly have limited formal training as language teachers
- are possibly inexperienced in language teaching
- are working in primary or secondary schools (with learners aged 5 to 16+)
- are working in countries or regions undergoing educational reform
- are working with less than perfect resources

Of course, this does not mean that *Teachers in Action* is unsuitable for teachers who do not exactly fit this brief profile, such as native speakers, teachers from different countries who are attending a short training programme in an English-speaking country, or teachers whose training or experience is not limited.

Finally, I hope that the book does not necessarily require the presence of a trainer, so that it is also suitable for teachers meeting in self-help groups, or indeed for highly motivated individuals.

General aims of *Teachers in Action*

It is important to state clearly at the outset that this book does not provide trainers with a series of methodological topics related to professional practice which have been already selected by me, for groups of teachers to work through and look up the answers in a key. Rather, the general aims of *Teachers in Action* are to provide in-service trainers with:

1 a broadly focused range of generative tasks and materials that can be used flexibly to meet the needs of different teacher education and development programmes
2 an accessible, flexible framework for helping teachers to investigate topics in their schools and classrooms which are relevant to them, in order to further their professional development
3 tasks and materials to help to develop teachers' professional knowledge, skills and attitudes, so they can educate their learners more effectively.

Effective in-service teacher education: background issues

I will now describe some important background issues concerning the provision of effective teacher education and development, which in very general terms I understand to mean helping practising teachers to develop their professional knowledge, skills and attitudes[1], in order to educate their learners more effectively. These issues include: teachers' identities, teachers' professional knowledge, skills, attitudes and feelings, education, and change and teacher learning.

TEACHERS' IDENTITIES

Teachers as individuals

A thumbnail sketch of practising primary and secondary teachers might characterise them as ordinary people who lead very busy, often stressful, but potentially rewarding working lives. They have families and other important commitments outside school. Teachers are also, of course, unique individuals, with their own personalities, idiosyncrasies, hopes and concerns. They have different personal and educational histories, and possess professional knowledge about the subjects they teach, as well as professional experience and skills. Significantly, they have beliefs, attitudes and feelings towards aspects of their work. All of these elements change over time.

---

[1]See Section 6.1 for further discussion of terms such as 'teacher education' and 'teacher development'.

2

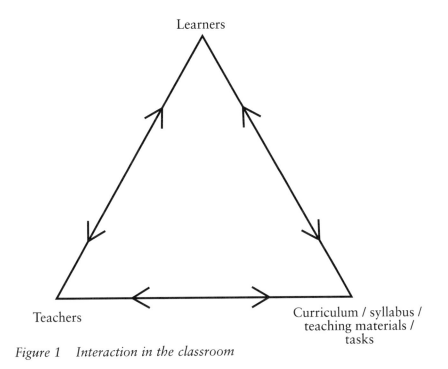

Figure 1   Interaction in the classroom

Teachers as social beings

In their professional practice, teachers are also social beings in that they interact with their learners and the curriculum in the classroom in a three-way process, as shown in Figure 1.

The classroom is clearly located within the more extended context of a school: a complex, constantly changing world full of exuberant children learning and playing, and colleagues busily attending meetings and talking to parents.

In turn, this context extends beyond the school gates, consisting of other 'layers', including the local community (a town or city with, for example, school inspectors, teachers' centres, higher education institutions); a region or country (with, for example, government ministries, publishers, national teachers' associations), and beyond this the international community at large (with, for example, organisations such as the European Union, the British Council, and international professional associations such as IATEFL or TESOL).

This social context is important in the present discussion, as the expectations of all the participants involved in the educational process exert an influence on a teacher's behaviour in school and in the classroom. The nearer the participants are to the teacher, the stronger their influence. See Figure 2.

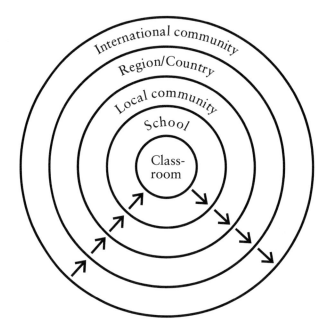

Figure 2   The social context of educating, teaching and learning

There is another crucial sense in which teachers are social beings, in terms of their own professional development. In this way, the tasks and materials in *Teachers in Action* are rooted firmly in the principles of 'social constructivism': on a training programme, a group of teachers explore and experience certain phenomena together, and as a result construct their own new meanings or personal understandings which did not exist before the programme began. See Section 6.2 for further discussion of this issue. In this social constructivist sense, *Teachers in Action* seeks both to help teachers to find their own individuality and to encourage them to interact and establish links with participants in the different layers of the educational community shown in Figure 2.

TEACHERS' PROFESSIONAL KNOWLEDGE

Teachers already possess professional knowledge when they join a training programme. This knowledge takes the form of 'personal theories', defined as a 'set of beliefs, values, understandings, assumptions – the ways of thinking about the teaching profession' (Tann, 1993: 55), and which take shape and develop as a result of individuals' experience as learners and teachers, and as a result of their previous training, to mention but a few sources.

One reason why these personal theories are important is that they help teachers to make sense of their past and present professional experience as educators and teachers. Making sense of experience would include the following: teachers' generalisations (e.g. 'For me a real curriculum contains...'), interpretations (e.g. 'The term "x" is really...'), principles (e.g. 'Schools should...'), feelings (e.g. 'Yesterday I felt pleased with...'), and priorities (e.g. 'We really need to improve...'). A second reason why personal theories are important is that they determine what teachers do in practice in classrooms, which has important implications for teacher education and development, which I outline below. A further important element of personal theories comprises individual teachers' understandings of so-called 'public theory', defined as 'the systems of ideas published in books, discussed in classes, and accompanied by a critical literature' (Eraut, 1994: 70). For English teachers, this might include ideas related to aspects such as what language is or how it is learned. (This idea of exploring public theory is included in aim 7 on p. 12, and in many of the tasks themselves.)

Of course, a teacher's personal theory may not necessarily be completely consistent or logical; perhaps there are gaps, or few connections between its different elements or components. It is also dynamic, changing over time, and highly individual, just as teachers are individuals. Significantly, personal theories are usually tacit or implicit.

One implication of this discussion concerning professional knowledge and personal theories is that an effective in-service programme should exploit fully the knowledge – as defined above – which teachers bring with them. *Teachers in Action* sets out to do so, for example, by deliberately encouraging teachers to reflect on their personal theories; to articulate them explicitly; to compare their own theories with those of their colleagues and so-called public theory; to relate their theories to their professional practice, and as a consequence to develop their own theories.

TEACHERS' PROFESSIONAL SKILLS

Teachers' professional knowledge – as outlined in the preceding section – is applied to their work in the form of skills, or routinised actions (although, naturally, not everything a teacher does is routinised). For the purposes of this book, I would like to highlight the relevance of the following: those skills related to subject matter, methodology and decision-making, as well as social and enabling skills.

Subject matter skills

Subject matter skills, such as language competence, or the use of the target language in class, are self-evidently of vital importance for language teachers. However, it is not a priority of this book to focus on subject matter skills directly, even though teachers often attach great importance to this. Instead, interested readers are recommended to consult such sources as Spratt (1994), Wright (1994), Bolitho and Tomlinson (1995), or Thornbury (1997).

Methodological skills

Of obvious importance to effective educating, teaching and learning, is the range of methodological skills required by teachers in the day-to-day world of schools, such as lesson planning, using a cassette recorder, or correcting learners' mistakes. A central feature of *Teachers in Action* is that teachers and trainers are encouraged to draw up shortlists of their own methodological priorities. What the book then does is to provide tasks and materials, for example, to help participants to analyse their current practice concerning these priorities, to read relevant books and articles, to exchange ideas about their priorities and to experiment in schools and classrooms with them.

Decison-making skills

These skills are defined as follows:

> Teachers are constantly confronted with a range of options and are required to select from among these options the ones they think are best suited to a particular goal. The option the teacher selects is known as a decision (Kindsvatter, Wilen and Ishler, 1988). Teaching involves making a great number of decisions.

(Richards and Lockhart, 1994: 78)

Richards and Lockhart go on to distinguish between different types of decision: planning decisions (e.g. 'What do I want my learners to learn from this lesson?'), interactive decisions (e.g. 'Are my instructions understood?') and evaluative decisions (e.g. 'Was this lesson successful?') (ibid. 78–89).

By encouraging teachers to involve themselves in decision-making about their own training programme, *Teachers in Action* deliberately seeks to develop teachers' ability to make decisions in their own schools and class-rooms, in categories such as those suggested by Richards and Lockhart.

Social skills

Teachers are social beings, and their social skills are of great importance for effective educating, teaching and learning. These social skills include inter-active skills, such as communicating and co-operating effectively with learn-ers, as well as with colleagues (e.g. discussing and sharing teaching ideas, problems or concerns), or with parents (e.g. explaining aspects of teaching and learning at parents' meetings), or with other participants in the educa-tional community. The social constructivist principles of *Teachers in Action* (see Section 6.2) explicitly encourage the development of such social skills.

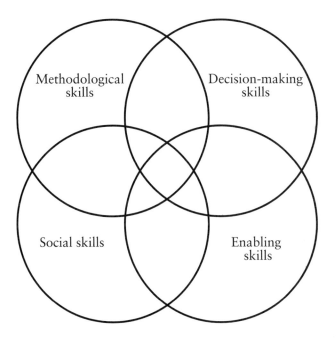

Figure 3 *The skills focus of* Teachers in Action

Enabling skills

Finally, I would like to highlight the importance of professional 'enabling skills' in *Teachers in Action*. Enabling skills are those which facilitate career-long teacher learning and include: professional reading skills, presentation skills, investigating, and the capacity to theorise, where the last is defined as the 'ability to acquire, refine, evaluate, and use theories for the improvement of practice' (Eraut, 1994: 73). Thus, *Teachers in Action* specifically aims to develop teachers' level of skills in four of the areas outlined in this section, that is to say, methodological, decision-making, social and enabling skills. See Figure 3.

TEACHERS' ATTITUDES AND FEELINGS ABOUT THEIR WORK

Naturally, teachers have attitudes and feelings about their work; by 'attitude' I understand a 'way of thinking that inclines one to feel and behave in certain ways' (Simons *et al.*, 1993: 239). Language teachers, then, feel or behave in certain ways about the language they teach, for example, or the goals and purposes of education; they are often influenced by social forces, such as the status and value of teaching in their region or country, the levels of pay, or the political structure of the school. Of course, many teachers have positive feelings, hopes, desires and dreams, and are keen to improve aspects of their professional practice, and to find out about new teaching ideas. However, experienced trainers know that teachers may also have many negative feelings, concerns, doubts and worries about their professional practice. For instance, they may have little time for catching up on professional reading, feeling guilty as a result. They may worry about the thorny issue of mixed ability classes, or their learners' motivation. Language teachers may sometimes have low self-esteem, and can be very self-critical about their own command of the language they teach.

Teachers in Action, therefore, deliberately seeks to help teachers to reflect[2] on and talk about such attitudes and feelings, both positive and negative. This not only enables them to obtain a balanced view of their professional strengths and weaknesses, but also encourages them to take action and identify opportunities to change aspects of their work. In the long term such an approach also helps to enhance teachers' self-esteem and develop their confidence in their own knowledge and skills.

EDUCATION

One question related to primary and secondary teachers' professional practice which is significant in the present discussion is 'What is education?', as there are parallels between the answer to the question and the underlying principles of *Teachers in Action* itself.

A determining characteristic of primary and secondary school teachers' practice is their involvement in the general education of their learners, a goal greater in scope than their specific responsibilities as language teachers. But how to define the purpose of education? Fullan (1993) records that two student teachers view the issue as follows:

> I hope my contribution to teaching, along with other good teachers' contributions, will help result in a better society for our future.... (10)

> I've always thought that if I could go into a classroom and make a difference in one kid's life ... then that's what I am here for. (11)

In addition to the rather idealistic purposes defined by these students, my own understanding of the term 'education' emphasises the following:

- developing the whole learner (the learner's knowledge, skills, attitudes, etc.)

---

[2]By 'reflect' I understand systematic, explicit and critical thinking about professional matters of importance to teachers. For a fuller discussion of the relationship between reflection and teacher development, see Roberts (1998: 47–60). See also aim 3 on p. 10 for an example of how reflecting in the above sense can be applied to teacher education and development.

- applying general and specific educational aims, as expressed in a curriculum, across the whole school;
- preparing learners for life-long learning

The tasks and materials in *Teachers in Action* reflect these priorities, in relation to both teacher education and development and the education of school-aged children.

CHANGE AND TEACHER LEARNING

In our daily lives we are surrounded by the shifting tides of change. Change is natural, varied and complex, simply a part of the way we live. For instance, there is political change when a new government is elected; technological change when a new computer software product is launched onto the market; environmental change when a forest fire pollutes the air with its smoke; and personal change when an individual begins a new job.

The field of education – the focus of this book – is no exception as regards change. Indeed, it is particularly susceptible to change, change of a constant nature. For example, change occurs when new curriculum plans are implemented by a ministry, granting schools more autonomy in running their own affairs. Naturally, learners themselves also change, for example, as they grow older and move up through the school, or as they respond to changes in society. For these and other reasons, therefore, teachers also need to change. If not, they risk being left behind, as the world around them moves on. Change for teachers takes place naturally; they may take on a new administrative role at school, use a new coursebook, experiment with a new idea recommended by a colleague, or apply new technology in class, such as video.

Further characteristics of change are that it is usually slow, as well as difficult, in that it always involves more work for teachers. An apparently simple decision to use video in class for the first time, for instance, requires an already busy teacher to find a time and a place to identify, view and select suitable materials before class.

Two important pre-conditions for change are that the educational system in which teachers are working actively promotes change, and that teachers themselves are ready to and want to change. Teachers must recognise a need to change, as it cannot be successfully imposed by others. Genuine change – in a teacher's knowledge, skills and attitudes – is also a long process, in effect, career-long, and not confined to an all too often short training programme.

Finally, just as with the social context of educating, teaching and learning, the contexts in which teacher education programmes take place are complex and unique, consisting of a variety of factors, including: Who is paying for the programme? Who is teaching on the programme? What resources are available? How is the programme structured? What incentives are there for the teachers to participate?

A training programme or training materials that work successfully in one context will not necessarily do so in others (see Section 6.3, for example, for two case studies of ineffective in-service training programmes). For this reason, the materials in *Teachers in Action*, whose aim is to deliberately help to facilitate change, need to be flexible to cater for differing contexts and needs, as well as to take into account the views outlined above with regard to the nature of change and teacher learning.

Specific aims of *Teachers in Action*

The following specific aims of this book state explicitly how it sets out to help trainers or teachers to develop or change:

1 *to improve the effectiveness of teachers' professional practice as educators and language teachers by developing their existing professional skills and developing new ones*

Of course, teacher education and development can hardly be said to be effective unless it helps teachers to do their work as educators and teachers better, by developing their professional skills (methodological skills, for example). Teachers come to a training programme with certain strengths and weaknesses in these areas, so a programme can develop or fine-tune existing skills, such as correcting learners' spoken language, or develop totally new ones, such as applying new technologies.

2 *to help teachers to make more informed, principled professional decisions in the future*

Teachers are required to be able to make the best professional decisions in their day-to-day lives, but in a changing world we do not know what kind of decisions they will need to make in the future. If teachers are well informed about the latest developments in their professional field, if they have reflected critically and systematically about their practice and have been involved in making their own professional decisions, they will be better equipped to cope with new and different problems that arise in the future.

3 *to enable teachers to reflect on, discuss and evaluate their current professional practice, and to help them to articulate and develop their personal theories of education, teaching and learning*

Educating, teaching and learning is a complex process. Each teacher comes to a training programme with different knowledge and concerns, and works in different circumstances. This complexity points to the need for teachers to understand better what happens in classrooms, or schools, which provides an important focus for *Teachers in Action*. The fact that practising teachers are in direct contact with learners in the classroom can be exploited, by encouraging teachers to consider what they already do in schools and classrooms, and by making their current practice explicit. For example, focusing on teachers' tacit personal theories is a vital part of their learning, as they need to reflect on and articulate, as well as analyse, their own (and others') professional ideas, practice and priorities. This is important because it:

- raises teachers' existing knowledge into consciousness
- helps teachers to examine and question their assumptions about education, language teaching and learning
- helps teachers in the long-term task of organising and clarifying their personal theories, and assimilating new information
- develops teachers' critical awareness
- allows trainers and other teachers to gain access to and understand individual teachers' theories

4 *to help trainers and teachers to explore, investigate and understand better what happens in schools and classrooms as an on-going process throughout their careers*

Teachers may consider or evaluate their current practice by identifying those aspects which they are satisfied with (but not 'throwing the baby out with the bath water'); identifying other aspects which they feel need improving, and by exploring and investigating alternative solutions and methods. However, I believe there are no 'right answers' to issues that arise in schools and classrooms, as such; any new understandings which come about as a result of teachers exploring and investigating are not fixed, as circumstances and the learning context change. For trainers and teachers alike, exploring, investigating and understanding is seen as an on-going process, to be sustained throughout their careers.

5 *to harness teachers' individual and collective knowledge and skills, and help them to co-operate more effectively with each other, as well as to join forces with other participants in the educational system*

Acknowledging and respecting the individual and collective knowledge and skills that teachers already bring with them to a training programme is an example of the important principle of 'starting where the teachers are'. It is a foundation of knowledge which can then be socially constructed in a gradual process, or built on together.

6 *to help teachers to select relevant goals for, manage the process of, and evaluate, their learning and professional development*

One way for teachers to construct new, personal meanings is for them to be involved in agreeing on the goals for their own development, and in selecting at least some of the topics to be investigated. *Teachers in Action* does not therefore prescribe *what* teachers investigate, but it does provide a framework for them to identify their own topics. Such an approach not only increases the relevance of a programme, but can also enhance teachers' sense of ownership of it. It is my view that such an experiential focus provides teachers with a potentially valuable level of learning, particularly when they are encouraged to assess the implications for their own teaching (see also Task 3.6, in particular the reference to Kolb).

7 *to provide teachers with a variety of pedagogical practices, materials, resources and ideas, as well as the opportunity to make sense of relevant aspects of the literature in their field, helping them to integrate this new experience and information with their personal theories.*

Of course, teachers delight in finding out about new teaching ideas and procedures, especially by taking part in them actively as learners. This provides opportunities for teachers to learn experientially. Exposing teachers to the thinking of others, that of their colleagues or the authors of professional books for example, is an important way of informing teachers of developments in their field, helping them to construct new meanings related to their professional practice. This can be attempted by helping teachers gain an overview of relevant aspects of the 'public theory', especially the critical literature.

8 *to help teachers to experiment with and evaluate new methods, materials and teaching ideas*

As important as the process of experiencing a variety of pedagogical practices, materials, resources and ideas is, it is not enough on its own for significant development to take place. Teachers also learn by assessing the implications of their experience as learners on a programme, and by experimenting in the classroom itself. So, *Teachers in Action* encourages teachers to select teaching ideas from those encountered, to implement them in class, and to evaluate the results.

9 *to seek to develop teachers' self-esteem, autonomy and confidence in their own ability to improve the effectiveness of their work*

Helping teachers to gain new knowledge or develop skills is relatively easy, compared with the more difficult challenge of changing teachers' often rather negative attitudes towards aspects of their work! But, without question, if teachers are to sustain learning throughout their careers, they will need certain qualities, such as high self-esteem, autonomy and confidence in themselves.

How this book is organised

The tasks and other resources in this book are presented in six chapters: Chapter 1, Exploring teachers' knowledge; Chapter 2, Identifying topics to investigate; Chapter 3, Exploring a topic; Chapter 4, Investigating in class; Chapter 5, Evaluating learning; Chapter 6, Resources for the trainer. Each chapter begins with an introduction. When taken together, Chapters 2–5 form a cycle, which is supported by Chapters 1 and 6 (see Figure 4).

Trainers may use the cycle in Figure 4 to sequence tasks and materials in a training session or sessions. However, the chapter headings and the investigating cycle itself are only intended to serve as a loosely structured guide. For example, some tasks might easily be placed in more than one chapter, while others deliberately forge links across different chapters.

So, I hope that trainers are able to pick and choose tasks in ways not suggested by the presentation and sequencing in the book, in order to suit their particular needs (see below 'Using the tasks', for more information).

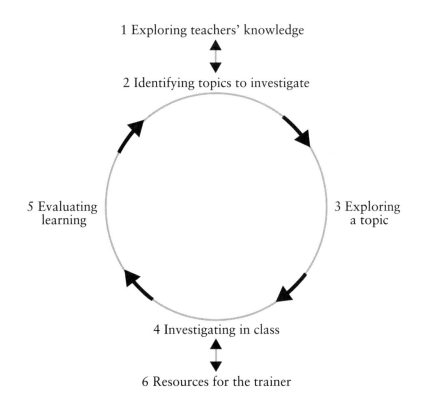

1 Exploring teachers' knowledge

2 Identifying topics to investigate

5 Evaluating learning

3 Exploring a topic

4 Investigating in class

6 Resources for the trainer

Figure 4   The investigating cycle in Teachers in Action

Investigating

In this section I will discuss issues related to my understanding of the term 'investigating', including references to relevant background literature, a practical example showing how teachers might go about investigating, as well as a description of some of its key features and benefits.

I use the term 'investigating' deliberately because it avoids some of the academic or technical associations of the term 'research'. 'Investigating' is also less ambitious than a 'stronger' form of 'classroom research' or 'action research', as it is designed to be less demanding of or threatening to trainers and teachers, who might not possess the resources and skills for a more rigorously applied research methodology. See Section 6.4 for information about a case study of a stronger form of action research in mainstream education (Hopkins, 1985).

There are two ways in which I use the term 'investigating' in this book. Firstly, in a general sense, I understand 'investigating' to be an open, questioning way of viewing education, teaching and learning, such that engaging in any of the tasks or any combination of tasks within the investigating cycle in this book (see Figure 4), constitutes 'investigating'. In a more specific sense, though, the focus in *Teachers in Action* is on helping teachers to develop their confidence and skills to investigate their work *in class*, as in the tasks in Chapter 4. This I refer to throughout the book as 'investigating in class'.

BACKGROUND

The approach to investigating in *Teachers in Action* has developed as a result of my discovery of action research in the literature of teacher education, and of the subsequent excitement I experienced when implementing such ideas with teachers (see Roberts, 1998: 258–74 for a detailed account and evaluation of such a training programme). The roots of action research can be traced back in the literature to such authors as Kolb (1984) , or Stenhouse (1975), who was concerned with curriculum development in mainstream education. There are numerous publications related to action research in education, including Carr and Kemmis (1983), Elliot and Ebbutt (1985), Hopkins (1985) and Wallace (1998).

In the specific literature of English language teacher education, Maley (1991) highlights the potential of action research as a future development in the field of English teaching practice:

> Increasingly both professional researchers and classroom teachers are becoming involved in pragmatically-rooted research 'at the chalk face'. Typically these research projects are designed to find answers to quite small-scale, specific problems. ...When carried out by teachers, they are a prime tool for teacher development. (29)

The literature also provides examples of different interpretations of the aims and nature of action research; personally, I find the following definitions clear and useful:

> *the systematic study of attempts to improve educational practice by groups of participants by means of their own practical actions and by means of their own reflection upon the effects of those actions.*
>
> (Ebbutt, cited in Hopkins 1985: 32)

> *small-scale intervention in the functioning of the real world and a close examination of the effects of such intervention.*
>
> (Halsey, cited in Bell *et al.*, 1984: 41)

Key terms here for my own understanding of investigating include: 'systematic', 'improve educational practice', 'groups of participants', 'practical actions' , 'small-scale', 'real world', which I will develop further in this section.

PRACTICAL EXAMPLE OF INVESTIGATING

How might the tasks in this book be used for investigating, as defined above in the general sense? Figure 5 on pp. 16–17 provides the reader with a guide in the form of a detailed, imaginary example of a full cycle of 'investigating' in practice. Please note that the example is illustrated with specific tasks from the book. The example features a group of twelve teachers who are attending a year-long in-service teacher education and development programme for secondary teachers of English. They meet once a week at a local teachers' centre, and are led by a native speaker (of English) trainer, Anne. English is used as a means of communication for the programme, although from time to time the teachers use their own language.

KEY FEATURES AND BENEFITS OF INVESTIGATING

I will now highlight some of the key features and benefits of investigating, referring to Figure 5 by way of illustration.

The teacher as protagonist

Teachers are the main protagonists in their professional development and educational change. In Figure 5, the topic for investigating, 'mistakes and correction', is selected because Françoise shows interest in it, rather than the topic being 'imposed' by the trainer. In the long term this encourages teachers to take responsibility for their development and change, promoting confidence in their own ideas and skills. Another important feature of investigating is that topics may be investigated with the teachers as protagonists (a) as a whole group, (b) in sub-groups, or (c) individually, as appropriate, or, indeed, by combining the three modes.

Identifying topics to investigate

One of the teachers, Françoise, becomes aware of the importance of oral mistakes and correction, as a result of the trainer's attitudes to and handling of the mistakes in English made by the teachers. Anne, the trainer, does not correct very much; Françoise realises that she does not like not being corrected. In comparison, she feels she corrects her own pupils a lot; she wonders whether this might inhibit their learning. In Task 2.1 Françoise reflects and writes about these and other related issues. Subsequently, in Task 2.4, she discovers that other teachers in the group are also interested in mistakes and correction. The topic is selected as a group priority alongside others, using Worksheet 18 to record these priorities (see Task 2.1). So the group decides to focus on this topic together in the coming weeks.

Exploring a topic

The teachers are also asked to look for articles in teachers' magazines and journals related to the topic, and share them. Despite her anxiety about reading a whole methodology book in English (she has never done so before), Françoise reads *Mistakes and Correction* (Edge, 1989), one of a collection of books provided for the teachers, and which was strongly recommended by a colleague in a review worksheet she had previously completed about the book (see Tasks 2.6 or 3.8). To Françoise's surprise, she finds the book very practical. The issue of mistakes and correction, and teachers' attitudes and assumptions, are then discussed, using both Task 3.1 and Task 3.9. Different technical terms related to mistakes and correction, such as 'error', 'fluency', 'interlanguage', etc., are clarified using Task 3.7, and a variety of correction techniques are demonstrated by the trainer and other teachers in the group, in a workshop in Task 3.6.

Investigating in class

The teachers are then encouraged to experiment with alternative correction technique(s) encountered in the previous workshop, and/or in their reading, in one class of their choice, over a period of two weeks. They organise themselves into three sub-groups, two with teachers working with 13-year-olds, the other with 14-year-olds. They describe what they wish to achieve by using the new techniques in terms of how their pupils might benefit. As they experiment, some teachers keep a teacher diary (see Task 2.7), while others take some photographs of their pupils in class involved in the activities, as in Task 4.3. One group also writes and uses a simple questionnaire in order to find out their pupils' attitudes to mistakes and correction, as in Task 4.4. Anne advises the teachers, answering their questions. Using Worksheet 40, the teachers are encouraged to summarise key points, implications and recommendations related to their investigations in class.

Evaluating learning

In a subsequent session, the sub-groups report back to each other, using ideas and materials from Task 5.7. The results of the questionnaire are presented, the completed worksheets, photos of learners, and key diary extracts are displayed on the walls. Several teachers report that their learners now appear more motivated than before. Following on from this, the teachers evaluate the work they have completed together on the topic of mistakes, using Worksheet 42. One teacher talks about how useful she found the learner questionnaire, and how surprised she was to find out about the pupils' perceptive insights into the topic. So the group of teachers decides to write another questionnaire together to find out about their pupils' views on another topic in the list of priorities which the group had drawn up before, which is ...

See also Section 6.5 for a further sequence of tasks, options and activities taken from this book.

Figure 5   A practical example of investigating

Teachers collaborate with trainers and other colleagues

So, although individual teachers are the protagonists, a vital feature is that the process of investigating takes place in a group, with the support of a trainer and colleagues. This social constructivist, collective orientation helps to develop a sense of what might be called a 'community of learning'. In Figure 5, Françoise discovers that other group members share her interest in mistakes and correction. They also work in sub-groups, focusing on learners of the same age. In addition, Anne, the trainer, is able to recommend suitable reading material, as well as helping teachers to write a questionnaire. Without such support, development would be much more difficult and require great determination. Indeed, if teachers are to help to bring about change in their schools, they will need to work together effectively, as well as with other participants in the educational system. A teacher education programme provides a splendid opportunity to develop such social skills.

Teachers improving practice

A specific aim of investigating is to help teachers to improve their practice with a clear emphasis on practical actions in the real world of the school and the classroom. How can teachers decide which aspects to improve, though? A simple yet effective way is for teachers to think of those aspects of their work that are important to themselves, their learners and their schools. For example, Françoise and other teachers sense that the way they currently deal with mistakes in class inhibits their learners, so by changing their correction techniques they hope that the overall motivation of their learners will improve.

Investigating by simple means

Techniques which teachers use for collecting information in classrooms, such as writing a short questionnaire, should not be too technical or demanding for them. After all, a teachers' main responsibility is to teach! Because of a lack of time, not all the teachers in Françoise's group are able to write a diary about their experiments, but they are able to take photographs of their learners in action or complete one of the worksheets. So the collection techniques presented in this book are deliberately simple, and seek to be non-threatening and accessible.

'Small is beautiful': being realistic

Individual teachers are recommended to select a specific topic to investigate, for example by monitoring the introduction of one teaching idea with one group of learners for a limited period of time, as my own experience convinces me that 'small is beautiful'. For instance, rather than investigating the topic of 'correction', a somewhat diffuse, vague focus, teachers might investigate the 'correction of oral mistakes in fluency activities' for two weeks, as in Françoise's group. Such a small-scale, 'narrow' focus enables teachers to maintain control of the process of investigating, while at the same time providing a framework for the analysis of more global educational issues, such as 'motivation' in Françoise's group. In the whole group, teachers could also cover more ground, as it were, by focusing on slightly different aspects of correction. Finally, Hopkins' advice to teachers as to the focus of classroom research should also be adhered to: 'do not tackle issues that you cannot do anything about' (1985: 47).

Being systematic

In their working lives, teachers do instinctively analyse their work, for example by reflecting on the effectiveness of a lesson while walking across the school playground after the lesson, as follows:

Now, was this lesson successful? Yes, the first activity worked quite well, although maybe next time I should....

However, it is unlikely that teachers keep a diary in which they regularly record such reflections, as they are encouraged to do in this book. Being systematic in this way will help Françoise and her colleagues to develop in an organised way, as well as helping them to monitor their learning.

The results of investigating are shared

One limitation of investigating is that it takes place in a specific local context, so any findings cannot claim to be valid beyond this context, or to contribute to a general body of professional understanding. However, the results of learning in *Teachers in Action* are deliberately made available to other teachers in the group, to the trainer, or possibly to other teachers in the same community, enabling them to join forces with and learn from the experience of the investigating teachers. For instance, Françoise and her colleagues record the conclusions reached about the topic of mistakes and correction on a worksheet which is displayed on the training room wall. It has been suggested that such classroom research by teachers enables them to acquire:

> more power over their professional lives and be better able to create
> classrooms and schools more responsive to the vision they and we have
> of our children's future.

(Hopkins, 1985: 129)

Teachers as reformers

Schön explicitly highlights strategies for teachers to gain the power advocated by Hopkins:

> If you train a teacher to be very independent, not only to look for the
> right answer, to face up to her own way of learning, who wishes to reflect
> in action, in her work with pupils and in her relationship with them, … this
> teacher will become a kind of reformer.

(in Sancho and Hernández, 1994: 92; my translation)

Teachers in Action seeks to develop the kind of teacher reformers described by Schön, that is to say, teachers who themselves can bring about change in classrooms and schools, in collaboration with their learners and others in the educational community.

The tasks

The tasks and other resources in this book offer the trainer pedagogic procedures for achieving the aims listed above. In this section, I will outline the following issues related to the tasks: background, using the tasks and the task format. See the contents list for a complete list of tasks.

BACKGROUND

Task-based materials for the language teacher trainer are already available in published form, such as Parrott (1993), Wajnryb (1992), Richards and

Lockhart (1994), and, for primary teachers, Pollard and Tann (1993). The literature concerning the use of tasks in language teaching and language teacher education, such as Nunan (1989), Ellis (1990) and Wallace (1991), has also been useful for me, by supplying the theoretical background, as well as key concepts such as tasks, input, activities, procedures, output and outcomes.

Expressed simply, teachers learn by 'acting', in the broadest sense of the word, that is to say, by being actively involved in processes such as reflecting, experiencing, experimenting, selecting, reading, discussing and theorising. In this respect, the word 'action' in the title of this book is also intended to highlight the crucial nature of teachers' own activity, whether physical, intellectual or otherwise, in their own development and educational change. The tasks in *Teachers in Action* therefore seek to involve and support teachers as actively, co-operatively and purposefully as possible in relevant, interesting and challenging activities related to their professional realities.

USING THE TASKS

Teachers in Action is intended to be used as a resource book, not as a training coursebook. Depending on the trainer's experience, skills, training context and needs, and the resources available, I hope that these flexible tasks can be used in one or more of the ways listed below.

Selecting individual tasks

The tasks are designed to be 'free-standing', allowing trainers to dip into the book. Trainers are therefore able to select and use individual tasks without modification, so that they fit in with other procedures which the trainers already employ. Of course, the chapters present the tasks in a certain order, but trainers are encouraged to enter this order at any point and select relevant tasks.

Adapting tasks

The tasks are designed to be generative. Trainers may wish to try to exploit this potential, by using the tasks as 'models' and adapting them, so that they are more closely tailored to their own contexts and needs. For instance, trainers might be attracted by Worksheet 31 used in the Task 3.7, for which teachers are required to examine terms related to the topic of language acquisition and learning. Trainers can then adapt this task by using the blank worksheet for the actual topic they wish to focus on with their own teachers. Some worksheets can also be used for several tasks; for example, Worksheet 27 may be used not only for Task 2.9, but for others, such as Task 3.1.

Sequences of tasks

The tasks may be combined in different ways. Trainers may use individual tasks, or they may wish to select and sequence several tasks. The book helps in this respect by providing suggestions for sequencing, as follows:

1 the order of tasks as presented in the chapters and the book
2 the sequences shown in Figure 5, or in Section 6.5
3 specific combinations of certain tasks suggested in the procedure for the tasks themselves

Alternatively, trainers may create their own sequences of tasks.

Other ways

I would be pleased if trainers find other ways of using this book that I have not anticipated.

TASK FORMAT

The tasks themselves address the trainer directly; the use of the imperative form underlines this point.[3] The task format is designed to present the input for each task, drawn from a wide range of sources, attractively, clearly and consistently. By way of example, the reader can look at Task 1.7 and Task 2.8, while reading the following detailed description of the task format.

There is an introductory text with a summary of relevant *background information* to the task, including, where appropriate, quotations from the literature.

This is followed by the *task aims*, which specify the purposes of each task; broadly these aims correspond to the specific aims for the book listed on p. 10.

There is information concerning any *preparation* the trainer will need to complete in order to do the task in a training session, such as the preparation of role cards. This is followed by a detailed guide to the pedagogic *procedures* for implementing the 'activities', the actual operations teachers are involved in for each task, presented in numbered stages for the trainer. Usually the procedures consist of the following pattern: after a brief whole-group discussion arousing teachers' interest and relating it to teachers' previous experience, there are notes which complement the aims and instructions on the actual worksheets (see also 'Using the worksheets' below). Finally, teachers are encouraged to report their findings after

---

[3] Although the information described above for each task is primarily addressed to trainers, it may also be used directly with teachers themselves. For example, when introducing a task, trainers may refer the teachers to aspects of the background information or the task aims.

completing a worksheet, by formulating action points, or some other future-oriented activity.

Where appropriate, there are also specific, cross-referenced suggestions for *combining tasks*, where this has not already been made clear in the text.

In addition, there are occasional suggestions for *further reading* for trainers to follow up specific interests (full details of books and articles in such sections are given in the bibliography).

Finally, many tasks also include one or more *options*, alternative activities for trainers to consider using at a specific point if they wish. The options are designed to be flexible, in that as well as being relevant for the task in hand, they are also intended for use in combination with other tasks.

The worksheets

The worksheets in *Teachers in Action* provide the material for direct use with teachers, and are located at the end of the book. The rubrics, instructions and aims on each worksheet are addressed directly to the teachers and written in plain English. Some worksheets also contain extra activities, designed for use by teachers who finish the worksheet ahead of the others. Such activities include questions relevant to the overall topic in question, but which are not essential for its successful completion. When processing the worksheet with the teachers, however, trainers may certainly elicit any responses to these extra activities. The worksheets are to be completed by teachers while engaged in a task, in a training session or at home in preparation for a session. They take various forms, including diagrams, drawings, questionnaires, checklists, partially completed sentences, etc. A complete list of worksheets is given on pp. 223–4.

The purpose of the worksheets is to:

- help teachers to focus and to marshall reflection, discussion and actions systematically
- enable teachers to personalise tasks
- help teachers to share and synthesise learning with each other and the trainer
- provide memorable, recoverable records of learning
- build a bridge between the present programme and future learning outcomes[4]

Where appropriate, authentic examples of completed worksheets by groups of teachers, or individual teachers, are provided for trainers, so that

---

[4] The term 'outcomes' refers to the the results of learning, that is to say, new knowledge, skills and attitudes applied in the teachers' professional practice in the future.

when they are considering using a certain task in their own training work, they can see clearly how real teachers have already responded. These examples are presented in Chapter 6.

USING THE WORKSHEETS

1 Trainers should make sure that teachers have access to the selected worksheet in one of the following ways:
   (a) teachers each have a copy of the book
   (b) where the trainer has access to a photocopier, worksheets can be copied for teachers in advance of a training session
   (c) worksheets can be copied onto an overhead transparency
   (d) worksheets can be written onto the blackboard, or onto an overhead transparency, by hand, so that teachers can also copy down the essentials
   (e) trainers can dictate key parts of the worksheet to the teachers

2 When using a worksheet, trainers should ensure that the teachers understand exactly what they have to do by pointing out the task aim(s) shown at the top of the worksheet. Teachers should be allowed enough time to read through the instructions; any unfamiliar terms employed on the worksheet should be explained. Examples of the responses required should be given, if teachers are not sure what is expected.

3 The worksheets are designed to be challenging, but also teacher-friendly for busy teachers, for example in terms of the time needed to complete them. So teachers should spend a realistic amount of time on a worksheet. To this end, approximate recommended timings are included on each worksheet (and in the procedures), or for different parts of it, but trainers may wish to negotiate more suitable times for their own teachers. Teachers should feel under no pressure to respond to *all* the questions or items on a worksheet, so stress that they need respond to only those items which are appropriate and/or of interest to them.

4 Trainers should make sure that the teachers know what will happen to the completed worksheets, *before* they start filling them in (see point 9 below).

5 The worksheets usually require teachers to reflect individually on a topic, and then respond in writing. Depending on the training context, teachers may do so in the training session itself, or between sessions. In the latter case, trainers may ask teachers to complete (parts of) worksheets at home for future training sessions. This gives them all-important time to mull over, or sleep on, ideas, a strategy which is particularly appropriate for the more challenging tasks requiring self-disclosure, or abstract thinking.

6 After reflecting, in a training session teachers are usually required to compare their response to a worksheet with that of colleagues, in pairs or sub-groups of three or four, depending on the size of the whole group. This is a vital element of the book, encouraging teachers to contrast their

23

own views with those of others, to agree and disagree, and to establish what they have in common with colleagues, helping them in the process to value their colleagues' views, as well as clarifying their own personal theories. As for the actual forming of pairs or small groups, trainers will establish criteria with the group which are appropriate for their own context, although they may wish to encourage teachers who work with learners of the same age, or who work in the same school, to collaborate. Trainers may help to reduce the potential imposition of dominant, outspoken teachers by insisting that both teachers in a pair, or all teachers in a sub-group, have the opportunity to contribute towards the task in hand. While teachers are working in pairs or sub-groups, trainers can 'monitor', that is to say, go around the room from sub-group to sub-group in order to check that everyone is on task, and/or to offer assistance where necessary.

7 Many tasks encourage trainers to take part actively as a member of the group, enabling them to establish contact with teachers on an informal basis (see Task 3.3, for example). Similarly, when teachers are writing responses to worksheets in a training session, trainers may also write, as a member of the group. This not only demonstrates to the teachers how important the task is to the trainer, but, where appropriate, also allows the text produced to be processed alongside the teachers' own texts.

8 When processing the results of a worksheet, trainers may encourage individuals or sub-groups to present their findings, either by inviting them by name, or asking for volunteers (see also Section 6.38.1). Depending on the size of your group, there may be time for all sub-groups to present, or only some, so trainers should be flexible about this. Whatever the case, teachers should be allowed to express any strong opinions that they might have about the topic. Trainers should try to elicit specific learning points (action points, recommendations, etc.), by extrapolating (using the information obtained by completing worksheets for making statements about teachers' professional practice, or about what is likely to happen), writing these up on the blackboard (whiteboard or overhead projector), or using a worksheet for this purpose. Teachers (individuals or sub-groups) can be encouraged to sign and date completed worksheets, so that they can monitor the development of and classify the worksheets and other material that they accumulate, and so that the material can be easily identified by the trainer or group members.

9 Completed worksheets can be employed in a number of practical ways:
   (a) certain worksheets record arrangements agreed by the whole group; these can be photocopied, where appropriate, so that teachers or groups of teachers each have a copy to refer to
   (b) worksheets may be displayed prominently and publicly on the walls of the training room for immediate or future comment, group discussion or reference (see the illustrated metaphors in Task 1.4, for example)

(c) worksheets may be retained for later reference/evaluation by individuals

(d) worksheets may be used as part of an on-going portfolio, or bank of materials, collected by an individual teacher during a programme (see Task 5.6 for further information regarding this strategy)

(e) worksheets may be read by (i) other colleagues (providing an opportunity for sharing ideas and receiving feedback on one's own ideas, or (ii) the trainer(s). The latter not only provides trainers with an opportunity to learn about teachers' professional knowledge and backgrounds, but, where appropriate, also provides a valuable opportunity for trainers to establish and maintain an on-going written 'dialogue' between themselves and individual teachers. In so doing, trainers can seek to encourage teachers, challenge their assumptions, raise questions and suggest alternatives or appropriate reading material, by pencilling in brief comments and questions on to the text, thus promoting further reflection (on some worksheets there are spaces for other teachers and/or the trainer to write such notes). This dialogue might also be followed up subsequently by teachers and trainers in individual tutorials, for example. Trainers can also read all the completed worksheets for a given task, and write a summary of how the whole group has responded to it, giving a copy to each teacher for reference (see, for example, the summary feedback letter in Task 3.5).

General suggestions

CREATING A SUITABLE ENVIRONMENT

Encouraging teachers to talk frankly about their professional practice, or to experiment with teaching ideas, may prove difficult, or even threatening to teachers, causing them to feel inadequate or anxious. So trainers need to look for ways of creating a safe environment characterised by trust, patience, support and encouragement. At the beginning of a training programme, trainers may discuss and establish a set of 'ground rules' with the group. For example, will the training programme be conducted in English? What is the status of the teachers' mother tongue? Is it acceptable for them to use it?

USEFUL AIDS

Trainers using this book may not be working with excellent resources, in terms of teaching aids and materials, such as photocopiers, computers, access to a library, etc. If they do have such facilities, all the better, but I have tried to make this book accessible to trainers working with less than perfect resources. The following aids will, however, prove particularly useful when using *Teachers in Action*: a blackboard/whiteboard, a selection of professional books, journals and magazines, a cassette recorder, files/ring-binders for teachers to keep and organise materials in, a notice-board on the walls of the training room, and an overhead projector.

TRAINERS INVESTIGATING

Trainers themselves can adopt an investigating attitude towards their own practice as trainers, which may act as a positive 'model' for participating teachers. It is also envisaged that by using this book the trainer will be able to develop professionally.

TRAINERS SHARING

A simple, effective way of informing teachers of recent developments regarding a topic being investigated is for trainers to give a brief lecture on it, lasting, say, 10–15 minutes. Although this book clearly places an emphasis on the participating teachers themselves researching, reporting and sharing their findings, there are still a number of reasons for trainers to give a lecture. For instance, they are more likely to know what to read with regard to a particular topic, and have more time to read than teachers who are busy teaching! Such a lecture might include an overview of background issues, as well as the trainer's own professional judgement on a topic, which teachers are often keen to find out about. If there are teachers in the group who are well informed about a topic, and who are also willing to give a mini-lecture, they can be encouraged to do so. See also Woodward (1992) for interesting ways of varying lectures.

A FINAL WORD OF ENCOURAGEMENT

Investigating has, I believe, untapped potential for helping to provide effective language teacher education and development, in itself a process without end. Teachers are capable of extraordinary achievements in learning! So I would be happy if this book helped trainers and teachers to realise their own learning aims, and possibly to surprise themselves and each other by how much can be learnt and achieved together. And, last but not least, while not forgetting that teacher education and development is a very important, serious matter, I also hope that this book helps trainers and teachers to experience the excitement of learning, *and* to have some fun. They deserve it!

Further reading

The following texts have been particularly useful in preparing this book, and/or are particularly recommended to trainers. Full details are given in the bibliography at the end of the book.

Eraut, The Acquisition and Use of Educational Theory by Beginning Teachers (a clear, stimulating article on the relationship between theory and practice).

Fullan, *Change Forces: Probing the Depths of Educational Reform* (one of the most stimulating books on education I have read for some time).

Griffiths and Tann, Using Reflective Practice to Link Personal and Public Theories.

Head and Taylor, *Readings in Teacher Development* (a book in Heinemann's excellent Teacher Development series).

Hopkins, *A Teacher's Guide to Classroom Research* (a book of great clarity I still go back to again and again, after using it for over ten years; particularly relevant for classroom research with school-aged children).

Lamb, The Consequences of INSET (it is a good idea to check *English Language Teaching Journal* regularly, where this article was published, or to check back issues, as each issue usually contains an accessible article on teacher education and development, usually with an international focus).

Pollard and Tann, *Reflective Teaching in the Primary School* (comprehensive, full of INSET ideas for mainstream education that can be adapted to other contexts).

Richards and Lockhart, *Reflective Teaching in Second Language Classrooms.*

Roberts, *Language Teacher Education* (an authoritative overview of the theory and practice of language teacher education, with useful case studies highlighting effective practice; it has been very helpful in providing a foundation to the Introduction to this book, and is strongly recommended to readers).

Wajnryb, *Classroom Observation Tasks* (excellent ideas related to observation and feedback, not dealt with in this book).

Williams and Burden, *Psychology for Language Teachers: A Social Constructivist Approach* (a valuable survey of learning theories).

Woodward, *Ways of Training* (ideas for livening up one's training).

1 Exploring teachers' knowledge

Introduction

Chapter 1 lies deliberately outside the investigating cycle of Chapters 2–5: (see Figure 1.1). A central issue related to Chapter 1 is that teachers bring with them on to an in-service teacher training programme a wealth of tacit individual and collective knowledge related to educating, teaching and learning in the form of personal theories (see also 'Teachers' professional knowledge', on p. 4). The tasks in this chapter therefore help teachers to explore and articulate their personal theories, as a foundation to building

Figure 1.1   The investigating cycle in Teachers in Action

on them, or developing them. This helps both teachers and trainers to gain access to this knowledge in order to harness it for other tasks, as well as developing teachers' ability to theorise.

Many of the tasks in Chapter 1 are challenging in that they require teachers to think in sometimes quite abstract terms about general issues related to educating, teaching and learning which may seem rather remote from the hustle and bustle of school and classrooms. Typical issues addressed are 'How can we learn together?', 'Why teach English?' and 'Reflecting about the nature of change in education'. Of course, by placing these challenging tasks at the beginning of the book, I am signalling to the reader how much importance I attach to them. In this respect, in my own training work, I take a kind of two-track approach. On the one hand, I seek opportunities to do some of the challenging tasks in Chapter 1, with teachers theorising about more abstract, general concerns. On the other hand, I demonstrate plenty of more concrete, practical activities based on specific classroom issues – located in other chapters in this book – as well as encouraging teachers to theorise about these activities. In this way, I metaphorically zig-zag from the general level to the specific level in a manner which I have found to be productive and generative, and which significantly helps teachers to construct a kind of scaffolding around which to structure their development. However, I am not necessarily suggesting that trainers using this book also work in the way I have described above; the tasks are designed to be generative, providing ways for teachers to explore their own knowledge, but I envisage trainers using the material in other, different ways which are appropriate to them. Whether, when or how trainers choose to use the tasks in Chapter 1 will depend on many factors, including whether there is enough trust in the group for participating teachers to reveal their personal theories about their work, and whether teachers are prepared to focus on the so-called theory of education, teaching and learning. Nevertheless, I hope that trainers will feel they *are* able to use the tasks, with patience and with sensitivity to the difficulties involved, as the processes these tasks promote are vital to bringing about genuine change.

Task 1.1 Getting to know each other: What do we expect from the training programme?

BACKGROUND FOR THE TRAINER

This task is designed for use at or near the beginning of a training programme, and includes Worksheets 1, 2 and 3, on pp. 225–8, as well as Options 1, 2 and 3 (see below), all of which trainers can choose from according to their needs and training contexts.

Getting a training programme off to a positive start is self-evidently important for its successful development, and there are certain needs common to all programmes, regardless of where and when they take place, and who is participating. For example, the trainer(s) will need to find out as much about the teachers as is realistically possible before or at the beginning of a programme; the trainer and the participating teachers, who are perhaps a little nervous, will need to get to know each other, to learn each other's names, and to begin to get used to working together. In addition to this, the teachers will want to find out how the programme is organised. This task offers a simple framework for meeting some of these needs.

TASK AIMS

- to enable teachers to describe and make explicit aspects of their own professional background, experience and day-to-day realities at school
- to enable trainers and teachers to find out about each other's background, experience and expectations regarding the training programme

PREPARATION

Have copies of the programme syllabus ready for the teachers, if there is one, and if they do not already have a copy of it.

PROCEDURE

Allow at least 45 minutes for this task.

1 Ask whether any of the teachers know each other. If they do, invite one to briefly tell the group something about their colleague, explaining that you wish to continue the process of getting to know each other by means of this task.
2 Follow the instructions on Worksheet 1. Allow about 20 minutes for Part 1, and 20 minutes for Part 2. Part 2 is a so-called information gap activity, where in pairs the teachers tell each other something about themselves that the other does not know. Ask the teachers to interview someone they do not already know, and to interact orally, rather than reading each other's completed column 1 on the worksheet.
3 After completion of Part 2 of Worksheet 1, invite one or two pairs to volunteer to report briefly to the whole group about their findings. Focus the feedback on the instructions in Part 2 ('something you have in common' etc.), but especially the teachers' expectations for the training programme. Write a shortlist of the teachers' expectations on the blackboard,[1] for example, 'We want to find out about new teaching ideas'; comment on these, and explain about the content of the programme, its

[1] Worksheet 2 may also be used by trainers and teachers after they have used Worksheet 1, enabling them to make a summary of the discussion.

organisation, etc., ideally referring to the programme syllabus for this purpose. Collect in the completed worksheets if you wish, to find out about the teachers' backgrounds, and return them at a later date. If you intend to do this, tell the teachers before they write.

Note: Worksheet 1 has a clear professional focus. You may, however, prefer a non-professional emphasis, by eliciting information about the teachers of a more personal nature (e.g. about their families, interests, likes, dislikes, favourite restaurants, music, etc.). This may be perceived by the teachers as a welcome relief from talking about aspects of their schools, and enable them to get to know each other more personally.

OPTION 1

Worksheet 2 provides a simpler version of Worksheet 1. Allow a total of about 40 minutes for the teachers to use the whole worksheet, and to process it.

1 Ask teachers in pairs to discuss the same topics as on Worksheet 1 (the subjects they teach, how long they have been teaching English, etc.); write these topics on the blackboard for ease of reference. Follow the instructions on Worksheet 2, with each pair of teachers using one worksheet. Ask the teachers to write their names and the date in the spaces provided on the worksheet. Allow 20 minutes.

2 After about 20 minutes, and where appropriate, display the completed worksheets on the training classroom wall. Invite teachers to stand up and read the worksheets, rather like looking at pictures in an exhibition, comparing their own worksheet with those of the other teachers. (Getting teachers up from their chairs and encouraging them to move around freely may relieve some initial nervousness.) Allow about 10–15 minutes.

3 Having asked teachers to sit down at an appropriate moment, focus a follow-up discussion on Worksheet 2, especially point 4, exactly as was done for Worksheet 1.

OPTION 2

The focus of Worksheet 3 is less factual and more exploratory than Worksheets 1 and 2. Allow about 30 minutes for teachers to complete this worksheet and to process it.

1 Use the partially completed sentences to elicit teachers' responses, following the instructions on the worksheet. Teachers could also complete the worksheet at home. Allow about 15 minutes.

2 Display the completed worksheets on the training room wall, as for Worksheet 2, and/or collect in the completed worksheets, and read them. Allow about 10–15 minutes. See the space at the bottom of the worksheet for trainers (or other teachers) to write encouraging remarks

related to the content of the completed worksheet. Later return the worksheets to the teachers.

An example of a completed Worksheet 3 is provided in Section 6.6.

OPTION 3 'FIND SOMEONE WHO...', BASED ON TEACHERS' BACKGROUNDS

Produce your own personalised 'Find someone who...' worksheet, based on the information obtained from Worksheets 1, 2 or 3, for use in a subsequent training session. See Task 3.3 for an example of a 'Find someone who...' procedure.

Task 1.2 How do I learn? How can we learn together?

BACKGROUND FOR THE TRAINER

This task includes Worksheets 4 and 5 on pp. 229–30.

It would be a mistake to assume that teachers attending a training programme have no experience of professional learning. Teachers also learn teaching, or about teaching, in very many ways (see Section 6.7). So trainers should try to relate the training programme to other ways in which teachers may already be learning, and support such ways of learning.

TASK AIMS

- to encourage teachers to reflect on how they learn about teaching, and to consider the effectiveness of these and other ways of learning
- to help the trainer to find out about the teachers' current ways of learning
- to help teachers to select relevant procedures for their own professional development as a group

PROCEDURE

Allow a total of about one hour for this task.

1 Ask the teachers about ways they have personally learnt about teaching, eliciting one or two examples, and writing these on the blackboard. Discuss briefly.
2 Follow the instructions on Worksheet 4. Allow about 10 minutes for the whole worksheet. Where appropriate, also refer teachers to the ways listed in Section 6.7. Encourage teachers to add to this list where possible. Later, you may also collect in Worksheet 4, if you wish, for your information, returning them to the teachers later.

3 After teachers have completed Worksheet 4 individually, have them form small sub-groups (a maximum of four teachers). Follow the instructions on Worksheet 5. Ask each sub-group to read and discuss each other's completed Worksheet 4. Emphasise to the teachers that they select the *main* ways in which they have learnt, and which will be effective when working *together* on the programme. Allow about 20–30 minutes.

4 Ask each sub-group to exchange their completed Worksheet 5 with that of another sub-group, look at it and compare it with their own. Ask the teachers to consider the following questions while doing so:

Are the completed worksheets similar or different?
Which ways of learning do both sub-groups have in common?

Allow about 10 minutes. When teachers have had enough time to read the worksheets, in a whole group discussion try to agree on a set/short-list of, say, 3–5, ways of working together, the content of which you and all the teachers agree to.

5 A final worksheet (using Worksheet 5 as a framework) may then be produced by the trainer, as a working agenda for the whole group. It can be displayed prominently in the training room, or copied by or for each teacher, for consultation when the effectiveness of a programme is evaluated. For example, teachers could later look back at this worksheet, as is required for Task 5.2. They can compare the suggestions the worksheet contains with the ways in which the group has actually worked together. Are they the same? Are they different?

FURTHER READING

See Roberts, *Language Teacher Education*, in particular, Chapter 1.1, 'Theories of learning and implications for teacher education'.

Task 1.3   Investigating: an overview

BACKGROUND FOR THE TRAINER

This task includes Worksheets 6 and 7 on pp. 231–3, and Option 4 (see below).

One of the specific aims of *Teachers in Action* is 'to help trainers and teachers to explore, *investigate* and understand better what happens in schools and classrooms as an on-going process throughout their careers'. A general way of defining 'investigating', as I understand and use the term, is that it is an open, questioning way of looking at education, teaching and learning, such that engaging in any of the tasks or any combination of tasks in this book constitutes investigating. Another more specific sense of the term refers to helping teachers develop their confidence and skills to investigate and understand better what happens in schools and classrooms, which I refer to as 'investigating in class'. This task, therefore, can be used for introducing teachers to the different stages of the process of investigating in *Teachers in Action*, as defined above, or more fully in the Introduction.

TASK AIM

• to give teachers an overview of 'investigating' their own professional practice

PROCEDURE

Allow about 30–40 minutes for this task.

1 Write a definition of the term 'investigating' on the blackboard, or dictate it to the teachers (use the information above or in the Introduction). Ask teachers what benefits there might be for them as teachers in investigating their work as defined above. For example, 'teachers are the protagonists in their own professional development and educational change', 'teachers collaborate with trainers and other colleagues', or 'teachers improve their practice' (for other possible answers, see the Introduction).

2 Follow the instructions on Worksheet 6. Allow about 10 minutes for Part 1, and about 10 minutes for Part 2. Finally, check the responses to Worksheet 6 with the whole group, trying to agree on an order of the different stages which everyone accepts. See Section 6.8 for one possible sequence. If teachers suggest a different sequence, discuss its merits. If appropriate, you may also refer teachers to Figure 1.1 for the purpose of clarification.

3 In order to move away from a general overview of investigating, and to begin to focus on the specific stages of investigating as described on Worksheet 6, discuss the questions from Part 2 of the worksheet:

Which of the eight stages do you think would be the easiest / most difficult? Why?

You could also discuss a particular stage in more detail if the group expresses an interest in doing so. For example, Stage E, 'Find a colleague(s) to work with'; you could start off on a positive note by pointing out that the group of teachers already provides colleagues to work with. A relevant question to address might be:

How can we share our ideas?

See also Task 1.2. Another possible action point would be to select a task from Chapter 2 in order to identify a topic for investigating.

FURTHER READING

See the suggestions at the end of the Introduction if you wish to read more about action research or classroom research, etc. Where appropriate, of course, you can recommend suitable reading to teachers.

OPTION 4 OVERVIEW OF INVESTIGATING: MATCHING STAGE HEADINGS TO THEIR DESCRIPTIONS

Instead of using Worksheet 6, with its jumbled sequence of stages, use Worksheet 7, where the headings for each stage have been omitted. Follow the instructions on Worksheet 7.

1 Give the teachers the missing worksheet headings by writing them on the blackboard. They then read the headings and match them to the corresponding descriptions of the stages. Ask the teachers to write the headings in the corresponding blank spaces. Allow about 10 minutes for teachers to complete the worksheet.
2 Check the sequencing of the stages of investigating with the whole group. See Section 6.8 for the 'key'.
3 Follow this up by selecting another task from Chapter 1, or elsewhere.

Task 1.4 'It's quite obvious the gardener's a teacher': exploring teachers' metaphors

BACKGROUND FOR THE TRAINER

This task includes Worksheet 8 on p. 234, and Option 5 (see below).

For Task 1.4, teachers are required to select and draw metaphors concerning aspects of educating, teaching and learning, as both a fun activity and a serious exploration into the 'expressions, meanings and organising ideas which underpin teachers' ways of thinking' (Griffiths and Tann, 1992: 75). As part of the fun, therefore, trainers should not underestimate the importance of the image or the visual aspect of the task. The resulting drawings provide a tangible focus for what might otherwise be rather general talk, as well as making attractive displays for the training room wall.

Teachers use images and metaphors when talking to each other or to their learners about their work, without even thinking about it. In this respect, I agree with the following statement:

> *Images – and the metaphors that help identify them – far from trivialising the search for alternative approaches, offer teacher educators a valuable tool: they are a powerful – perhaps the most powerful – force for change, and should be of critical interest to those whose business is educational change.*

(Thornbury, 1991: 197)

In what specific ways might images or metaphors be of critical interest to trainers and teachers? I believe that they help:

- teachers to see, or to re-frame, the very familiar world of schools and classrooms from different perspectives
- to promote lively, memorable discussions about education, teaching and learning
- trainers to find out about the type of language teachers use to talk about their work, as explained by Griffiths and Tann:

> *the notion of image, as it relates to metaphors, can be a powerful way into the expressions and meanings and the organising ideas which underpin our way of thinking about teaching and learning.... The images and allusions that surround key words of a practice are essential to the thinking and understanding which will form future actions.*

(1992: 75)

By way of illustration, see the above example of a gardening metaphor for the teaching and learning process, produced by a small group of teachers. In Section 6.9.1, there is the transcription of a discussion related to this metaphor led by one of the teachers.

TASK AIMS

- to help teachers to consider and discuss the appropriateness of different metaphors for aspects of educating, teaching and learning

- to help teachers to begin to articulate, understand and discuss their personal theories of educating, teaching and learning

PREPARATION

For this task you will need large (A3) sheets of paper, one sheet for every group of three or four teachers, as well as plenty of coloured pens.

PROCEDURE

Allow a total of about 90 minutes for this task.

1 In a brief whole-group discussion, show the group the drawing of the teacher as a gardener, and ask them to suggest what they think the teacher is thinking or saying. Prompt discussion about the roles of the teachers, the learners, etc., in educating, teaching and learning, by using the following types of question:

What role does the teacher have here? (A gardener.)

If the teacher is a gardener, what's the classroom? (A garden.)

How would you describe the processes which take place there? (The learners are plants; growth is slow, requiring sunshine and water, etc.)

Establish that the gardener, garden, etc. are examples of metaphors, representing different aspects of educating, teaching and learning. Ask the teachers whether they see their school or classroom as a garden.

2.1 Follow the instructions and example on Worksheet 8. Use Worksheet 8 to fill in information about and focus on the gardening metaphor, by copying it on to the blackboard or photocopying it on to an overhead transparency.

2.2 Ask teachers to think of their own metaphors, and share them in groups or pairs, allowing them about 5 minutes to do so. Use the grid on Worksheet 8 to elicit, record and discuss other metaphors suggested by the teachers. See also Section 6.9.2 for some examples. Perhaps encourage teachers to consider outlandish metaphors (e.g. the classroom as a hairdressing salon), for fun, although, of course, the activity is serious!

3 In sub-groups of three or four, teachers select an appropriate metaphor from the list compiled by using Worksheet 8, and illustrate/draw it on a large sheet of paper (e.g. A3 size). While the groups are in the process of selecting, monitor the activity carefully, trying to ensure, where possible, that different metaphors are chosen by each sub-group, so as to provide for variety. When drawing their metaphor, teachers may use different coloured pens, speech bubbles, captions, etc. in order to bring their drawing to life and to explain the different parts of the drawing. (See example of the gardening metaphor above.) Allow about 40–45 minutes for this.

4 When they have finished their drawings, ask teachers to pin them up on the training room wall. They then stand up and mill around, looking at the different drawings, as in an art exhibition. Where appropriate, representatives from sub-groups may volunteer to comment on and explain their drawing to the group, with the other teachers standing or sitting around it, asking questions about the metaphor in question. Allow at least 15–20 minutes for this.

5 Leave the completed grid for Worksheet 8, and the illustrated metaphors, on the training walls, allowing the group to refer back to them in subsequent training sessions, as and when appropriate. Teachers may also be encouraged to look out for, collect and share other metaphors that they come across in their reading, etc., as the training programme progresses, adding these to the original grid list.

OPTION 5 DIFFERENT WAYS OF USING METAPHORS

1 Encourage teachers to focus on metaphors for other related aspects of educating, teaching and learning, such as: the school, a lesson, the language learning process, language, educational change, teacher education and development, new teaching ideas, etc. See Section 6.9.2 for some examples.

2 Audio-record the discussion which takes place while teachers are looking at the illustrated metaphors exhibited on the training room walls, for your own future reference, and that of the teachers. See Section 6.9.1 for a sample discussion.

Task 1.5 Mapping the whole: developing conceptual frameworks for educating, teaching and learning

BACKGROUND FOR THE TRAINER

This task includes Worksheet 9 on p. 235, and Option 6 (see below); it is particularly suited for use at or near the beginning of a training programme.

I can trace the development of this task back to a need I felt while participating on a course as a learner to relate the individual components of the course to each other, as well as locating them all on a mental map. How, for example, did the component 'syllabus design' relate to 'testing', and how could these be located on the rather incomplete, fragmented map in my head? This mental map is what I now call a 'conceptual framework'. This task encourages teachers to make explicit – by committing themselves to paper – the mental frameworks of 'concepts' related to education, teaching and learning (where the term 'concept' is understood to mean an idea related to a particular subject or a particular view of that subject). As a result, teachers will also gain more intellectual control over concepts, and be able to use them more effectively throughout a training programme. Where appropriate, the task may be repeated at a later stage of the training programme, allowing the original frameworks to be modified by, for example, adding new under-standings and meanings acquired by teachers, or relocating concepts.

TASK AIMS

- to develop teachers' capacity to theorise and to prepare them for articulating their personal theories of educating, teaching and learning
- to help teachers to anticipate, organise and use key concepts related to a training programme

PREPARATION

Before the training session, select, say, 20–25 key concepts related to your training programme. See Section 6.10.1, for a sample list of concepts. Write the concepts on to sets of 20–25 small cards, so that there is one complete set for each sub-group of three or four teachers (plus 5 blank cards per group). You will also need one large sheet of A3-sized paper for each sub-group, reusable adhesive, sticky tape, etc.

PROCEDURE

Allow a total of about 45 minutes for this task.

1 Explain that you have made sets of cards which feature key concepts for the training programme, referring the teachers to the training pro-gramme syllabus, if appropriate. You may also ask teachers what the key concepts might be before you tell them.

2 Give each sub-group a set of the same 20–25 cards, on which the key concepts are written. Follow the instructions on Worksheet 9. Monitor the group work, double-checking that teachers understand the concepts you have included. Allow at least 30 minutes for Part 1.

3 When the teachers have completed Part 1 of the worksheet, they may move around the room looking at the different frameworks laid out on the tables. For Part 2, let the activity run its own natural course, or bring it to an end at a suitable moment.

4 Once the teachers have sat down again, ask if the frameworks were similar or different, and discuss. Make sure the teachers have a copy of their own sub-group's framework to take away, for future reference. You may also decide to display the frameworks, or some of the frameworks, on the training room walls, for reference in future sessions, allowing the group to modify the frameworks in the light of new experience and learning. They could also be asked specifically to bring their frameworks

to a subsequent training session when evaluating the training programme, to consider any changes in them. In this sense, this task could be combined with others in Chapter 5, for example Task 5.4.

FURTHER READING

See Wright, *Investigating English*, pp. 9–10, for a similar approach to exploring the English language.

OPTION 6 DIFFERENT WAYS OF USING MAPS/CONCEPTUAL FRAMEWORKS

1 *Producing a whole-class map for educating, teaching and learning*
Prepare a large space on the training room wall, with a large sheet of paper or card; in the middle write 'Educating, teaching and learning in the language classroom', in large letters. In this space, teachers produce a conceptual framework which all the teachers agree with, by placing cards one by one on to the wall (by means of self-stick notes, reusable adhesive, or drawing pins).
Note: this option is very valuable and thought-provoking, leading to much heated discussion, but it may take a long time!

2 *Evaluating published conceptual frameworks*
As well as eliciting teachers' own conceptual frameworks, show teachers ones which already exist, such as Richards and Rodgers (1982: 165), 'Method: approach, design and procedure, a framework for the systematic description and comparison of methods', or others that you know of. See the Richards and Rodgers model in Section 6.10.2.

3 *Producing maps for teacher education and development*
Teachers may produce frameworks describing the process of their own professional development, or learning, as well as, or instead of, educating, teaching and learning, comparing them with published models, such as Wallace's 'Reflective model for teacher education' (1991: 15). See the Wallace reflective model in Section 6.10.3.

Encourage the teachers to comment on such published frameworks critically from their own experience, and/or to modify them.

Task 1.6 Why teach English? Reflecting on the goals of educating, teaching and learning in the language classroom

BACKGROUND FOR THE TRAINER

This task includes Worksheets 10 and 11 on pp. 236–7, and Options 7 and 8 (see below).

It is perhaps axiomatic that an important part of effective educating, teaching and learning is that teachers are clear about the long-term goals, as well as the general and specific aims, of their professional activity, and that they able to plan their work accordingly. Such planning might be reflected specifically in terms of curricula, syllabuses, schemes of work (planning over periods of months and weeks) and lesson plans. Sometimes, however, teachers are not clear about, or have forgotten, what they wish to achieve by teaching their subject. So this task provides a structure for groups of teachers to reflect on and discuss the general, long-term goals of their work, and to decide where they agree or, indeed, disagree. Teachers – even those working within the same school – may have different ideas concerning the goals of foreign language teaching and the place of language teaching within the curriculum as a whole. 'Disagreeing' in teacher development, in this sense, I feel is very important, as supported by Fullan, who states that 'educators are particularly susceptible to groupthink' (1993: 82), where 'groupthink' is defined as 'the uncritical acceptance and/or suppression of dissent in going along with group decisions' (ibid. 82). I do not wish to suggest that trainers deliberately provoke disagreement or dissent, but I find the following advice on this issue offered by Fullan sensible: 'Taking a questioning stance, especially at the early stages of a change initiative, is healthy not heretical' (ibid. 83).

TASK AIMS

- to help teachers to consider and to clarify the goals of educating, teaching and learning in the language classroom and their place in the curriculum, deciding what they agree on and what they disagree on
- to encourage teachers and trainers to explore and exploit official curricular documents, where appropriate

PROCEDURE

Allow about one hour for this task.

1 Write 'Why teach English?' on the blackboard and, in a brief general discussion, ask the teachers to describe the role of English teaching in the school curriculum in their situation, eliciting one or two examples, and writing these on the blackboard. Show or read them either or both of the statements which follow, made by two student teachers, inviting comments from your teachers' perspectives:

> *I hope my contribution to teaching, along with other good teachers' contributions, will help result in a better society for our future. I care about children and the way that children are learning.*
>
> (Fullan, 1993: 10)

I've always thought that if I could go into a classroom and make a
difference in one kid's life...then that's what I am here for.

(Fullan, 1993: 11)

Ask the teachers if they think of their work as 'making a difference' to their learners' lives, or helping to produce a better society. See also Worksheet 10, for information about other possible reasons for teaching English, and the extract from 'A curriculum for the future' (Wragg, 1997: 22) in 6.11.1.

Note: much of the content for Worksheet 10 is adapted from *Core Curriculum, Foreign Languages, Primary and Secondary Education* (Ministry of Education and Science, 1995: 27–33).

2 Follow the instructions for Worksheet 10; allow about 30 minutes for its completion.

3 Ask for feedback from the sub-groups once they have completed Worksheet 10, and draw up a list of what the whole group agrees or disagrees about, either on the blackboard or by using Worksheet 11. Follow the instructions on Worksheet 11; allow about 15 minutes for its completion. This worksheet may be used to record the whole group's choices for their priorities, or indeed the sub-groups' choices, following the use of Worksheet 10. It may also be used for other topics; simply write the name of the topic in the space provided on the worksheet. Teachers may then take home a photocopy of the completed worksheet, or copy one into their own notebooks by hand, for future reference. Alternatively, display the completed worksheets prominently on the training room wall.

COMBINING TASKS

This task leads on neatly to Task 2.2, in which teachers reflect about their ideas and priorities concerning educating, teaching and learning, but in greater detail. See also the sample of a summary feedback letter in Task 3.5.

FURTHER READING

Fullan, *Change Forces*, Chapter 2, 'Moral Purpose and Change Agentry'
White, *The ELT Curriculum: Design, Innovation and Management*, Chapter 3, 'Language Curriculum: Values and Options'
Wragg, *The Cubic Curriculum*. See extract in Section 6.11.1, entitled 'A curriculum for the future', from Chapter 1 of this book

OPTION 7 CONSULTING LOCAL OFFICIAL CURRICULUM DOCUMENTS

If you have copies of local official curriculum documents related to the goals and aims of educating, teaching and learning in the language classroom, where these are available, or copies of syllabuses for the local context or for particular schools (teachers may of course also have access to such documents), these can be employed usefully. Where appropriate, copy extracts from such documents for the teachers to examine. You could show these to teachers either before or after they use Worksheet 10, in order to tailor the discussion more closely to the local context. Two example curriculum documents are shown in Sections 6.11.2 and 6.11.3.

OPTION 8 PYRAMID DISCUSSION

For this option, I will imagine that there are 16 teachers in the whole training group, and that teachers are already working in sub-groups of four with Worksheet 10. Once the teachers have finished the worksheet in their sub-groups, ask them to:

1 Join up with another sub-group so that all the sub-groups are now working in groups of eight teachers, and compare their choices made for the worksheet with those of the other sub-group. Together they then select **five reasons for teaching English that both sub-groups agree about**.

2 Coming together in the whole group of 16 teachers, this time try to select **five reasons that the whole group agrees about**.

Task 1.7 Are we speaking the same language? Understanding general terms related to educating, teaching and learning

BACKGROUND FOR THE TRAINER

This task includes Worksheets 12 and 13 on pp. 238–9.

Naturally, teachers are familiar with the world of schools and classrooms, and probably feel comfortable with the language they use to talk about this world, in the staffroom, for example. However, the so-called academic discourse of public theory found in professional books and journals or heard at teachers' conferences may be unfamiliar, confusing or even alienating to teachers. Trainers can underestimate teachers' difficulty in making sense of such academic terms in English, and perhaps in their own language, too. Moving from one type of discourse to another, from an informal staffroom to academic discourse, for example, requires much learning and interpretation. But in a more immediate sense, a group of teachers learning together also needs a metalanguage, enabling them to 'speak the same language', in order to share and discuss ideas clearly and effectively, and to interpret and gain intellectual control over what are often new terms and concepts. This task provides a practical, supportive framework to help teachers with such a challenge.

TASK AIMS

- to help teachers to agree on, understand and use selected general terms and concepts related to education, teaching and learning in English
- to encourage teachers to collect key terms related to relevant aspects of education, teaching and learning in the form of glossaries
- to develop reference skills such as the systematic recording of information related to professional reading (noting sources, publication, author, page reference, etc.)

PROCEDURE

Allow about 40 minutes for this task (excluding Worksheet 13).

1 Ask teachers whether they can suggest examples of professional terms in use in English or the teachers' mother tongue, and which are important for schools, teachers and learners. (Think of some topical terms yourself, in case the teachers do not contribute any.) Write one or two terms on the blackboard and try to define them with the group. (Later, use the space at the bottom of Worksheet 12 to enter such terms, if appropriate.) Explain that it is important that certain key terms, such as the ones focused on in the worksheet, are understood by everybody, if the group is to work together effectively. See also the sample list of concepts in Section 6.10.1, used for Task 1.5.

2 Follow the instructions on Worksheet 12, allowing about 30 minutes for its completion (including checking). When the teachers have completed Part 1, check the correct answers with the whole group. Encourage teachers to try to use these terms in order to talk about their own experience. Alternatively, use the format of Worksheet 12, but generate your own activity by selecting terms that are particularly suited to your situation. See the key to Worksheet 12 in Section 6.12, for information.

3 Follow the instructions on Worksheet 13. Teachers can be encouraged to make personal records of new key terms that they encounter in their reading or from other sources, by using Worksheet 13. Alternatively, teachers may simply write their glossaries in their notebook.

3.1 Agree on an appropriate, uniform format for recording the bibliographical information for the worksheet with the group. See also Section 6.20.1 for further information about bibliographies.

3.2 Where appropriate, ask teachers to complete a personal glossary worksheet by a particular date, for example after reading methodology books; or teachers can complete a certain number of worksheets regularly over a certain period of time, say, once a month.

3.3 In a subsequent training session, these worksheets could then be shared with other colleagues, with teachers explaining why they think the terms selected are important for schools, teachers and learners.

Instead of personal glossaries, a blank worksheet(s) can be kept on the training room wall, for teachers to record terms on, as and when they are discovered, as a group glossary.

COMBINING TASKS

See Task 3.7 for a further idea for helping teachers to make sense of terminology.

FURTHER READING

You are recommended to consult published glossaries such as Seaton (1982) and Richards, Platt and Weber (1985), both of which are general in focus, or Wallace (1991: 44–7), Lightbown and Spada (1993: 119–25), and Pinker (1996: 473–83), all of which have a specific focus. Of course, you may use other glossaries that you know of. Encourage teachers to use these glossaries, too, where appropriate.

Task 1.8 Reflecting on the nature of change in education: What helps us to change?

BACKGROUND FOR THE TRAINER

This task helps teachers to reflect on the nature of change in education from their personal perspectives; it includes Worksheets 14 and 15 on pp. 240–2, and Option 9 (see below).

The theory and practice of change in education, whether change in the system as a whole, in teachers, learners or some other aspect, is a fundamental issue with regard to teacher education and development. No matter what aspects of educating, teaching and learning trainers and teachers concern themselves with on a training programme, the notion of change is never very far away. See also the Introduction, 'Change and teacher learning', as well as Task 1.9, which is closely related thematically to the present task.

TASK AIMS

- to help teachers to make sense of relevant aspects of the theory and practice of educational change
- to help trainers and teachers to explore their attitudes to educational change and consider their own future role in promoting it

PREPARATION

Prepare a pile of slips of paper before the training session (each measuring about a fifth of a sheet of A4); you will need enough slips for each teacher to have one or two.

PROCEDURE

Allow about 60–75 minutes for the whole task.

1 Ask teachers if they can think of any important changes that have taken place in the educational system of their country or in their schools in the last year, or the last few years. Be ready to give examples, in case the teachers are not able to suggest any. Focus on such aspects as what the changes were, why, when and how they came about, and how the teachers themselves were affected. Where appropriate, you may also explain and discuss the following key terms:

change 'Change is considered to be any alteration in something between time 1 and time 2. Change can occur spontaneously and does not involve conscious planning or intention'. (White, 1988: 114)

innovation 'an idea, object or practice perceived as new by an individual or individuals, which is intended to bring about improvement in relation to desired objectives, which is fundamental in nature and which is planned and deliberate'. (Nicholls, cited in White, 1988: 114; see also Task 1.9)

change agents refers to the people who act as a link between different participants involved in change in a system. For example, a teacher might be a link between learners and a school director, and therefore, a change agent.

top down refers to change promoted by a change agent who holds a higher position in the system hierarchy. For example, a college of education teacher trainer tells a student teacher the 'right way' to correct repeated oral mistakes in class during her initial training.

bottom up refers to change which is brought about by those directly involved and affected, e.g. teachers.

tides of change refers to tendencies, or shifts in society at large, which may have an influence on a system. For example, the phenomenon of information technology is currently exerting a major influence on the way we live, communicate, and learn.

2.1 Follow the instructions on Worksheet 14, allowing about 45–50 minutes for its completion. Allow the teachers time to read through the quotations fairly quickly, and check that they understand the gist of each one before they begin to respond. For Part 2, give pairs of teachers two or three slips of paper to write their suggestions on. You may also need to leave a little time to answer any questions from the teachers related to the quotations.

2.2 Collect in the teachers' completed slips, read them immediately and write the factors suggested by the teachers on the blackboard. Then use Worksheet 15 to record the final list agreed with the teachers. This worksheet (or, if appropriate, a transparency or poster) may be copied for the teachers to take away for reference, or displayed on the training room wall. See also Section 6.13 for an example of a list of factors which will help teachers to change and/or innovate, produced by a group of teachers.

COMBINING TASKS

Worksheet 15 can also be used for Task 1.9. See also Task 5.5, which encourages teachers to consider realistic strategies for their future professional development after the completion of a training programme.

FURTHER READING

Fullan, *Change Forces*
Wragg, *The Cubic Curriculum*, in particular, 'How do schools and teachers change?', pp. 111–15

OPTION 9 MY OWN FUTURE ROLE IN PROMOTING PROFESSIONAL CHANGE AND/OR INNOVATION

Ask teachers to choose one (or more) of the points on the completed Worksheet 15, which they feel especially important or relevant to their own school, etc., and to write about it from their perspective. Encourage teachers to be constructive, by considering ways in which they could help personally help. For a recommended procedure for this option, see Task 3.5.

Task 1.9 Innovation in our schools: How can we help to promote it?

BACKGROUND FOR THE TRAINER

This task includes Worksheet 16 on p. 243, and Option 10 (see below).

No matter what aspects of educating, teaching and learning trainers and teachers concern themselves with on a programme, the notion of change is never far away: see the Introduction, 'Change and teacher learning'. This task focuses on a particular aspect of change: 'innovation', that is to say, change of a planned and deliberate nature, in the context of teachers' schools. See also Task 1.8, which is closely related thematically to the present task.

TASK AIMS

- to help teachers to analyse an educational innovation they are familiar with
- to help teachers to consider their own future role in promoting innovation in education

PROCEDURE

Allow at least 50 minutes for this task, possibly over two training sessions.

1 In Session 1, define the term 'innovation' by showing the teachers the following quotation (or another suitable one that you know of). 'Innovation' is:

> an idea, object or practice perceived as new by an individual or individuals, which is intended to bring about improvement in relation to desired objectives, which is fundamental in nature and which is planned and deliberate.
>
> (Nicholls, cited in White, 1988: 114)

At this point you may wish to contrast this definition of 'innovation' with that of the term 'change' in Task 1.8, although, of course, you need not be too technical about distinguishing between 'change' and 'innovation' with the teachers.

2 Ask the teachers if they can suggest any important recent innovations that have taken place in education in their local context. Be ready to give examples, in case the teachers are not able to suggest any. Focus on such aspects as what the innovation was, why, when and how it was introduced, and who was involved.

3 Follow the instructions on Worksheet 16, allowing about 20–25 minutes for its completion. Ideally, ask teachers to complete the worksheet at home, by a certain date, for a future training session. See Section 6.14.1 for an example of a completed Worksheet 16 questionnaire, written by a teacher.

4.1 Before Session 2, collect in and read the completed worksheets, where appropriate, responding to points raised by the teachers, by writing in comments on the worksheets (see Introduction, 'Using the worksheets', for suggested strategies for doing this).

4.2 By way of summary, prepare a list of 'Factors which will help us to innovate', by collating the teachers' responses to Question 8 from

Worksheet 16. (You can use Worksheet 15, for this purpose.) See also Section 6.13 for an example of a list of factors which will help us to change and/or innovate.

5.1 In Session 2, give the teachers a copy of the list you have drawn up, inviting comments. If there is an example(s) of a particularly successful innovation that a teacher has been involved in personally, and that you have read about on a completed worksheet, perhaps ask the teacher in question to describe the innovation more fully for the group.

5.2 Discuss the following question:

What are the implications of our findings about innovation for our own future professional development and practice?

Suggest to teachers that they keep their copy of the list of factors in a safe place, in order to monitor any future developments in terms of change and innovation which they are involved in.

COMBINING TASKS

See Task 5.5, which encourages teachers to consider realistic strategies for their future professional development after the completion of a training programme.

FURTHER READING

White, *The ELT Curriculum*, in particular, Chapter 8, 'Language Curriculum Design: Process and Management', and Chapter 9, 'Innovation: Managing and Evaluating'.

OPTION 10 READING ABOUT LOCAL INNOVATION PROJECTS IN EDUCATION

1 Find an example from your local or national press, or educational journals and magazines, of projects promoting educational innovation (not necessarily directly related to language teaching and learning).

2 Ask the teachers to read and summarise the article, by focusing on the What?, Why?, Who?, When? and How? of the innovation in question.

See Section 6.14.2 for an example of such an article. Where appropriate, teachers may also look at the previously compiled list, 'Factors which will help us to change and/or innovate' (see above in Procedure), and modify it accordingly, in the light of the information from the article they have read. If two articles about innovations in the local context are available, put the teachers in pairs, asking each teacher to read one of the articles, and then report to their partner regarding the content of their own article. Invite teachers to confirm in which ways the projects are similar, and/or different. Of course, teachers themselves may be able to suggest articles to read.

2 Identifying topics to investigate

Introduction

The principal aim of all the tasks in Chapter 2 is to help trainers and teachers to identify topics for investigating (see Figure 2.1), for example by reflecting on and discussing their personal theories of educating, teaching and learning. Deciding which aspect(s) of educating, teaching and learning should form the content of a training programme is, naturally, an important issue. In this respect, *Teachers in Action* does not predetermine *what* trainers and teachers investigate, though it does provide suggestions as to how they may work together on the topics they themselves identify.

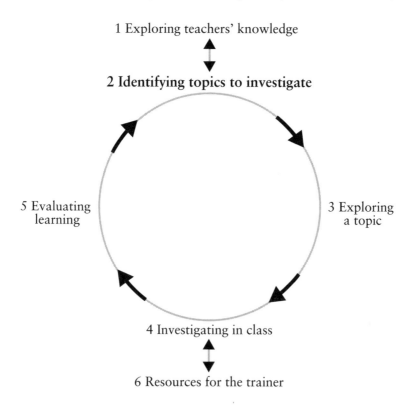

1 Exploring teachers' knowledge

2 Identifying topics to investigate

5 Evaluating learning

3 Exploring a topic

4 Investigating in class

6 Resources for the trainer

Figure 2.1   The investigating cycle in Teachers in Action

So who decides which aspects to investigate? The trainer? The teachers? Someone else? In reality, perhaps a mixture of all three. For example, a trainer may already have decided on the topics, or at least some of the topics for a training programme. This may be because the course sponsors or providers (those paying for the programme, e.g. a ministry) have particular requirements in this respect, or because the trainer knows from experience how teachers will best benefit. However, there is a danger that the content may, in the teachers' eyes, be 'imposed' insensitively and/or irrelevantly, even by a well-meaning trainer.

So, *Teachers in Action* assumes that the trainer is willing and able to leave space on a programme timetable for teachers themselves to select topics. The advantages of this are that teachers perceive the programme to be more relevant to their needs, and their sense of 'ownership' of the programme is enhanced.

However, this approach may prove difficult for trainers, especially those who are inexperienced, and this is for many reasons. For example, where should they start looking for topics? Chapter 2 provides the trainer with help in the form of starting points. These encourage the trainer and teachers to train their magnifying glass, so to speak, on where the teachers are at the moment: on their current personal theories, as well as their professional practice, their schools and classrooms. As a result, groups may draw up lists of general priorities, enabling them to go on to focus on these priorities in more detail, for example by considering practical recommendations for any given topic.

A further crucial question relates to what exactly constitutes a topic. How broadly or how narrowly should a topic be defined? These questions can be answered only by the group of teachers in question, although I wish to emphasise two points:

- suggestions for topics should, as far as possible, come from the teachers themselves, although you may guide the teachers or help them to define the topics
- once a general topic area has been identified, it should be broken down into more manageable, concrete aspects, for investigation. For example, the general topic of 'self-esteem' may be broken down into the following aspects: learner self-evaluation, listening to learners, learners taking risks, projects, considering attitudes when planning, praising learners, etc. (see Task 2.9 and the practical recommendations for enhancing learners' self-esteem in Section 6.23.2). Otherwise, the process of investigating can get out of hand; remember that 'small is beautiful'.

Finally, another emphasis in Chapter 2 is very much on teachers initially investigating a topic together as a group, or different aspects of the same topic in sub-groups, giving each other support and spreading the workload in the process. Of course, this does not exclude the possibility of teachers going on to investigate individually, especially when they have developed the necessary skills and attitudes to do so effectively.

Task 2.1 Examining critical incidents

BACKGROUND FOR THE TRAINER

This task includes Worksheets 17 and 18 on pp. 244–5.

Gaining access to teachers' beliefs, values and assumptions can be difficult, but 'critical incidents' provide a way forward in this respect. But what precisely is a 'criticial incident'? It may be defined as follows:

> The term 'critical incident' comes from history where it refers to some event or situation which marked a significant turning-point or change in the life of a person or an institution...The vast majority of critical incidents, however, are not at all dramatic or obvious: they are mostly straightforward accounts of very commonplace events that occur in routine professional practice which are critical in the rather different sense that they are indicative of underlying trends, motives and structures. These incidents appear to be 'typical' rather than 'critical 'at first sight, but are rendered critical through analysis.
>
> (Tripp, 1993: 24/25; my emphasis)

How precisely might critical incidents be used in teacher education and development, then? Critical incident techniques can be used to elicit teachers' contextualised knowledge. When asked to comment on such material, experienced teachers generally reveal a rich, episodic knowledge resource which is readily related to classroom situations (Calderhead, 1990: 158).

The starting point for creating a 'critical incident' is a commonplace event, an observation or comment that teachers make about their everyday practice. Tripp (1993: 18) gives examples, such as a teacher who says: 'John didn't finish his work today, must see that he learns to finish it.' Tripp suggests that, through systematic questioning about events, teachers are challenged on the premises of their comments, bringing to light their under-lying beliefs and values, allowing their personal theory to develop, as they understand the basis for their beliefs and modify them in the light of their professional learning in general. The questions employed are diagnostic, reflective, critical and practical in nature.

It is the move away from the immediately practical questions of *how* to do something towards *why* teachers do it that is the strength of using critical incidents. The fact that the incidents start with things that teachers them-selves have noticed ensures that the analysis is meaningful to them. The involvement of another person (a teacher or trainer) means that assumptions that an individual may be unaware of can be explored, and that the teacher can be brought to relate their incident to aspects of 'public' (as opposed to their personal) theory. The systematic nature of the questioning ensures that analysis of an event does not remain superficial, or insignificant, taking the teacher through a cycle of description of the event, explanation of it in its immediate context, and interpretation of it in a wider context.

TASK AIMS

- to encourage teachers to reflect on, exchange information about, and analyse their own critical incidents
- to help teachers to examine their assumptions about educating, teaching and learning
- to help teachers to organise and clarify elements of their personal theories of educating, teaching and learning, and to see connections between these elements

PROCEDURE

Allow a total of about 60–75 minutes for this task.

1 Describe an example of a critical incident from your own professional experience which 'called basic professional values into question, or raised questions of hidden assumptions' behind your way of working (Griffiths and Tann, 1992: 72). In order to structure your description, you may use the questions on Worksheet 17 as a general guide. For clarification, I include in Section 6.15.1 an example of a critical incident related to a Basque language class I attended with colleagues, for which I used the questions on Worksheet 17. After providing your own example of an incident, explain to the teachers that you have given them an example of a critical incident, possibly showing them or reading aloud Tripp's definition above.

2 Follow the instructions on Worksheet 17. Allow at least 20 minutes for Part 1, and 20 minutes for Part 2. Elicit teachers' critical incidents by using this worksheet. Check that the teachers understand the questions on the worksheet before they begin. See also the sample critical incident from a teacher in Section 6.15.2.

   Part 1: Teachers reflect on the question at the top of the worksheet in silence, so that each participant identifies an incident. Refer back to your own incident as an example, if the teachers are still not sure what is required. (Where appropriate, teachers may complete Part 1 at home for a subsequent session.)

   Part 2: Note that the prompt 'We now realise that…' on the worksheet may help if teachers are reluctant to contribute and need encouragement.

3 Set up a whole-group discussion by eliciting teachers' responses to the questions in Part 2 of the worksheet and writing (some of) them on the blackboard, or on a large sheet of paper. For example, the following new understandings were elicited from a group of teachers I worked with in this way:

We realise now that…
- *we underestimate learners' difficulties*
- *learners' needs change, therefore we need to change*
- *we should show learners how clever they are!*

4 This task might help teachers to identify a topic for investigation, for example, 'How can we help our learners to see how clever they are?', taken from the above list. See Worksheet 18, which can be used to record the group's choice of topics; the completed worksheet can then be displayed prominently in the training room. The group could then select a task from Chapter 3, for example Task 3.2, to focus in more detail on the topic identified. As an alternative follow-up activity, you could also ask teachers to write about their critical incidents, see the sample critical incident from a teacher in Section 6.15.2.

FURTHER READING

Tripp, *Critical Incidents in Teaching. Developing Professional Judgement.* This book inspired me to explore the potential of critical incidents.

Task 2.2 Effective educating, teaching and learning in the language classroom (1): What are our priorities?

BACKGROUND FOR THE TRAINER:

This task includes Worksheet 19 on p. 246, and can be combined profitably with Task 2.3.

> *No matter how concerned teachers may be with the immediate practicalities of the classroom, their techniques are based on some principle or other which is accountable to theory.*
>
> (Widdowson, 1984: 87; my emphasis)

The principles that Widdowson refers to form part of a teacher's personal theory of educating, teaching and learning, as discussed in the Introduction. Personal theories are defined by Tann as a 'set of beliefs, values, understandings and assumptions – the ways of thinking about the teaching profession' (1993: 55). It is important for teachers to uncover the principles, beliefs, values, understandings, assumptions, insights and priorities underlying their practice. This is part of teachers' general capacity to generate their own personal theories, or to theorise, defined by Eraut as the ability to acquire, refine, evaluate, and use theories in order to improve their practice (1994: 73).

When teachers uncover their principles, it helps them to:
• raise their existing knowledge, beliefs, etc. into consciousness;
• organise and clarify their knowledge, and assimilate new information

When theorising is undertaken in groups, as is the case for this task, it also:

- helps to reduce the potential anxiety experienced by individual teachers when focusing on theory on their own, particularly if they are unfamiliar with such activity
- develops the skill of listening to and understanding other teachers' ideas;
- provides a collective impetus towards individual teachers articulating their own individual theories (see Task 2.3)

TASK AIMS

- to help teachers to uncover and articulate their personal theories of educating, teaching and learning
- to encourage teachers to establish shared priorities
- to prepare individual teachers for establishing their own priorities for their future professional practice

PROCEDURE

Allow a total of about 90 minutes for this task.

1   Ask teachers what they understand by the term 'theory' related to language learning and teaching, and what relevance it has to their professional lives. (Allow teachers to let off steam a little at this point, if they wish!) Ensure that the teachers understand what is meant by the term *'personal theory'*, and suggest that there is always a reason why we do what we do in class, even though we may not think about it consciously.

2.1 Explain that teachers are going to discuss the following question in sub-groups, writing it on the blackboard:

Effective educating, teaching and learning in the language classroom: what are our priorities?

2.2 Draw a triangle on the blackboard, explaining that the educating, teaching and learning process can be reduced to an interaction between three basic elements: learners, the teacher and the curriculum / syllabus / teaching / materials / tasks: see Figure 1 in the Introduction. Note: of course, Figure 1 shows only one way of representing the process schematically, and is also necessarily a simplification of this process, but it does provide a starting point. For groups who have also completed Task 1.6, they may prefer to use their professional goals recorded on Worksheet 10 as an alternative starting point to this task.

3   Follow the instructions on Worksheet 19, allowing at least 40 minutes for its completion. With the co-operation of the teachers, decide which of three different elements each teacher is to focus on, that is to say,

the role played by: (a) learners, or (b) the teacher, or (c) the curriculum / syllabus / teaching materials / tasks and ask teachers to copy the corresponding element, e.g. 'Learners', into the blank space on the worksheet. (Refer them to the triangle diagram once again, if necessary, making sure they understand the terms 'curriculum', 'syllabus', etc.) Allocate the three elements mentioned above evenly among the participants. For Part 2, organise the teachers into sub-groups of three or four; if there are three sub-groups, each concentrates on one of the elements; if there are six, two sub-groups consider each element. Teachers can be asked to complete Part 1 at home in preparation for a future training session, allowing them to 'sleep on' the activity. Encourage teachers to express their priorities in terms of appropriate attitudes, behaviours, characteristics, skills, activities and techniques.

Note: the use of 'should' on the worksheet encourages teachers to express what they aspire to professionally in the future, as opposed to describing current practice; you may, however, prefer another emphasis. If necessary, elicit one or two examples of priorities before the teachers begin the group work. I have found that asking for 5–10 items on the worksheet works well, as it obliges teachers to select and prioritise, but you could request fewer. Make sure each teacher completes a worksheet. For information, see the sample responses to Worksheet 19, completed by a group of teachers, in Section 6.16.

4.1 On completion of Part 2, ask the teachers to form new sub-groups with representatives from each of the original sub-groups, and to read and compare their responses to the worksheet.

4.2 Explain that they should now select at least one high-priority item *for each of the three elements*. Encourage teachers to copy down what they have agreed in their sub-group for reference. Allow at least 20 minutes for this.

5 In a whole-group discussion, with the co-operation and agreement of the teachers, select one or more popular priorities from the previous discussions, for example 'Learners should be encouraged to self-evaluate'. These can be recorded on Worksheet 18, for example. Then address the question: 'In what practical ways can we achieve this?', possibly using Worksheet 27 for this purpose. A task from Chapter 3 could then be selected.

Task 2.3 Effective educating, teaching and learning in the language classroom (2): What are *my* priorities?

When we use the expression 'teaching principles', we are referring to a broad number of features or elements which take on an important role in the classroom; the students, the teachers, the syllabus and some external elements such as parents or educational authorities. These 'principles' have suffered an important change in recent years due to a new, modern way of considering the learning process. The students' role has turned into an active one, that is to say, our students are more involved in the activity of learning than we were. The teacher is not the centre of the world – considering the classroom as the world – any longer. From my point of view, it is worthwhile considering that most of us teachers weren't taught in this way and that a broad reflection has been made and must still be made among us to change both teaching beliefs and attitudes.

(extract from a teacher's pedagogic manifesto)

BACKGROUND FOR THE TRAINER

This task includes Worksheet 20 on p. 247, and Option 11 (see below).

Trainers are recommended to read and complete Task 2.2 before attempting Task 2.3, which helps *individual teachers* to reflect on and write about their own priorities for their future professional practice in the form of a 'pedagogic manifesto'. Worksheet 20 – completed for Task 2.3 – represents an intermediary, supportive link or stage between the group discussions held previously for Task 2.2 and a teacher's individual manifesto, which may differ in detail from the group perspective, as a result of personal histories, circumstances, teaching style, etc. It is my experience that teachers very much benefit from this intermediary stage as preparation for writing their manifesto.

TASK AIM

- to help teachers to organise and clarify their knowledge, and provide a record against which they may compare any future modifications, adjustments, realignments or additions in their personal theories and professional practice

PROCEDURE

1 Having completed Task 2.2, suggest to teachers that they interpret or fine-tune from their own personal viewpoint the priorities agreed on by the group of teachers, by writing a 'pedagogic manifesto'. See the brief extract from a teacher's manifesto reproduced above, or more of the manifesto in Section 6.17.

Note: writing a manifesto might be intimidating to teachers, as it lays them open to criticism from others. Tell the teachers it is important not to worry about whether their ideas are 'correct' – as *all* ideas are valid. Stress that the manifestos will not be criticised negatively, but that you may provide some constructive feedback on them, and that it is also acceptable and natural for them to wish to change their minds about their priorities at a later date.

2 Follow the instructions on Worksheet 20, allowing at least 30–40 minutes for its completion. The procedures for this task span a number of training sessions.

3 Collect the completed worksheets, take them away, read them and write in constructive comments in the space provided. Return the worksheets to the teachers in the next training session.

4 At home, teachers write up their ideas in prose in the form of a one- or two-page 'pedagogic manifesto', using Worksheet 20 as a scaffolding or foundation.

5 In another session, or at another arranged time, collect in the manifestos, and/or allow teachers to read each other's texts, if they are in agreement (decide with the group beforehand). See Introduction, Using the worksheets, point 9, for suggestions for what to do with the resulting texts. The manifesto could help individual teachers to identify a topic for investigating which is of particular interest to them, the appropriateness of which you can discuss with them. Alternatively, you may wish to produce a summary feedback letter; see Task 3.5, for suggestions as to how to do this.

OPTION 11 PRODUCING A SUMMARY OF PERSONAL THEORY, 'HELPING YOU TO LEARN'

One immediately practical application of the manifesto produced for Task 2.3 is for teachers to produce a summary of their manifesto for use with their learners. In spoken or written form, this text, which could be called 'Helping you to learn', explains to learners, especially learners of secondary-school age, a teacher's priorities, and is particularly useful at the beginning of a school year with a new class. Depending on the situation, this text could be in the learners' mother tongue, or in English.

Task 2.4 Our current professional practice: strengths, weaknesses, opportunities and benefits

BACKGROUND FOR THE TRAINER

This task includes Worksheet 21 on p. 248, and Option 12 (see below).

This is an open-ended task designed to help teachers to identify topics for investigating, by encouraging them to consider specific aspects of their current professional practice. But knowing precisely what aspects of practice to begin with can prove a difficult enterprise. So the constructive framework of this task encourages teachers to consider their strengths, weaknesses, opportunities and the potential benefits of given topics with reference to their schools, as well as to themselves and their learners.

TASK AIM

- to help teachers to identify topics for investigating together on their training programme

PROCEDURE

Allow a total of about 45 minutes for this task.

1 Follow the instructions on Worksheet 21, allowing about 15 minutes for the completion of Part 1. Allow about 15 minutes for Part 2. You may collect in the completed worksheets if you wish, in order to take them away, read and return them to the teachers, for information.

   Part 1: The initial focus of Worksheet 21 on strengths is, of course, deliberate, and is designed to direct teachers' attention towards positive aspects of their professional practice. This is because I have often found that there is a perhaps natural tendency for groups of teachers to dwell on negative aspects, problems, etc., and not to value their own ideas (see also Task 2.9).

2 In a whole-group discussion, elicit responses to both prompts in Part 2 at the bottom of the worksheet: strengths and priorities. (If teachers are not forthcoming in providing descriptions of strengths, or successful practice, you may need to encourage them to respond, with patience. Encourage teachers to explain any such examples in some detail for the benefit of the other teachers.)

3 Select a shortlist of, say, three topics, which are considered high priority by the group, and which can be used as a subsequent focus for training sessions, perhaps using Worksheet 18 for this purpose. The group could select one of the three topics and 'get down to action' immediately by, for example, selecting one of the tasks in Chapter 3, with reference to a topic which has been selected.

OPTION 12 TEACHERS SELECT TOPICS FROM THE TRAINER'S SHORTLIST

Of course, trainers are sometimes formally required to cover certain topics on programmes, for example as the result of requests by institutions funding training; trainers may also have their own personal preferences for topics, based perhaps on previous experience. This option presents a more focused framework than the main, open-ended approach to Task 2.4, by helping groups to select topics based on institutional or trainer preferences.

1 Pre-select a shortlist of topics that you know or feel to be potentially relevant to teachers in your training context, and which you are willing and able to focus on. See the sample list of topics to investigate in Section 6.18, for information.

2 Divide the teachers into sub-groups (a maximum of four teachers per group). Give the teachers the list of possible topics by writing them on the blackboard, for example, checking that each item on the list is understood.

3 Ask the teachers to select a certain number of topics from the list that they consider to be priorities for the whole group, say, three. In whole-group mode, select and rank these priorities for the whole group. Worksheet 18 may be used for this purpose.

Task 2.5 My best lesson / teaching idea

BACKGROUND FOR THE TRAINER

This task includes Worksheet 22 on p. 250.

Teachers the world over learn from the informal exchanges, such as in the following imaginary staffroom dialogue:

TEACHER 1: Has anyone got any ideas for teaching 'x' at level 'y'?

TEACHER 2: Well, actually, last week I tried out this idea I heard about at a Teachers' Conference last term, and it worked quite well, …

TEACHER 1: Hmmm, how does it work?…

This task provides a more systematic version of the communication between teachers above, exploiting the sometimes overlooked treasure trove of teachers' own teaching ideas as a force for change.

TASK AIM

• to help teachers to share their own teaching ideas and to encourage them to experiment with these

Encouraged to tell tales

© Jacky Chapman/photographer

Carol Ward: picking out key points gives children a skill many adults use for public speaking

MY BEST LESSON

CAROL WARD

Some years ago our Years 5 and 6 were lucky enough to have a series of visits from a storyteller. After she had left, I devised this lesson to give children a method for remembering main events in order to tell a story orally. It has always worked well and since then, it has proved useful in helping pupils to summarise what they have heard or read, to select main points and to plan story writing of their own.

◆ Children are organised in groups (mixed ability is fine as a scribe can be appointed if necessary).

◆ Provide lots of small pieces of paper to each group.

◆ Tell or read a short story – a traditional one is always successful.

◆ Ask every child to write one thing that happens on one piece of paper. Emphasise that it is only an event you want, not a description.

◆ Let them carry on putting one event per piece of paper until they have finished or you call time. If all the children can write well enough unaided, work individually and in silence at this point.

◆ Get the group to arrange the papers in a sensible order, discarding any duplicates and adding any omissions. There will be lots of good discussion here. You'll appreciate the previous silence!

◆ Check the list as a class to agree the outline. On the first occasion, I make a large-class plan like a flow diagram and let individuals and groups use it

to retell the story in any way they choose. The plan provides the "hooks" for their memory and they are encouraged to add the "frilly bits" themselves to make an interesting version. The least confident have enough prompts to ensure success and everyone can enjoy themselves at their own level.

Most junior classes will enjoy the lesson and with some practice in the method, children can become quite proficient in picking out and ordering key points for a variety of purposes. It is an invaluable study skill, and one which many adults use when preparing to speak publicly. It's only a small step to the little pile of index cards nestling in a handbag or inside pocket!

Carol Ward is former head of English at Linslade Middle School, Leighton Buzzard, Bedfordshire

61

PROCEDURE

Allow several hours for this task, over two or more training sessions.

1 The teachers read the article 'Encouraged to tell tales', reproduced above. Then lead a general discussion based on the article, by asking questions such as: 'Is this a good teaching idea?', or 'Do you use stories in your teaching?'

   Note: You may like teachers to read 'In her element', an article by Klein and Neumark about secondary science teacher Julie Fleetwood's lessons (see Section 6.19), as well as, or instead of, the article 'Encouraged to tell tales'. I hope that the science article provides language teachers with a stimulating, general educational perspective, away from the immediate concerns of language teaching. Reading this article would allow teachers to discuss similarities and differences between language teaching and science teaching, for example.

2 Before using Worksheet 22, ask the teachers to exchange ideas informally in pairs about their own successful lessons / teaching ideas, for about 5 minutes (they may need some encouragement here if they are not immediately forthcoming).

3 Follow the instructions on Worksheet 22, allowing about 20 minutes for its completion. Introduce the worksheet by suggesting that teachers use it to write about their teaching ideas, so that they can be shared in the group by making copies for a special file, to be kept in the training room.

   Note: before looking at the worksheet with the teachers, you could ask them what kinds of information would be useful to include about their teaching ideas. (Refer to the content of their previous discussions in pairs, or the article(s) included in this task. Elicit such information as: the name of the activity, how the teacher found out about it, age of learners, classroom management, aids and resources required, why it is a good idea, etc.) Teachers may complete the worksheet either in class or at home.

4 When the worksheets have been completed, the teachers read each other's texts in a training session. While reading, the teachers should try to find a new idea to experiment with in their own teaching. You can either organise this activity in small groups or ask the teachers to display their worksheets on the training room wall, allowing others to read them. (Because the author of each worksheet can be easily identified, teachers may also speak directly to a teacher whose lesson interests them, for further information, if this is required.) Ensure that each teacher selects an idea in order to experiment with it in class. Worksheet 40 (see Task 4.8) could be used for this purpose. (You could also lead a discussion about why they think that certain teaching ideas described on the worksheets were successful, possibly eliciting a set of principles of effective teaching ideas).

5 A follow-up session could then be held when teachers had had time to experiment in class with the idea they had selected from those described

on Worksheet 22. In this session, the teachers exchange information and recommendations regarding the teaching ideas they have tried out. (Note that teachers may also provide the authors of the worksheets with valuable feedback regarding their experiments, by writing comments in the space provided on Worksheet 22 and/or by talking to the teacher in question.)

6 Collect in the worksheets and put them in a file, to be kept in the training room, where possible. Encourage teachers to complete worksheets for ideas they try out throughout the training programme, which they can also continue to use as a source of teaching ideas. See the Introduction, 'Using the worksheets', point 9, for other suggestions as what to do with the texts.

Task 2.6 General reading survey: a class library, bibliography and open forum

BACKGROUND FOR THE TRAINER

This task includes Worksheets 23 and 24 on pp. 251–2, and Option 13 (see below).

Task 2.6 assumes that the trainer has available a selection of professional literature – books, journals, magazines and articles related to educating, teaching and learning – for use with teachers. The task helps to structure general, exploratory reading on a training programme, especially when first introducing the idea of reading as a way of learning. (Please note that for this task I use the term 'book', but also mean journals, etc.)

It is probably true to say that busy primary and secondary teachers have little opportunity for professional reading, due, among other reasons, to a lack of time, and/or the feeling that such reading might not meet their day-to-day needs. While it is also probably true to say that most teachers will have read professional literature at some point in their initial training and/or during their careers, they might:

- be out of touch with recent educational publications in general, and in particular in the field of educating, teaching and learning in the language classroom
- not be used to, or confident in, reading professional literature (in English)
- not have access to the professional literature
- not know which books to read, given the wealth of material available to teachers

Perhaps because of such factors, reading on a training programme can be a powerful stimulus for learning. It also enables teachers:

- to be exposed to the thinking of others, in this case, authors, and, as a result, to acquire new understandings, in the constructivist sense
- to develop the 'enabling skill' of reading professional literature (potentially encouraging them to continue reading during and after the training programme)
- to cover a wide range of books in the group within a short space of time (otherwise impossible for individual readers; see below)

TASK AIMS

In addition to helping teachers to identify topics for investigating, and to gaining the benefits listed above, this task aims:

- to help teachers to make sense of relevant aspects of the professional literature in their field
- to encourage teachers to explore and exploit professional publications available in their own region or country

PREPARATION

Bibliography and class library: where appropriate, either (a) select and/or buy the books you wish to use on the training programme, or (b) identify the books available in a library that the group has access to. Ideally produce a bibliography which gives details of the books that have been selected. See Section 6.20.1 for suggestions on producing a bibliography and Section 6.20.2 for a sample bibliography. If you are able to buy or obtain books for use with the group, try to provide at least one book for each teacher in the group in order to make a class library. Obtain duplicate copies of especially relevant texts, but otherwise obtain as many different titles as possible. Of course, easy access to the books in the training room encourages teachers to read more. So put all the books in a box, to be kept in the training room, complete with a file containing a sheet on which teachers can record when they borrow and return materials, as well as a copy of the bibliography. The file can also be used to keep the teachers' reviews in (see below). Where there are no funds available for buying books, and where appropriate, you could collect an agreed sum of money from each teacher, buy a list of different books with this money, allowing the teachers access to a variety of books during the programme. At the end of the training programme, each teacher can then keep one of the books.

PROCEDURE

Allow several hours for this task, over several training sessions.

1   Generate a brief general discussion related to the potential benefits and practical issues related to reading professional literature, perhaps using the following questions:

Can busy teachers learn by reading? What are the advantages/disadvantages of reading? Where are books available locally (libraries, The British Council, school, home, etc.)?

See the list of some potential advantages or benefits of reading professional literature in the 'Background for the trainer' above. See also Option 13 below as a way of introducing this task.

2   Follow the instructions on Worksheet 23. Allow at least 20 minutes for this worksheet. Give each teacher a copy of the bibliography you have prepared, letting them read through it for a few minutes, and answering any questions they have. Where appropriate, each teacher has a number of blank copies of Worksheet 23 (as many copies as you think they can realistically use in the time you are working together on the training programme). This will enable teachers to complete an agreed number of review sheets over a certain period of time, by a certain date.

3.1 If you have a class library as described above, show the group the box of books, and the file you have prepared, suggesting that teachers keep in it records of when they borrow and return materials, as well as their completed worksheets. Explain that by reading the review sheets in the file, teachers can then find out about and learn from other teachers' recommendations. (If a previous group of teachers has produced reviews on file, these can be shown to the teachers, by way of example.) Emphasise the labour-saving benefits of this task, as teachers only read one book, but find out about many more without having to read them all first.

4.1 Perhaps introduce a selection of key titles briefly. The teachers then select one title each from those available, with guidance from you where necessary; allow plenty of time for this.

4.2 Suggest that the teachers should: (a) read their book, and complete a worksheet for it by a certain date, when they will present their books to each other in a training session, and (b) bring the completed worksheet and the book with them on this agreed date.

   Note: tell teachers that it may not be necessary to read *all* of their book, just those sections or chapters which are relevant to their experience or situation, and to bring back a book immediately and exchange it for another if it proves unsuitable. Where appropriate, several teachers can read the same book, and review it together. You may also like to read and review a book from the bibliography yourself. If you do not have a class library, inform the group where the books can be found (for example, in a library). See Section 6.20.3, for an example of a review sheet completed by a teacher (Worksheet 23). See also Worksheet 24, an alternative review sheet, which may be used instead of Worksheet 23.

5   Open forum: allow about 45 minutes for this. On the agreed date, in a training session, the teachers sit in a circle, with you or another teacher

acting as chair. Do everything you can to make the atmosphere as relaxed as possible. The teachers take it in turns to tell each other about the books they have read, using Worksheet 23 or 24 as a guide, and answering any questions about the books from other members of the group. Allow a few minutes for each teacher's contribution. In this way, teachers can recommend to each other further reading material, and can also mark relevant books on their own bibliography.

6 The teachers put their completed review sheets in the review file so that other teachers can find out about the others' recommendations whenever they wish. Suggest that when looking through the reviews on file, they comment on other teachers' reviews, by making notes in the space provided on the review sheet, signing their comments. You may also do this, of course. Subsequently, teachers may borrow materials and return them to the box freely.

7 Discussion: ask the question:

Have we identified topics for investigating as a result of our reading?

The group selects topics from those emerging from the open forum. The following example is taken from the teacher review sheet in Section 6.20.3:

I want to know how I can do different activities with 8–9-year-old children who have just started learning English and don't know some of the verbs or expressions that appear in many songs.

In this case, the group might agree to investigate the use of songs, by selecting a task from Chapter 3.

OPTION 13 BOOKS WE ARE READING, OR BOOKS FROM OUR PAST

You could introduce Task 2.6 by bringing to the training session a copy of a professional book that you are reading at the moment:

1 Show the book that you are reading to the teachers. Tell them about such aspects as:

How you found out about the book; where you got it (did you buy it, borrow it from a library or a friend, etc?); who the author is; when, where it was published and who by; whether it is theoretical or practical, or both; whether you would recommend it. Why? Why not?

2 Ask if the teachers are reading anything professional at the moment, or if there is something they have already read, even if this was some time ago, which they would recommend to the others, or wish to read again themselves. Invite a few teachers to briefly tell the group about such books. One of my own favourite books in this category is *How Children Fail* (Holt, 1982).

Task 2.7 Keeping a classroom diary

> *Tuesday, February 12th*
> *2nd Part of the morning*
>
> *After the break we worked on different ways to express disagreement. In fact, Peter gave us 15 and we had to decide what they had in common. It was a very abstract work, at least, for me.*
>
> *Fortunately, the task became more practical, clear and useful when we had to use these different forms of disagreement discussing with a partner some statements about 'Learning a language'. Personally I prefer practical exercises to theory, although I think theory is necessary, but sometimes it's very hard.*
>
> *Well, as it was a busy day for all of us and we were tired, we spent the last part of the morning watching TV (Sky Channel), it was a very interesting and useful activity, even if we didn't understand very much. I think we should do it often, in order to improve our listening skills and to be able to understand average English speakers.*

BACKGROUND FOR THE TRAINER

This task includes Worksheet 25 on p. 253, and Option 14 (see below).

Encouraging teachers to write regularly about a class of learners they teach, sometimes called keeping a log or journal, helps them in the sometimes difficult enterprise of describing and evaluating what happens in their schools or classrooms. Self-disclosure of the type required when writing a diary may not come easily to teachers, so this task provides a supportive framework to overcome this difficulty. The diaries can be written in private, or as a social activity, where teachers share the contents of their diaries. But why keep a diary? It helps teachers to see the familiar world of their school and classrooms from a different perspective, and to re-frame their perceptions or assumptions about it. Further benefits include that it:

- provides time for teachers to consolidate / reflect quietly on their learning

- provides teachers with practice in describing and evaluating in writing (in English) their professional practice and development
- develops and acknowledges teachers' own insights into aspects of their professional practice
- provides an opportunity for teachers to examine their assumptions about their professional practice
- helps teachers to develop their critical awareness of aspects of their professional practice
- helps teachers to organise and clarify their ideas
- provides a reference point for future discussions, learning and investigating

TASK AIMS

See above.

PROCEDURE

This task is designed to take place over a number of sessions; for more information regarding timing, see below.

1 Follow the instructions on Worksheet 25. Please note that Worksheet 25 can be used for Tasks 2.7 and 2.8. Having suggested the idea of the teachers keeping a diary based on (a) their own teaching (Task 2.7), or (b) the training programme itself (Task 2.8), focus on point 1 from Worksheet 25 for a discussion of the teachers' own previous experience of diary-writing. Suggestions: (see numbered points on the worksheet):

- Worksheet 25, point 2. How long to keep the diary? Avoid 'overkill' by limiting the period of diary-keeping; it is a difficult activity in itself and can easily become tedious for teachers. Agree how long the diary will be kept for. Depending on such factors as the frequency of the teachers' classes or training sessions, an ideal period might be one or two weeks. There is a space on the worksheet to fill in the number of days the diary is to be kept for. (If the task proves successful, it can always be repeated later in the programme.) As far as the choice of language is concerned, asking teachers to write their diaries in English might prove attractive in terms of the language learning potential, but do not insist on this. They could use their own language, if reluctant to use English.
- Worksheet 25, point 3. Benefits of diaries: Elicit some benefits of keeping a diary, selecting from those quoted in the 'Background for the trainer' for this task; the teachers can list some of these in the spaces provided on their worksheet.
- Worksheet 25, point 4. Organising the diaries: Before starting, agree with the group what to do with the diaries once they have been written. There are a number of possibilities (see Option 14).

- Worksheet 25, point 5. What you can write about: The teachers may be uncertain as to what to write about in their diaries and especially find it difficult to get started, so provide help by judiciously selecting a few prompts from the worksheet, such as, *Today in class I noticed that…* or *Something that worked well was…*. A fuller list of prompts is given in Section 6.21. It is important, however, that teachers write what they wish to write, so take care not to 'overstructure' their diary-keeping.

2 See Option 14 below for other ideas as to what to do with the diaries after they have been written.

3 At the end of the diary-writing period, lead a discussion (see Option 14, point 2, for a way of structuring this) in which you elicit feedback from the teachers' diaries, for example in the form of the prompts from the worksheet: '*Today in class I noticed that…*', etc. Find out if there are any suggestions from the teachers' feedback for topics to investigate. A topic selected could then be investigated by means of a task from Chapter 3.

4 To conclude, you may evaluate the usefulness of this task briefly with the group by looking again at the list of the benefits of diary-keeping recorded on the worksheet. Ask questions such as:

How useful has the task been? Would the group like to repeat the experience later in the programme? If so, why? If not, why not?
(see also Task 5.1).

OPTION 14 KEEPING A DIARY: VARIOUS OPTIONS

1 Show the diary to others: once the diaries have been written, teachers may show them to a trainer or to colleagues (providing an opportunity to respond to the diary-writer orally or in writing, and potentially commencing a dialogue with the teacher in question in the process).

2 Select extracts from the diaries and discuss: once the diaries about the participants' classes have been written, teachers may select extracts of particular significance for discussion with other teachers in a training session. (See Task 2.8 for a full description of this procedure.)

3 Keep diaries completely confidential: teachers may write their diaries but not show them to anybody. This option clearly loses out on the social dimensions of dialogue and discussion in the first two suggestions above. However, it still includes some of the benefits of diary-writing, as well as the fact that teachers might write more candidly.

4 Learner diaries: consider the possibility of the teachers' *learners* keeping diaries about their classes. This could be done as a follow-up activity once the main task has been completed, providing an alternative way of investigating learner perceptions (see also other tasks in Chapter 4).

Task 2.8 Our experience of the training programme: discussion based on diaries

BACKGROUND FOR THE TRAINER

Task 2.8 includes Worksheet 25 on p. 253, and Option 15 (see below).

Trainers are encouraged to read Task 2.7, which is closely related, before attempting Task 2.8; the latter is suitable for use once a training programme has been running for some time (say, at least five sessions).

Briefly, teachers keep a regular diary, for an agreed period of time, which is based on their individual perceptions of the experience of the training programme in which they are participating (see the sample diary entry on p. 67). Keeping a diary provides a valuable opportunity to step back from the programme, and to try to make sense of it from a personal perspective. In a subsequent discussion in a training session, the teachers compare key extracts they have selected from their diaries, and try to describe and evaluate the common experience of the programme together, an example of experiential learning through social interaction.

TASK AIM

- to help teachers to reflect on, describe and evaluate the pedagogic practices, materials, resources and ideas employed on their training programme, in order to identify topics for investigating

PREPARATION

Prepare 5–10 slips of paper for each teacher, each measuring approximately one fifth of a sheet of A4 paper.

PROCEDURE

This task is designed to take place over several sessions. For more information about the timing, see below.

1 Follow the instructions on Worksheet 25. Follow the procedures described in Task 2.7, but with the teachers focusing on their training programme, not on their own teaching at school. You may wish to modify the diary prompts on the worksheet (point 5), or those in Section 6.21, in order to focus more on the teachers' experience of the programme. Explain to the group what is involved in the diary-keeping and in the subsequent discussion in a training session, agreeing on how long the teachers will keep the diary for (days or weeks), how long they are to write for (minutes), preferably at the end of any given session, and when they will compare the diaries in a training session.

Note: teachers may also write a diary outside the actual training sessions, if time cannot be found in the sessions themselves. Naturally, you may also participate by writing a diary.

2 The teachers keep their diary during the agreed period of time and, when they are finished, bring them to a training session.

3 Teachers select extracts from diaries: in a training session, the teachers are each given the slips of paper you have previously prepared. They are asked to re-read their diaries and copy brief extracts about significant events, thoughts, insights, etc. on to the pieces of paper. Try not to be too specific about the criteria for selecting extracts, as this might prompt the teachers to think along certain lines. Allow at least 30 minutes for this activity. Where appropriate, this could also be completed at home; if so, tell the teachers to bring the extracts to a training session on a certain day for comparison with other teachers' diary extracts.

4 Group discussions: divide the teachers into sub-groups of, say, four or five teachers so they can discuss their extracts as follows. In each group discussion, the teachers:

- read out their extracts to each other, and/or read each other's extracts in silence
- try to understand each other's extracts, if necessary by asking the author of a given extract questions about it
- compare each other's extracts, determining what, if anything, they have in common
- try to classify similar extracts into 'categories', using a paper clip to keep all the slips in each category together, and give each category a name

Allow at least 30 minutes for this discussion. The following is an imaginary example of the kind of discussion I expect to take place:

TEACHER 1: OK. I'll begin. My extract reads like this: 'At the beginning of the course I felt a bit nervous, but happy because I'm going to be a student again'.

TEACHER 2: Yes, I've got something similar, listen: 'A student again! I was nervous and expectant'.

TEACHER 1: Has anybody else got similar comments? We could call these 'first feelings'.

TEACHER 3: Actually I have, too. I wrote: 'Being back in class as a student has been great, away from the children and away from school'.

An example of a category might therefore be 'First feelings', which, when classified, might look something like this:

First feelings

- At the beginning of the course I felt a little bit nervous, but happy because I'm going to be a student again.
- A student again! I was nervous and expectant.
- Being back in class as a student has been great, away from children and away from school.

See Section 6.22 for a fuller sample of classified diary extracts collected from a group of teachers.

5 One or two sub-groups report to the whole group on the categories that they have selected in their discussion. Write a list of the teachers' categories on the blackboard, and ask the following types of questions about them:

Which category is the most frequent? Why?

What are the implications for the rest of the programme?

Is there a category that we could investigate in our schools and classrooms?

For example, a topic for further investigation could be:

Given the feelings we have about our training programme, what kind of feelings do our learners have about their lessons, and how can we find about these feelings?

(See discussion and data cited above for the source of this idea.)

A task from Chapter 3 could then be used for investigating this topic or other topics.

OPTION 15 PRODUCING A SUMMARY OF TEACHERS' PERCEPTIONS ABOUT A PROGRAMME (BASED ON DIARIES)

1 After the period of diary-writing, the teachers submit all their slips of paper to you, classified into named categories, each category held together by a paper clip (make sure that the teachers know this will happen before they select their slips).

2 This information is then typed up in the form of a summary, and a copy given to each teacher to read at home. This is a valuable source of material for:

- the trainer to monitor the teachers' participation on the programme (as a kind of detailed feedback on the development of the training programme); or for the trainer to consider when planning and working on future training programmes
- the group, or part of the group, to follow up later in the training programme, for example by selecting and investigating as topics other categories included in the summary

Task 2.9 'We can do it!' Self-esteem, us and our learners

BACKGROUND FOR THE TRAINER

This task includes Worksheets 26 and 27 on pp. 254–6, and Option 16 (see below).

This task is intended to form a link between the tasks in Chapter 2, which are designed to help teachers to identify topics for investigating, and those in Chapter 3, which are intended to help teachers to focus on the individual topics selected. Task 2.9 is different from others in Chapter 2 in that it already focuses on a topic, albeit a very broad one, that of 'self-esteem', examining its role in teachers' professional practice and development. Why 'self-esteem'? I believe that it is a central issue in education, and as such a particularly rich framework within which teachers can identify more concrete aspects for investigating. By 'self-esteem' I understand an affective process defined by Lawrence (1987: 1–4) as the individual's evaluation of the discrepancy between 'self-image' and 'ideal self'. 'Self-image' refers to individuals' awareness of their mental and physical characteristics, whereas 'ideal self' refers to the ideal characteristics, standards of behaviour and particular skills which an individual *should* possess. See also Task 2.4, the constructive framework of which is closely related to the principles underlying this task.

TASK AIMS

- to identify ways of enhancing learners' self-esteem, providing topics for investigating
- to enhance teachers' confidence in their own ability to make changes in their work

PREPARATION

Before the training session, reflect on and complete Part 1 of Worksheet 26 yourself (adapted from Kahn, 1993) with regard to your own professional experience.

PROCEDURE

Allow a total of about one hour for this task.

1 Follow the instructions on Worksheet 26, allowing about 45 minutes minutes for its completion. Start the session by telling the group about your own response to one or two of the sentences from Part 1 of the worksheet. See Section 6.23.1 for a sample response to a prompt on Worksheet 26.

2 In a whole-group discussion, process the teachers' responses to Worksheet 26, and in particular Part 3, by focusing on the following question:

In what practical ways can we enhance our learners' self-esteem?

Elicit recommendations from the teachers and write a list on the blackboard. Worksheet 27 may be used for recording teachers' recommendations – for this task or, indeed, for others in the book. Simply complete the title of the worksheet appropriately by writing, for example:

Practical recommendations for enhancing learner's self-esteem.

Note: there are five spaces on the worksheet for recommendations, enabling the group to select a maximum of about five of recommendations. This number encourages teachers to select those which are most relevant to the group, and results in a number which is manageable for the group to process. For future reference, either make enough copies of the completed Worksheet 27 for each teacher to have one, or display one completed copy on the training room wall.

3 The group may then choose one of the recommendations for investigating. See the practical recommendations for enhancing learners' self-esteem in Section 6.23.2. An example of these recommendations which could be investigated might be: 'Reviewing learning achievements at the end of coursebook units'.

FURTHER READING

Lawrence, *Enhancing Self-Esteem in the Classroom*. Interesting and slim enough for busy trainers, from outside immediate English language teaching circles, containing many practical ideas.

OPTION 16 FURTHER READING: 'IT'S TIME WE ALL STOOD UP FOR TEACHER' AND 'STRATEGIES TO HELP YOU FIGHT STRESS'

Tim Kahn's article 'It's time we all stood up for teacher', reproduced in Section 6.23.3, caught my eye and was instrumental in focusing my attention on the issue of 'self-esteem'. (The prompts in Part 1 of Worksheet 26 are adapted from this article.) You may, of course, ask teachers to read the article, perhaps considering the following question as they do so:

What practical ways does the author suggest to enhance teachers' and learners' self-esteem?

If appropriate, teachers may also read and discuss Anne Cockburn's article 'Strategies to help you fight stress', also reproduced in Section 6.23.3.

3 Exploring a topic

Introduction

For the nine tasks in Chapter 3, it is assumed that a topic(s) for investigating has already been identified, for example by means of a task(s) from Chapter 2. The tasks help teachers to explore a topic by probing, examining and clarifying their ideas related to it. In most cases the tasks also help teachers to break down the topic in question into more teacher-friendly practical action points or recommendations for the classroom. These form a kind of bridge between Chapters 3 and 4, the emphasis in the latter being on the classroom itself, and encouraging teachers to implement action points previously identified in Chapter 3.

1 Exploring teachers' knowledge

2 Identifying topics to investigate

5 Evaluating learning

3 Exploring a topic

4 Investigating in class

6 Resources for the trainer

Figure 3.1   The investigating cycle in Teachers in Action

Task 3.1 Why, why, why? Examining our assumptions and beliefs about a topic

BACKGROUND FOR THE TRAINER

This task includes Option 17 (see below).

Several tasks in this book encourage teachers to explain aspects of their ~~~y~~ answering the question *Why?*. For example, see Task 1.6, 'Why ~~~nglish?~~', or Task 3.2. Task 3.1 is very much in keeping with this ~~~ch~~, although it helps teachers to *systematically* and *persistently* ask and answer the question Why?, with regard to a particular topic which has been selected for investigating. This process of questioning may eventually lead to the revealing of a deeply held assumption or belief related to the topic, where 'assumption' is understood to mean something taken for granted, something accepted or supposed true without proof or demonstration (Simons *et al.*, 1993: 239).

TASK AIMS

- to help teachers to examine and question their assumptions and beliefs about a particular topic
- to help teachers to identify action points concerning a particular topic for implementing in school and class

PREPARATION

Before a training session, read the (abridged) extract from Tripp (1993: 46–48), 'Reading: The *Why?* Challenge' below. If you decide that the topic you wish to investigate with your teachers lends itself to the treatment described in the extract, follow the procedure for this task.

The *Why?* Challenge

[A] simple form of analysis that can be far-reaching and sometimes quite devastatingly dramatising in its effects, is, like Socrates, to ask, and go on asking, the question, Why? When we do this, we do not go on forever, but we may go on for a long time…. In effect, the end point is the same: we see that things are as they are because we choose to make them that way. In practical terms, if we ask Why? for long enough, we end up saying either, 'Because that's how it ought to be.' or, 'Because that's how it is.' In the former we have to recognise that we are operating from a deeply held belief which may or may not be appropriate to our work or consonant with other beliefs; and in the latter that something we take for granted and as a part of the natural order of things and therefore unchangeable, may in fact be a social construct and therefore open to change. Either way, it is our responsibility.

(ibid.: 46)

Tripp tries out the '*Why?* challenge' on himself about the issue of plagiarism by university students, in answer to the question 'Why is plagiarism so important?':

> Why?
> Because it's cheating.
> Why?
> Because it's not their work.
> Why?
> Because they've copied someone else's work.
> Why?
> Because they want to pretend it's their own.
> Why?
> Because they want to get out of doing their work or get a better mark.
> Why?
> Because a mark is an indication of how well you've done.
> Why?
> Because you have to have measures of how good people are, and that's one we happen to use. (ibid.: 47)

A second challenge was a dialogue between Tripp and a teacher, who had complained he could not get his nine-year-old children to stop talking while they wrote:

> What do you mean by not talking? Do you require all talking to cease?
> Of course.
> For how long?
> About 20 minutes.
> Why do they have to stay in silence for so long?
> Because you can't concentrate when you or others are making a noise.
> Why?
> Because you keep looking and listening to what the others are doing.
> Why?
> Because it's more interesting than writing, and not such hard work.
> Why?
> Because writing is less interesting than talking to people and it's hard work.
> (ibid.: 48)

Tripp goes on to state that, as a practical consequence of this dialogue, 'many teachers would wish to work on the matter of making writing more interesting' (ibid.: 48).

PROCEDURE

Allow about 45 minutes for this task.

1   Ask for a volunteer teacher to talk in front of the other teachers about his or her own experience with regard to the topic selected for

investigating, and demonstrate what is required for this task by leading a 2- or 3-minute dialogue with the volunteer in front of the group. Gently, sensitively and supportively 'probe' about what the teacher does in class with regard to the topic, by asking 'Why?', as in the two examples in the Tripp text.

Note: where appropriate, if you feel this might be too difficult for a teacher, volunteer to be interviewed yourself. Allow a teacher to persistently ask you 'Why?', 'Why?' with regard to a topic (you could be interviewed about the same topic as that being investigated by the group, or about a different topic). Of course, the teachers may also read the Tripp text in order to understand better what is required of them for this task.

2.1 Following the above demonstration, where appropriate, ask the teachers to make notes individually about their current classroom practice with regard to the topic (what they themselves do, what their learners do, etc.). If, for example, the topic is 'developing leaners' writing skills', a teacher might note down: 'I usually get learners to write their essays at home', or 'I collect the work in and then correct it ready to return it in the next lesson', or 'I use a system of correction symbols in the margin of my learners' essays'. Allow the teachers 5 minutes to make such notes.

2.2 In pairs, the teachers exchange their experience in a discussion based on their notes by interviewing each other as in the demonstration extract, asking each other why they do what they do in class. Allow 15–20 minutes for this activity; tell the teachers to time themselves, so that they each have a turn to speak. Tell them to be ready to share any deeply held assumptions or beliefs that have been revealed in their discussion with the others.

3.1 In whole-group mode, ask the teachers to share the content of their exchanges with the others, especially any suggestions for assumptions or beliefs that have been revealed. List any such suggestions on the blackboard. For example, in the second dialogue of the Tripp extract, the last sentence is:

Because writing is less interesting than talking to people and it's hard work.

If a group of teachers were focusing on the topic of 'writing', and the dialogue of one pair of teachers had ended with the above statement and been included in the teachers' list of suggested assumptions, the whole group could consider examining and questioning this statement further, collectively or individually. They could do this by trying to answer the following types of questions, in order to suggest specific action points concerning the topic:

Is this statement true?

Is this reality open to change?

What can we do to change this situation?

What can we do to make 'x' / writing more interesting?

3.2 Worksheet 27 on p. 256 could be used to record any practical recommendations that emerge from such a discussion. Other beliefs or assumptions listed could be investigated at a later point in the training programme, if appropriate.

COMBINING TASKS

As a possible follow-up, select a task from Chapter 4, for example Task 4.4, encouraging teachers to produce a learner questionnaire in order to investigate their learners' attitudes to the topic being investigated.

OPTION 17 WHY IS THIS TOPIC IMPORTANT?

A simple, alternative way of focusing on a topic at the beginning of a training session – see, for example, stage 1 of the procedures for Task 3.1 – or indeed at the end of a session as a summary, is to ask teachers why they think the topic is important for them (to investigate).

1 Give each teacher a slip of paper on which they note down their response to the following partial statement:

This topic is important because...

Allow the teachers a few minutes to do this.
2 Collect in the slips and read them immediately for your information. Perhaps read out some of the slips to the group of teachers and encourage discussion as to whether the teachers agree or disagree with the suggestion you have read out.
3 Move on to stage 2 of the procedure for Task 3.1, or another suitable activity.

See Section 6.24 for two sample sets of responses for Option 17, for the following topics: 'The correction of learners' oral errors is important because…', and 'Project work in the English classroom is important because…'. If you are able to type up the statements that teachers produce as in the two sample sets, this provides a very useful document for the group to refer back to.

Task 3.2 What do we understand by the topic 'x'? (What? Why? Who? etc.)

BACKGROUND FOR THE TRAINER

Task 3.2 includes Worksheet 28 on p. 257, and Option 18 (see below).

This task encourages teachers to answer systematically so-called *wh-* questions concerning the topic selected for investigating, as follows: *What?*, *Why?*, *Who?*, *Where?*, *When?* and *How?* I will illustrate this task by focusing on the topic 'Using English in class', as if it were being investigated by a group. I have deliberately chosen this topic, as I have found it to be crucial for many non-native-speaker teachers I have worked with on training programmes. (See Section 6.25.1, summary of a workshop I gave at a teachers' conference', for practical recommendations and advice concerning the topic 'Using English in class'.) I hope, however, that the framework for this task lends itself to discussing other topics that teachers wish to focus on, such as: 'What do we understand by "group work and pair work", by "correcting oral errors", or by "learner autonomy"?'

TASK AIMS

- to help teachers to explore aspects of a specific topic by defining it
- to help teachers to identify any difficulties they experience concerning a topic

PROCEDURE

Allow at least 45 minutes for this task.

1.1 Introduce the task by saying something like the following:

> *Like many aspects of education, the topic 'Using English in class' (insert the name of your own topic) may mean different things to different teachers. Together let's try to define what we mean by 'Using English in class', before investigating it in more detail. So what do you think it means?*

1.2 Allow the teachers to discuss this question in pairs for about five minutes. Suggest that they note down any key terms, concepts or ideas which they associate with the topic, and which they think they will use in investigating it together.

1.3 Ask one or two pairs to share their ideas with the whole group, and comment on these briefly. (Depending on the nature of the topic, it may also be useful to produce a working definition of it with the group; for example, 'Learner autonomy is…'. Write up this definition in the form of a poster for prominent display in the training room; this could then be modified in the light of subsequent experience and reading.)

2 Follow the instructions on Worksheet 28, allowing teachers at least 15 minutes to complete it (either at home or in a session). Ask teachers to write the name of the topic in the space provided. See the example of a completed Worksheet 28 for the topic 'Using English in class' in Section 6.25.2. (For item 3 on Worksheet 28, 'Why is this topic important?', see also Option 17 on p. 79 for information.)

3.1 After teachers have completed the worksheet, ask them to form sub-groups of three or four teachers, in which they read through each other's worksheets point by point, paying special attention to point 8, *'What I find difficult about this topic'*. Ask each sub-group to select one of their difficulties which they think would be useful to investigate together further; encourage them to frame their suggestion as follows:

What we find difficult about this topic is... .

Allow 10–15 minutes for this activity.

3.2 In whole-group mode, elicit the sub-groups' difficulties, and list them on the blackboard. Choose one difficulty of high priority for the whole group. For example, point 8 on the sample worksheet in Section 6.25.2:

Sometimes, quite often, actually, I don't know how to say something in English, especially when giving instructions...

Ask the question:

How can we make this easier for ourselves or our learners?

COMBINING TASKS

Task 3.6 could be then used to focus a workshop on 'Giving instructions in class'. Subsequently, Task 4.8 could be used to structure teachers' own experiments with ideas related to giving instructions in class, with some teachers perhaps monitoring the implementation of their ideas by means of a diary (see Task 2.7). Other items on the list of difficulties drawn up above could be investigated at a later point in the training programme.

OPTION 18 ADVANTAGES AND DISADVANTAGES OF A TOPIC

When focusing on a specific topic in a training session, and once teachers have a clear idea of what is meant by the topic, a simple yet effective way of brainstorming is to ask teachers to think about the advantages and dis-advantages of it. They may do this from the viewpoint of their schools, and/or themselves as teachers, and/or their learners. For example, see Section 6.25.3 for a sample list of advantages and disadvantages for the topic 'Using computers with learners'. Subsequently, the group of teachers could try and provide solutions to the difficulties identified under 'dis-advantages'. For example:

I am not sure what material there is (for computers).

Naturally, this option also lends itself to other topics, such as the advantages and disadvantages of using coursebooks.

Task 3.3 What do we already do in school or class regarding the topic 'x'? (Find someone who...)

BACKGROUND FOR THE TRAINER

This task includes Worksheet 29 on p. 258.

'Find someone who...' is probably a familiar 'warmer' or 'ice-breaking' activity to many teachers and trainers. Applied to teacher education and development in this task, it is a means of helping a group of teachers to focus on a topic together for the first time. In addition, the task may well lead to a little fun, as well as providing a change in interaction patterns and physical activity.

TASK AIMS

- to help teachers share, contrast and compare their current professional practice regarding a specific topic
- to identify practical recommendations related to a topic for implementing in school and class

PREPARATION

See Worksheet 29. Before the training session, prepare your own worksheet by using Worksheet 29 as a model and writing in the name of the topic in the space provided, as well as at least five partially completed sentences related to the topic identified. (You could of course include more items, which would mean that it would take longer to complete and to process afterwards.) See Section 6.26 for a sample of a completed Worksheet 29 on the topic of 'Helping our learners to work effectively in pairs and groups'.

Note: I have found it best not to use too many different verb forms / tenses in the sentences/questions on the worksheet, as this can lead to confusion. Restrict yourself to a maximum of two forms: for example, 'Do you...?'; 'Have you...?' (see the sample worksheet in Section 6.26).

PROCEDURE

Allow about 30 minutes for this task.

1 Give each teacher a copy of Worksheet 29, which you have previously prepared. Follow the instructions on the worksheet. Before beginning, possibly give examples of the type of questions the teachers will need to ask for the activity, for reasons of clarity, e.g. 'Do you...?' Allow about 10–15 minutes for this activity. You may join in the activity, if you wish!
2 After the whole-group mingle activity has finished, the teachers sit down.

(The activity may end naturally, with everyone choosing to sit down when they are ready, or you can invite the group to be seated at a suitable moment.) Begin a discussion related to the activity, perhaps by eliciting or providing feedback related to it in one or more of the following three ways:

1 Open questions (the teachers decide who contributes):

> TRAINER: *Who can tell the group something they learnt about another teacher from this activity?*
>
> VOLUNTEER TEACHER: *I discovered that Brigitte uses group work and…, etc.*
>
> TRAINER: *I see, thank you. (Develop discussion.) And Brigitte, what about you? What did you learn from someone else?*
>
> BRIGITTE: *Well, I spoke to Alexandra, who…, etc.*

2 Ask teachers by name (you decide who contributes):

> TRAINER: *Wolfgang, tell me something that you discovered in common with another teacher, after having done the activity.*

3 Feedback from the trainer: If you participate in the 'Find someone who…' activity yourself, *you* can begin the discussion afterwards by telling the group something that you learnt about the topic:

> TRAINER: *Well, I found out that Alexandra uses...*

3 Try to lead this discussion towards specific, practical ideas / action points. For example, ask:

What practical tips can we recommend to each other about the topic?

Worksheet 27 on p. 256 can be used to list such emerging ideas. With the group, select one idea from this list which could be further investigated, by means of a task from Chapter 4, for example.

COMBINING TASKS

See Option 3 on p. 32 for another suggestion for using the 'Find someone who....' activity.

Task 3.4 Do we agree that…?

BACKGROUND FOR THE TRAINER

This task includes Worksheet 30 on p. 259, and Option 19 (see below).

Once a topic for investigating has been identified, one way to focus on related key aspects is to find out what the teachers already know about the topic in general terms (their attitudes, knowledge, ideas, etc.), thus stimulating reflection and subsequent discussion. This task provides a simple framework for doing this.

TASK AIMS

- to explore and establish what teachers already know about a particular topic
- to identify practical recommendations related to a topic for school and the classroom

PREPARATION

Prior to a training session, read through this task and decide if the topic you have in mind lends itself to the procedures proposed. Select the statements which you wish to show the teachers, type them up in the form of a handout and make one copy for each teacher. Then copy the blank Worksheet 30. (Although there is only space for three statements on the worksheet, you could of course select more and ask teachers to write their responses on another sheet of paper.) See Section 6.27 for sample statements, my comments and practical recommendations for Worksheet 30 for the topic 'Helping our learners to listen to English in class'. Be prepared to tell the teachers your own views regarding the statements and to provide practical recommendations.

PROCEDURE

Allow about 40 minutes for this task.

1   Give each teacher a copy of the statements you have selected as well as a copy of Worksheet 30, and follow the instructions. Part 1 can be completed at home or in a training session. Allow a total of about 20 minutes for Parts 1 and 2.

2.1 When the group has had time to complete the worksheet, lead a general discussion, helping the whole group to agree (or 'to agree to disagree') on the items in Part 1, giving the teachers your own views about the statements. See, for example, my own comments regarding the items in Part 1 of the sample worksheet in Section 6.27.

2.2 Elicit the teachers' practical recommendations for your topic (see Part 2 of the worksheet) and write them on the blackboard, for example:

When getting learners to listen to English in class, we should..."

Use Worksheet 27 on p. 256 for this purpose. See the list of ten practical ways of helping learners to listen to English in class in Section 6.27. See also Worksheet 11 on p. 237, which could be used at this point to record the group's views.

2.3 Select one or more of the teachers' recommendations for the group or individuals to investigate further, e.g.:

How can we help our 'learners to reflect on and discuss the process of listening'?

(See the first recommendation in the list in Section 6.27.)

3　Select a task(s) from Chapter 4 to further investigate the specific recommendation selected.

OPTION 19　REFLECTIVE LISTENING

Reflective listening forms a permanent part of my repertoire as both teacher and trainer. Below I illustrate how it could be specifically used in conjunction with Part 2 of Worksheet 30, but it also works well as a general way of exchanging or brainstorming knowledge, information and ideas. This option lends itself particularly well to the topic of 'Helping our listeners to listen to English in class', the topic chosen to illustrate Task 3.4, as there is an obvious thematic link between the topic itself and the actual methodology employed (see the sample worksheet provided in Section 6.27, especially the first statement). Allow about 10–12 minutes. Make sure that you explain the instructions of the activity carefully, especially the first time you attempt it with a class, but it sounds more complicated than it actually is!

1　The teachers read and respond individually to Part 1 of Worksheet 30 (for example).
2　The teachers then process Part 1 of the worksheet in pairs as follows:
2.1 Teacher A has *two minutes* to tell Teacher B about his or her ideas related to the points on the worksheet, while Teacher B listens without speaking. You keep time throughout, and tell the teachers to stop when the time is up.
2.2 Then Teacher B has *one minute to reflect back* to Teacher A what he or she has just heard from Teacher A, and Teacher A listens without speaking.
2.3 The procedure at Stage 2.1 and 2.2 is repeated, but now it is Teacher B who has two minutes to tell Teacher A, etc.
3　After the group has finished, ask for a volunteer pair to provide a little feedback on their reflective listening, focusing on the content of their exchange. You may also focus on teachers' experience of the actual reflective listening procedure itself:

Was it easy / difficult? Why? Were you good listeners? etc.

Note: I first came across 'reflective listening' in a workshop held by Mario Rinvolucri at a TESOL-Spain conference.

Task 3.5　Writing about a topic: organising, developing and clarifying my ideas

BACKGROUND FOR THE TRAINER

This task encourages teachers to write about a topic individually, promoting the process of personalising related issues, and uncovering personal theories.

TASK AIMS

- to help teachers to organise, develop and clarify in writing their ideas related to a topic
- to provide a way for the trainer to give feedback on teachers' ideas
- to identify practical recommendations related to a topic for school and the classroom

PROCEDURE

Allow about one hour for this task, over two training sessions.

1 With the whole group, brainstorm the topic you have selected by getting the teachers to suggest key issues, ideas, questions, problems, etc. related to it. Use some of the following questions:

What is your personal experience regarding the topic?

How do you feel about the topic?

What key terms do you associate with the topic?

How can this topic help you in school or in class?

What is, or would be, good practice, regarding the topic in your opinion?

Write all the suggestions on the blackboard.

2 Give teachers the instructions for the activity 'Fastwriting' as follows, asking them to write for about 15 minutes on whatever aspects of the topic occur to them after the brainstorming, as follows:

> Fastwriting is a technique not unlike brainstorming in that it depends on speed and lack of inhibition. However, whereas brainstorming produces lots of individual ideas, fastwriting is concerned with developing and relating them. In fact, fastwriting can follow brainstorming, the writer now developing one or more ideas produced during the brainstorming phase. Because speed is important, it is best to have a time limit of between 10 and 20 minutes for fastwriting.
>
> (Select a topic and give the teachers the following instructions.)
>
> 1 Concentrate on ideas, not on language, grammar or punctuation.
> 2 Write as quickly as you can and don't stop writing.
> 3 Don't stop to cross out or correct mistakes.
> 4 If you can't think of a word or a phrase, either write it in your native language, or leave a blank or write 'something'.
> 5 Return to the blank spaces or the words in your native language when you have finished writing, and then, using a dictionary or thesaurus, add or translate the words and phrases concerned.
>
> (adapted from White and Arndt, 1991: 46.)

Note: before the teachers start writing, discuss what to do with the texts which they will produce. If the group agrees, you can collect in the texts, but be careful to tell the teachers that you will not make value judgements about the content of their texts. You may also write about the topic while the teachers are writing.

3   Follow the instructions in 3.1–3.3 in order to produce a summary feedback letter. See the example reproduced below, which was written by the trainer for a group of teachers focusing on the issue of 'Me as a teacher and/or educator'. The letter provides teachers with written feedback related to texts they produce, as in the procedure for this task.

3.1   Collect in the teachers' texts and read them before the next training session.

3.2   Select extracts from these texts in order to compile a set of quotations related to key issues, and write a question to accompany each quotation.

3.3   Write all the quotations and questions up in the form of a letter to the teachers and duplicate it.

4.1   In the next training session, give each teacher a copy of the letter. The teachers then read and discuss the questions you raise in it.

4.2   As a result, the group and/or individual teachers may identify a specific topic(s) for investigating further that emerges from the discussion of the letter, such as:

How can we help learners to show an attitude of respect to other languages, countries and cultures?
(See item 1 in the sample letter.) Elicit the teachers' recommendations for your topic, writing them on the blackboard and/or using Worksheet 27 on p. 256.

5   The group could then select a task from Chapter 4 to investigate the recommendations further in the classroom. Return the original texts completed at stage 1 (above) to the teachers.

COMBINING TASKS

For further detailed consideration of the topic 'the teacher as an educator', see also Task 1.6, especially Worksheet 10 on p. 236. The feedback letter in Task 3.5, complete with notes made by an individual teacher, might provide the basis for a discussion between the teacher in question and the trainer in a tutorial; see Task 5.6 for information.

SAMPLE OF A SUMMARY FEEDBACK LETTER

Topic: 'Me as a teacher and/or educator'

This is a copy of summary feedback letter I have used with a group of teachers.

Dear Teacher,

You will remember that in a session last week I asked you to write about the topic 'Me as a teacher and/or educator', and that I collected in your texts. Your texts made very interesting reading, so I include below five extracts, and some related questions or points of my own, for you to read. Consider my questions from your own perspective, making notes if you wish. Spend about 15 minutes on this activity.

1 *I have an important role as an educator to show students an attitude of respect to other languages, cultures and countries.*

My question: *How can we help learners to show an attitude of respect towards other languages, countries and cultures?*

2 *I really don't know if I am only a teacher and sometimes an educator too, or just a teacher. The reason for my doubts is the differences between teaching young learners and older ones. With young children it is easier to be both teacher and educator, but with older children it's the other way round.*

My question: *Why is it more difficult to 'educate' older children than younger ones?*

3 *I want to find ways of helping learners to find out about themselves and about their classmates.*

My question: *What kinds of things can learners find about about themselves and their classmates? And how?*

4 *Some parents think that teachers should educate students; it's supposed to be the teacher's main work, so parents 'delegate' education on teachers.*

My question: *In what practical ways can we help parents to understand what we are trying to do in terms of children's education?*

5 *When I decided to do this course, I thought of myself as an empty vessel which wanted to be filled with lots of theory, practical ideas. I think, I thought, that I would get most of that information from our trainer(s) (I had never heard of the word 'educator' applied to teachers), and then that I would comment with the other participants on what we did. But I thought we would get the rest of it from our trainer. Now I must say that I've changed my previous point of view (fortunately). Although it is true that I am learning from our trainer, the actual fact is that I am learning even more from our groupwork, our teamwork. (....) Now I know where I want to direct my path; though I know that it will be hard work, I will try with the help of others.*

Evaluate your own participation on this programme with reference to this statement.

Thank you. When you have all read this letter, we can compare our views in a discussion, Peter.

Task 3.6 Workshop: experiencing teaching ideas as learners

BACKGROUND FOR THE TRAINER

This is a key task in *Teachers in Action* and includes Option 20 (see below).

Broadly speaking, Task 3.6 follows the structure of the experiential learning cycle devised by the educational theorist D. Kolb, defined as:

> *a flexible and helpful framework for formal and informal teacher learning. It suggests a structure for the design of teacher learning activities: cycles that integrate experience, reflection and discussion, access to public knowledge and opportunities for experiment*

(Roberts, 1998: 33)

In my experience, teachers delight in one type of experiential learning: finding out about language learning activities by participating in them as learners, with the trainer playing the role of teacher. (Note that the activities might not be new to the teachers, as in some cases teachers may have known about or indeed used these activities in their own teaching in the past, but for some reason no longer do so. Experiencing the activities first-hand, therefore, helps them to recall them.)

In keeping with Kolb's cycle, after direct contact with teaching activities by means of a demonstration, teachers require help in (a) reflecting on and evaluating these activities; (b) making generalisations or abstract conceptualisations about them, as well as (c) considering possible applications for experimenting in their own teaching. This task therefore provides a framework for meeting these needs, and lends itself in particular to what I might call 'practical' topics. For example, I have used a similar framework for focusing on the following topics: correction techniques for oral mistakes, warmer activities, developing writing skills, developing listening skills, using English in the classroom, teaching vocabulary, and learner autonomy.

TASK AIM

- to give teachers an opportunity to experience as learners different language teaching activities and ideas related to a topic selected, and to evaluate their applicability to their own teaching situation

PREPARATION

Prior to the training session, select, say, three or four teaching ideas or activities related to the topic in question. Choose activities that you feel or know from experience teachers might be able to and wish to try out in their own classrooms following the workshop.

PROCEDURE

Allow about one hour for this task.

1   Select another task in Chapter 3 or a similar activity of your own choice in order to introduce the topic in question.

2   Demonstrate to the teachers the pre-selected activities one after the other as if the teachers were themselves language learners, ensuring that each activity is given a name, so as to facilitate identification of these later. Write up the names of the activities on the blackboard for reference.

   Note: where time is short, an alternative to actually demonstrating the activities is to provide a description of them; ask teachers to discuss and select those activities which are suitable in their own teaching situations. See 'Workshop' in Section 6.5 for an example. Another valuable, popular alternative or extension to the trainer demonstrating is 'peer teaching'. If the teachers themselves know of any other relevant teaching activities for the topic, invite volunteers to demonstrate these activities to the rest of the group.

3.1 Ask teachers to evaluate the activities demonstrated in the workshop by individually considering (some of) the following questions, and making notes:

   1 *What did the activities have in common?*
   2 *In what way(s) were the activities different?*
   3 *Which activity(-ies) involved you the most as a learner? Why?*
   4 *Which activity(-ies), if any, could you consider using in your own teaching? (Would you need to adapt it? How?)*
   5 *What might be the long-term effect on the learners of using this activity?*

   Allow the teachers 10 minutes for this stage.

3.2 Then ask the teachers to form sub-groups to exchange their responses to the above questions for about 10 minutes.

4   In a whole-group discussion, elicit teachers' views regarding the above questions, in particular number 4. Write a list of the practical activities or recommendations emerging from the discussion, using the board and/or Worksheet 27 on p. 256. Encourage teachers to experiment with one of the activities in their classrooms, perhaps using Worksheet 40 on p. 274 to evaluate the experiment.

5   In a subsequent training session, provide the teachers with an opportunity to give feedback on their experiments.

FURTHER READING

See Roberts, *Language Teacher Education*, pp.35–5, for information about Kolb and experiential learning.

OPTION 20 TEACHING MATERIALS WORKSHOP

Another profitable way to structure a workshop is to encourage teachers to develop teaching materials which they can then use directly with their learners (if this is appropriate to the topic you are focusing on). Such materials form a kind of bridge between the training programme and the classroom; they are also likely to be popular with teachers, especially if it is possible to photocopy the materials produced and keep them in a file for a rainy day! Such a workshop also promotes the teachers' materials development skills.

1   Materials may be prepared in sub-groups, in which teachers share the same particular interest regarding the topic, or where they teach learners of the same age group. For example, if a group is investigating 'reading skills', you might choose one reading text from a coursebook used by the teachers in their schools. With the same text, teachers have to devise different activities and lessons which they can actually go on to employ in the classroom. You may, of course, lend assistance and guidance when it is required.

2.1 A follow-up training session can then provide an opportunity for teachers to compare and discuss the implementation of the materials developed in the workshop.

2.2 The teachers may also be encouraged to draw any general conclusions related to the topic, as a result of using the material in the classroom. For example, they could reflect on the principles underlying effective teaching ideas experimented with, and then attempt to compile a list of the characteristics of an effective or successful activity.

Task 3.7 Understanding key terms related to a topic

BACKGROUND FOR THE TRAINER

This task includes Worksheet 31 on p. 260.

Naturally, teachers are familiar with the world of schools and classrooms, and probably feel comfortable with the language they use to talk to each other about this world. However, the so-called academic discourse of public theory – that used in the professional books and journals or heard at teachers' conferences – may be unfamiliar, confusing or even alienating to teachers. Trainers – and I speak from personal experience – can underestimate teachers' difficulty in making sense of such academic terms in English, and perhaps in the teachers' own language, too. Moving from informal staffroom discussion to academic discourse may require much learning and interpretation by teachers. This task provides a framework for meeting this need, and will potentially enable teachers to go on to investigate a topic more effectively. See also Task 1.7.

TASK AIMS

- to help teachers to make sense of and be capable of using specialist terms related to a specific topic
- to encourage teachers to collect key terms related to relevant aspects of education, teaching and learning, in the form of glossaries

PREPARATION

Before the training session, select 5–10 key terms related to the topic you are investigating with the teachers, ensuring that you yourself are able to define the terms clearly. (Perhaps have definitions already prepared on an overhead transparency.)

See the sample list of ten specialist terms and definitions for the topic of language acquisition and learning below. I have chosen to illustrate this task with this perhaps rather difficult topic because in my experience teachers often find in it a new set of stimulating ideas from public theory.

SAMPLE LIST OF TEN SPECIALIST TERMS AND DEFINITIONS

Topic: Language acquisition and learning

comprehensible input	A term introduced by Stephen Krashen to refer to language which a learner can understand. The language may be comprehensible in part because of clues such as gestures, situations, or prior information.
developmental error	An error in learner language which does not result from the first language influence, but rather reflects the learner's gradual discovery of the second language system. These errors are often similar to those made by children learning the language as their mother tongue.
formulaic patterns or routines	These are expressions which are learned as unanalysed wholes of 'chunks' (for example, 'How old are you?').
fossilization	*Interlanguage* patterns which seem not to change, even after extended exposure to or instruction in the target language.

input	The language which the learner is exposed to (either written or spoken) in the environment.
interlanguage	The learner's developing second language knowledge. It may have characteristics of the learner's first language, characteristics of the second language, and some characteristics which seem to be very general and tend to occur in all or most interlanguage systems. Interlanguages are systematic, but they are also dynamic, continually evolving as learners receive more input and revise their hypotheses about the second language.
language acquisition	This term is most often used interchangeably with *language learning*. However, for some researchers, most notably Stephen Krashen, acquisition is contrasted with learning. According to Krashen, acquisition represents 'unconscious' learning, which takes place when attention is focused on meaning rather than language form.
language learning	A learner's developing knowledge of the target language. In Stephen Krashen's terms, however, 'learning' is contrasted with 'acquisition' and is described as a 'conscious' process which occurs when the learner's objective is to learn about the language itself, rather than to understand messages which are conveyed through the language.
overgeneralization error	This type of error is the result of trying to use a rule in a context where it does not belong, for example, a regular *-ed* ending on an irregular verb, as in 'buyed' instead of 'bought'.
transfer	Learners' use of patterns of the first language in second language sentences. Also called 'interference'.

(Lightbown and Spada, 1999: 171–9)

PROCEDURE

Allow about 45 minutes for this task.

1   Begin by writing one of the key terms that you have previously chosen on the blackboard. Ask the teachers if they understand it and/or can define it in their own language or in English. When the group has arrived at an acceptable working definition of the term, explain that you wish to examine other key terms related to the topic being investigated.

2   Follow the instructions on Worksheet 31. Ask teachers to write the name of the topic in the space provided. (Where appropriate, Part 1 could be done at home.) Write the remaining terms you have selected on the blackboard or on an overhead transparency, so that teachers can transfer them to the corresponding columns of the worksheet grid. Allow 5–10 minutes for Part 1 and 5–10 minutes for Part 2.

   Note: if you have copies of relevant published glossaries or specialised dictionaries, you may make them available to teachers in the training room (see 'Further reading' for Task 1.7 for some possible sources).

3.1 Once the teachers have completed the worksheet, check the meaning of the terms being focused on with the whole group, until satisfactory working definitions are agreed on.

3.2 The teachers may then copy down such definitions from the blackboard or an overhead transparency, using Worksheet 13 on p. 239 for this purpose, where appropriate. If there is a particularly important term for the teachers, display it along with its definition in the form of poster in a prominent position in the training room.

4   Definitions arrived at may, of course, be modified at a later date, in the light of subsequent experience, either individually or collectively.

5   As a follow-up activity, teachers may be encouraged to make personal records of new key terms related to other topics they investigate on their own, by using Worksheet 13.

Task 3.8 Targeted reading: key extracts

BACKGROUND FOR THE TRAINER

This task includes Option 21 (see below).

Teachers may learn a great deal about a particular topic by reading as much about it as possible. See also Task 2.6. Where plenty of published material is available for the topic being investigated, you may organise a targeted reading survey related to it, by adapting the procedures recommended for Task 2.6. Task 3.8 provides another way of structuring targeted reading, in the shape of a jigsaw reading activity, which involves teachers reading different, selected input on a given topic, as a springboard for reflection, discussion and possible action in the classroom.

TASK AIM

- to identify and discuss specific issues related to a topic for investigating in the classroom

PREPARATION

Prior to the training session, select different short extracts from key articles or books focusing on your topic which you feel will generate reflection and discussion, and make them all available to the teachers in the form of one handout, with each extract numbered, as in the sample selection below. Make as many copies of the handout as there are teachers in the group.

SAMPLE SELECTION OF READING EXTRACTS FOR THE TOPIC 'LEARNER AUTONOMY'

Read *one* of the following five texts on 'learner autonomy', following your trainer's instructions, and be prepared to summarise its content to your colleagues.

1 A careful analysis of the teacher–student relationship at any level, inside or outside school, reveals its fundamentally narrative character. The relationship involves a relating Subject (the teacher), and patient, listening objects (the students). The contents, whether values or empirical dimensions of reality, tend in the process of narration to become lifeless and petrified.

(Freire, 1972: 45)

2 A language is a highly complex set of systems, structures, and rules, and consequently the process of learning is fairly complicated. So, while any reasonably intelligent person can learn more about gardening or motor car maintenance fairly easily by reading, the same is not the case with language teaching. Because of its complexity, the person who wishes to continue learning a language independently has to first learn how to do it, and has to build up his or her confidence in their ability to do it.

(Dickinson and Carver, 1980)

3 Not long ago 'autonomy' and 'individualisation' were terms typically more widely acceptable to the 'lunatic fringe'. They are no doubt more widely acceptable now, but they are still, I think, terms typically associated with a radical re-structuring of our whole concept of language pedagogy, a re-structuring that involves the rejection of the traditional classroom and the introduction of wholly new ways of working.

(Allwright, 1988)

4 Five negatives:

a. Autonomy is not a synonym for self-instruction; in other words, autonomy is not limited to learning without a teacher. b. In the classroom context, autonomy does not entail an abdication of responsibility on behalf of the teacher; it is not a matter of letting the learners get on with things as best they can. c. On the other hand, learner autonomy is not something teachers do to learners; that is, it is not a teaching method. d. Autonomy is not an easily described single behaviour. e. Autonomy is not a steady state achieved by learners.

(Dam, 1991)

5 Autonomous learners:

1 can identify what's being taught / are aware of the teacher's objectives.
2 can formulate their own learning objectives.
3 can select and implement appropriate learning strategies.
4 can identify strategies that are not working for them and use others.
5 are involved in self-assessment/monitoring their own learning.

(Dickinson, 1993)

PROCEDURE

Allow 30–40 minutes for this task.

1 If, for example, you have selected five extracts for your handout, as in the above sample, put the teachers into sub-groups of five.

2.1 Ensure that each teacher has a copy of the extracts, and within the sub-groups randomly give them each a number from 1 to 5. Then ask each teacher to read their corresponding extract on the handout; for example, if they are Number 1, they read extract 1. (If in one sub-group there is not exactly the right number of teachers to cover all the extracts, ask an individual teacher to read more than one.)

2.2 Tell the teachers that as they read they should consider whether their extract reflects their own beliefs and experience; they should also be ready to summarise the contents of their extract for the others. Encourage teachers to make notes on the text, if they wish. Allow about 5 minutes for this activity.

3 Having read their extracts, each sub-group member in turn summarises the content of their own extract for the others in the sub-group, until all the extracts have been covered. Ask them to refer to key ideas and terms in their extract, but without reading the text aloud. This procedure should lead to general, yet focused, discussion of the topic within each sub-group. Allow about 15 minutes for this activity.

4 In a brief whole-group session, encourage teachers to suggest one of the issues raised in the sub-group discussion which they regard as high priority as a topic for investigating further in their classrooms. For example, with reference to extract 5 in the selection reproduced for this task, teachers could select an issue such:

How aware are our learners of our teaching objectives?

5   Teachers could then follow this up, by selecting another task from Chapter 3, for example Option 17 on p. 79. Alternatively, a task from Chapter 4, such as Task 4.5, could be used.

OPTION 21 EXAMINING COURSEBOOKS

Another profitable way of encouraging teachers to read is for them to examine how certain topics are handled in the different language coursebooks which are used in local schools.

1   Have copies of different coursebooks available in the training room (I have found that publishers are pleased to make such teaching material available, knowing that in this way teachers will find out about the material, and consider using it in their schools). I suggest you select both well-known and recently published titles.

2   In sub-groups, teachers examine one of the coursebooks with regard to the topic in question (where appropriate, encourage teachers to examine a coursebook they don't know very well). For example, teachers might consider how a certain book deals with the topic of 'learner autonomy', or whatever topic is being investigated. You can, of course, structure the teachers' reading. For example:

In what ways does the coursebook promote learner autonomy? Select one or two examples to tell the other teachers about...

Worksheet 23 on p. 251 could also be used to structure teachers' feedback on coursebooks.

3   The different sub-groups can then report their findings to the whole group.

3.9 Debate: understanding the wider implications of a topic

BACKGROUND FOR THE TRAINER

This task includes Worksheet 32 on p. 261.

Understandably, teachers often consider a topic from the viewpoint of their own particular school or learners, because this is the viewpoint they are familiar with. As a consequence, teachers may find it difficult to consider the implications or ramifications[1] of a topic in the wider social context beyond their classrooms or schools. (See Figure 2, in the Introduction.) Task 3.9 addresses this difficulty by encouraging teachers to discuss a topic

---

[1] A 'ramification' is one of the many consequences or developments that complicate a decision, idea or plan, especially the indirect consequences that are not at first obvious to you.

and consider in a formal debate its implications and ramifications, with participants taking on views which represent a broad cross-section of the educational community. Although, of course, there is a serious purpose to the debate, it should be approached in a spirit of fun!

TASK AIM

• to help teachers to explore a topic by formally debating an issue(s) related to it

PREPARATION

Before a training session, prepare both a 'motion' for debate (i.e. the precise issue which is to be debated), related to your topic, as well as a set of roles for the debate audience (for teachers who are not on the debating teams). See Section 6.28.1 for a sample motion for debate with accompanying roles which I have used with a group of teachers. Allow a maximum of four members per debating team, but make sure you prepare enough other roles so that each teacher has one – either on a team or as a member of the audience. I also suggest that you write the roles for the members of the audience on cards. Where appropriate, also prepare name-cards to place on the tables in front of each member of the audience to aid identification. See also Section 6.28.2 for suggestions for other motions for debate.

PROCEDURE

Allow at least 75 minutes for this task.

1   A role-play provides a way of breaking the ice before the actual debate, by brainstorming related issues and language (vocabulary, etc.), as follows: the teachers work in pairs; one teacher plays the role of an English teacher who is for the motion you prepared, and the other against it (for example, for and against 'testing' learners). The teachers defend their own positions. Allow about ten minutes for this role-play. (Alternatively, introduce the training session by means of a task from Chapter 3, or another activity of your choice.)

2.1 After the role-play, elicit and make a list on the blackboard of the arguments for and against the motion suggested by the teachers.

2.2 Follow the instructions on Worksheet 32, which teachers should read carefully before the preparation begins. Allocate the roles on the debating teams first, by asking for volunteers or by selecting teachers yourself. Then read out the prepared role-cards for the members of the audience one by one, and ask teachers to volunteer for a role. Go around helping the different sub-groups' preparation, taking time to ensure that: (a) the debating teams fully understand whether they are defending or opposing the motion, and that (b) the members of the audience are formulating provocative questions, preferably helping each other in pairs or small groups. Allow about 30 minutes for the preparation.

3.1 You can moderate the debate, if you wish; alternatively you can ask for a volunteer teacher to play this part. Also appoint a teacher to time the debating teams' opening interventions. Ideally, for the debate itself, teachers sit in a circle or semi-circle, with their name-cards in front of them on the table. Build up the atmosphere by getting the group to applaud the teams before and after they present. Allow 30 minutes for the debate.

3.2 After the debate, the teachers vote for the team that has best argued their case, not the team with which they agree! The winning team is applauded, and the losers consoled.

4 This task may be followed up by another in Chapter 3, for example Task 3.5, for which teachers are asked to summarise the debate in writing – from their own viewpoint or from that of another participant in the debate. Alternatively, a group could select a task from Chapter 4, for example Task 4.4 or Task 4.5, with reference to the topic they have debated. If the debate proves successful, the group may consider debating other topics later in the training programme.

4 Investigating in class

Introduction

Chapter 4 forms a crucial part of *Teachers in Action*, as it encourages teachers (a) to investigate in the classroom itself – within the social context of the school – by experimenting and collecting evidence with regard to topics being investigated, and (b) to evaluate and learn from this experience in class.

Practising teachers are busy people who are probably not skilled in – nor do they have time to develop – rigorous classroom data collection methods such as interaction analysis and observation schemes. Therefore, another

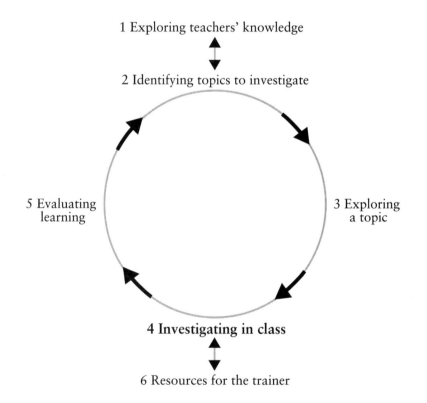

Figure 4.1   The investigating cycle in Teachers in Action

principal aim of Chapter 4 is to develop teachers' confidence and skills to investigate aspects of their work by giving them practice in different, teacher-friendly ways of collecting classroom evidence or data.

A further defining feature of the tasks is that they help teachers to investigate in their classrooms, but with the full support of the training group: the trainer and other colleagues. Investigating in class in this way is a key enabling skill; it potentially equips teachers with the necessary attitudes and skills to continue investigating autonomously in their future professional practice after the completion of a training programme.

Task 4.1 The benefits of investigating in class: teachers' perspectives

Investigating in class has helped me to recognise some practice contrary to my principles, for example, my excessive concern about grammatical correctness.

(teacher statement)

As a result of investigating in class some of my previous intuitions have become real.

(teacher statement)

BACKGROUND FOR THE TRAINER

This task includes Worksheet 33 on p. 262.

In my experience, teachers sometimes doubt their own abilities to investigate in class, even when offered help and encouragement to do so; they may also be put off by negative associations related to educational research. So this task, suited for use before teachers actually begin to investigate in class, is designed to overcome the above problems by presenting a selection of teachers' statements related to their own investigating in class. (These statements are extracts from formal reports written by a group of teachers, part of which required them to evaluate the experience of investigating.) See also Introduction, 'Key features and benefits of investigating', and Task 1.3.

TASK AIMS

- to familiarise teachers with the potential benefits to them of investigating in class
- to enhance teachers' confidence to investigate in class

PROCEDURE

Allow about 20–25 minutes for this task.

1   Explain to the teachers the meaning of 'investigating', or 'investigating in class' (where appropriate, refer to Task 1.3). Draw the teachers' attention to the quotations above, explaining that they show potential benefits of teachers investigating in class, as expressed by real teachers. Ask the group if they can think of any other benefits.

2   Follow the instructions on Worksheet 33, allowing about 5 minutes for its completion.

3.1 When the teachers are ready, and where appropriate, ask them to work in pairs to compare their responses to the worksheet.

3.2 Check the teachers' responses in whole-class mode. See Section 6.29.1 for the key. For the extra activity on the worksheet, check whether teachers have thought of any further benefits.

3.3 In addition to discussing the benefits of investigating, and in the interest of presenting a balanced picture, you may also wish to refer to some of the difficulties in investigating in class. For example, the teachers might lack data collection skills. See Section 6.29.2 for a list of five such potential difficulties and advice for trainers. Naturally, you may draw on this information while discussing difficulties with teachers. However, in the process of doing so, be careful not to exaggerate the problems so as to put teachers off becoming involved altogether!

4   If you feel that the task aim of enhancing teachers' confidence to investigate in class has been achieved, teachers may now attempt other tasks in Chapter 4, or other related activities, with reference to a relevant topic.

FURTHER READING

Teachers may also be recommended further reading related to investigating, or teacher-directed classroom research. See, for example:

Edge and Richards, *Teachers Develop Teachers Research*
Head and Taylor, *Readings in Teacher Development*
Hopkins, *A Teacher's Guide to Classroom Research*

Task 4.2 Which data collection method?

BACKGROUND FOR THE TRAINER

This task includes Worksheet 34 on p. 264.

While investigating in class, for example by means of the tasks in Chapter 4, teachers are encouraged to collect and to select significant data in terms of the aims set for the topic being investigated. Teachers can then use this data when presenting the results of their work in their classroom, for example in informal presentations in a training session, or in a talk given at a teachers' conference. Task 4.2 assumes that teachers are about to start investigating in class; it is designed to help teachers to find out about different ways or methods of collecting data and to consider the appropriateness of these methods. See Task 1.3., which defines the terms 'investigating' and 'investigating in class', of which the latter is particularly relevant to the task in hand. See also Section 6.8 for the key for Worksheets 6 and 7, as Task 4.2 focuses on stage 5 of the sequence referred to in this key, 'Decide which data to collect'. In addition, Task 4.2 is closely related to Task 4.1, which outlines the potential benefits of investigating in class.

TASK AIMS

- to familiarise teachers with some data collection methods
- to help teachers to select suitable data collection methods for investigating in the classroom, and to evaluate these

PROCEDURE

Allow approximately 30–40 minutes for this task (not including the optional evaluation stage: see stage 3 below).

Note: it is assumed that the teachers know *what* it is they wish to observe or investigate in class, which will obviously be influenced by the nature of the topic. For example, if the teachers are investigating 'group work', they will perhaps collect data on what happens while their learners are engaged in group work.

1   Ask the teachers in what ways they could collect data or evidence related to the topic selected while investigating it in the classroom. Elicit examples such as 'writing a questionnaire', and write these on the blackboard. At this stage you might also wish to give the teachers some general advice about investigating, for example:

- The data collection method you use should not be too technical or demanding. If it is too complex or ambitious, it will interfere with your teaching, which is your main responsibility!
- Small is beautiful. Limit your data collection to one group of learners, for a limited period of time. Choose a narrow focus to investigate; instead of investigating 'correcting', for example, select a more manageable focus, such as ' the correction of oral mistakes in fluency activities'.

(See Introduction, 'Key features and benefits of investigating'.)

See also Section 6.29.2 for a discussion of potential difficulties when investigating in class and advice for trainers, in particular the sections on teachers' unfamiliarity with the idea of investigating in class and teachers' lack of data collection skills.

2.1 Use Worksheet 34 to (a) provide the teachers with a fuller list of possible collection methods, supplementing the examples you have already elicited from the teachers and written on the blackboard, and (b) help the group select data collection methods which they would like to experiment with regarding the topic being investigated. Allow approximately 30 minutes for the the group to complete the worksheet. Supplement the brief description of each method on the worksheet by providing more information about each one that is of interest. Beforehand you may wish to consult the background information for the individual tasks in Chapter 4 or the cross-references on Worksheet 34 between each of the nine methods and the corresponding tasks or options in other parts of the book. Of course, you may also like to add information about other methods not included on the worksheet.

2.2 Decide with the group on a timetable for implementation of the methods selected, in other words, who will try out what and when. Ask teachers to fill in the relevant names of teachers and the corresponding dates in the appropriate worksheet column. Once the worksheet has been completed, it will help the teachers to know who is doing what and to monitor the progress of all the activities.

Note: in principle, it will be easier for everyone concerned if the group selects one method or a small number of methods, as this will make the whole process more manageable. You could ask either (a) different teachers to try out different methods at the same time, over a certain period of time, or (b) all the teachers to try out each method selected at the same time, one after the other, over a certain period of time. Whichever way you choose, organise the teachers into subgroups, once they have decided on suitable methods, so that they can work together, providing each other with mutual support. In addition, if for some reason an individual teacher is not able to try out a method in class, he or she will still be able to work closely with teachers in the same sub-group who can.

3 One follow-up activity available is to use the final column of Worksheet 34 in a later training session to help teachers to evaluate the various methods tried out. In order to prepare teachers for this in advance, tell teachers before they start collecting data in class that they will also evaluate the method at a later stage. Ask the teachers to fill in the corresponding column on the worksheet before the training session in question. Use any such teacher entries on the worksheet as a starting point for a whole-group discussion/evaluation.

COMBINING TASKS

Once a group of teachers has decided on a method(s), you may then use the corresponding task from elsewhere in the book, for example in Chapter 4. See cross-references on Worksheet 34 between each method and the corresponding tasks and options.

FURTHER READING

See Hopkins, *A Teachers's Guide to Classroom Research*, Chapter 6, 'Data gathering', in particular pp. 82–3, 'Taxonomy of classroom research techniques', in which a summary of the advantages and disadvantages of different methods is clearly presented.

Task 4.3 Our learners in action: using photographs of learners

© Julie Houck / CORBIS

© Ted Spiegel / CORBIS

105

© Bob Rowan; Progressive Images / CORBIS

© Keren Su / CORBIS

BACKGROUND FOR THE TRAINER

This task includes Options 22, 23 and 24 (see below).

A relatively simple way of collecting classroom data with regard to a particular topic is for teachers to take photographs of their learners, if appropriate in the training context. Most people are used to taking snapshots in their personal lives, so taking photographs of a reasonable quality as part of investigating does not require specialised skills. Using photographs for teacher education and development is: (a) a way of bringing the real world of schools, classrooms and learners into the training room (personally I have learnt a lot, often in great detail, about the realities of teachers' schools by looking at teachers' photographs, information I am sure it would be difficult to obtain by other means); (b) a powerful stimulus to help teachers to reflect, discuss and learn; and (c) a way of supporting other types of classroom data, such as lesson plans, diaries or questionnaires.

TASK AIM

- to encourage teachers to take photographs of their learners as a way of collecting classroom data about a topic

PROCEDURE

Allow about 30–40 minutes for this task over two training sessions.

1.1 By way of introduction, the teachers individually consider the photographs of learners reproduced for this task, perhaps using the following prompts:

What similarities or differences are there between the photographs?

What similarities or differences are there between these photographs and your own teaching situation?

Choose a photograph(s) you particularly like, or one you dislike, and say why.

Allow 2–3 minutes for this activity.

1.2 The teachers compare their responses in pairs. Allow five minutes for this activity.

1.3 In a whole-group discussion, elicit some of the teachers' responses to the photographs.

2.1 Suggest to the teachers that they take photographs of their own learners in action in their schools and classrooms, and bring them to a future session. This is best done with regard to a particular topic which is being investigated by the group, or by an individual teacher. For example, if the group is investigating 'group work in the classroom', teachers could take photographs of their learners involved in group work in order to support other forms of data they collect. Ask teachers to photograph learners involved in activities related to the topic which they regard as significant in terms of their teaching principles and/or teaching aims. If appropriate, teachers could also take photographs of their school, the classroom or themselves instead of, or as well as, their learners.

Note: it is not necessary for all the teachers in a training group to take photographs, as some might not have a camera, or might not feel comfortable using one in class, for example. Also recommend to teachers that as far as possible they try to take photographs in which learners are behaving naturally, not posing artificially for the camera.

2.2 Agree on the date of a future training session when teachers can bring and share their photographs, allowing plenty of time for teachers to take the photographs and have them developed.

3.1 In the agreed training session, the teachers show each other their photographs in small groups in one of the following ways:

1 play the game '20 questions' (see Option 23)

2 compare and discuss their photographs (see questions in stage 1.1 above);

3 select significant ones, categorise them, or find links between them

Allow 10 minutes for this activity.

3.2 Lead a brief whole-group discussion in which you elicit feedback from stage 3.1 and ask the group to select some of the photographs for display on the training rooms walls, allowing the material to be referred to in future training sessions.

3.3 As a means of evaluating the effectiveness of this task, you may also wish to elicit from teachers practical recommendations for taking photographs, using Worksheet 27 on p. 256 as a means of recording these. For example:

It's a good idea to tell your learners why you are taking photos. Photos can be used to show others what happens in your class, for example parents.

4 Encourage teachers to use photographs of learners together with other forms of data when giving a presentation to other teachers in the future: see Task 5.7. Photographs may also be used to bring to life reports or articles related to teachers' work investigating: see Task 5.8.

Note: instead of devoting a substantial part of one training session to using photographs, encourage teachers to bring their photographs on an individual basis, as and when they have been developed. Individual teachers could then take a few minutes at the beginning of different sessions to show the group their photographs, comment on and discuss them.

OPTION 22 USING PHOTOGRAPHS OF LEARNERS FROM THE LOCAL CONTEXT

As an alternative, or in addition to, using the photographs reproduced for this task, pre-select photographs featuring learners in different contexts published in the local educational press, where appropriate, or taken by local teachers. Use these photographs with the teachers as in the procedures described for Task 4.3 above. Build up your own collection of such photographs for use with teachers and/or ask teachers themselves to collect photographs from the local educational press, in advance of a training session.

OPTION 23 20 QUESTIONS: INTRODUCING A TOPIC BY MEANS OF A PHOTOGRAPH

Choose a photograph which is relevant to the topic being focused on in a training session, but do not show it to the teachers. Hold it in front of you in such a way that the teachers cannot see it. They then have to ask you a fixed number of *yes/no* questions – say, 20, 15 or 10 – in order to find out as much about the chosen photograph as possible. For example, typical questions might be as follows:

Are the learners working in groups?
Is the teacher standing?

Finally, show the teachers the photograph.

OPTION 24 USING OTHER VISUAL DATA: VIDEO AND DRAWING

1 *Teacher-produced video materials*
  Teachers can also **video record** their learners in action in class, where appropriate. Teachers who choose to do this might wish to view the resulting video themselves but not show it to other colleagues. But where teachers agree, such material could be valuable for use in training sessions to demonstrate to other teachers how certain ideas or activities could be introduced into class. This would allow other teachers to see with their own eyes a teaching idea being implemented in the local situation; perhaps as a result they will be convinced of its effectiveness, and be inspired to experiment with it themselves in their own classes.

2 *Published video material*
  Instead of using locally produced video material, you may like to make use of published material which features teachers at work, such as the excellent, internationally focused: *Looking at Language Classrooms* (1997), produced by Bampfield.

3 *Drawing*
  I have also organised interesting training sessions where teachers have been asked to **draw** their schools and/or classrooms – a quicker, more immediate and personalised alternative to taking photographs. Teachers will almost certainly need much encouragement in putting pencil to paper in order to draw their schools, but I have found that it is worth it!

Task 4.4 Consulting our learners (1): using a simple questionnaire

Investigating has helped me to value my learners' judgement and to make up my mind to ask for their opinion about our classroom practice more often and more formally than before.

While listening to the pupils' opinions and suggestions, it's possible to detect and sometimes choose a better way of working together.

BACKGROUND FOR THE TRAINER

Task 4.4 includes Worksheets 35 and 36 on pp. 266–9.

This task assumes that the group of teachers has already selected a topic for investigating. Finding out what learners, even quite young ones, think about a particular topic can often be the source of surprising insights for teachers. One way of doing this is for learners to respond to a questionnaire written by the teacher. However, writing an effective questionnaire may prove difficult for those with little or no prior experience, so this task provides teachers with guidance and practice in this respect. It is important to understand that in this task, questionnaires are not intended to be a rigorous, technical research method. Rather, trainers are offered a non-threatening, teacher-friendly way of helping teachers to co-operate in the planning, administering and evaluating in small groups of a simple learner questionnaire. While trying to decide whether the use of questionnaires is feasible or worthwhile in your teachers' teaching context, trainers may like to consider the summary of the advantages and disadvantages of using questionnaires to collect classroom data in Section 6.30. See also Task 4.5 for a similar, yet possibly less demanding, way for teachers to consult learners.

TASK AIMS

- to encourage teachers to consult their learners by means of learner questionnaires as a way of improving the effectiveness of their professional practice
- to develop teachers' skills in writing and using simple learner questionnaires

PROCEDURE

Allow at least three hours for this task over two training sessions, between which teachers administer their questionnaires in class. Follow the instructions on Worksheet 35, allowing at least one hour for the first session, the planning stage of the worksheet.

1.1 By way of introduction, refer the teachers to the teacher quotations at the beginning of this task, and ask if such views reflect their own experience. Explain that one way of finding out about learners' opinions is to ask them to respond to a questionnaire. Suggest that the teachers consult classes of learners of their choice about the topic selected by writing a brief questionnaire in small groups, giving it to the learners, and then presenting and evaluating the resulting data in a future training session.

Note: I recommend that the questionnaires in one group of teachers should all focus on the same broad topic, but that sub-groups can focus on different aspects of it, if they wish. For example, if the whole group is investigating 'correction', some teachers could examine specific techniques for learners' oral mistakes, while others consider techniques for correcting learners' written work.

1.2 Explain any technical terms related to questionnaires that you think will be necessary for this task, such as: 'to administer a questionnaire'; 'to collect data' (information); 'respondent' (the reader of the questionnaire); 'structured or open questions'; 'to pilot' (to try the questionnaire out); 'to collate the results'; as well as 'bar graphs' and 'pie charts'. (For the last two you are recommended to show the group examples, possibly by displaying on the training room wall those produced by previous groups of teachers.)

1.3 Before asking the teachers to write their questionnaires, lead a brief general discussion, focusing on one or more of the following points:
   - Elicit and discuss any benefits of using questionnaires as a way of consulting learners (for more information, see Section 6.30).
   - Elicit a list of the characteristics of an effective questionnaire, and/or refer to the list on Worksheet 36.
   - If you have copies of questionnaires written by other teachers in the local context, the present group may, if appropriate, evaluate the questionnaires, using the information in Worksheet 36 as criteria for this purpose.

2   While the teachers are planning their questionnaire, help each sub-group, where appropriate. Pay particular attention to the clarity of aims of each questionnaire by helping teachers to formulate precise questions, as well as getting them to agree on how to report the questionnaire results (choosing from overhead transparencies, posters and handouts, or from bar graphs, pie charts, etc.). Ensure that each teacher who is able to conduct a questionnaire in class leaves the first training session with a copy of a questionnaire (handwritten or photocopied). Recommend strongly that teachers pilot their questionnaire with a teacher who is not involved in the investigating before they conduct it with pupils. Agree on the date of a second training session with the teachers, when together they can analyse, interpret and discuss the data collected, first in sub-groups, and then with the whole group.

3.1 In Session 2, the teachers evaluate in their sub-groups the results of the questionnaires administered, following the instructions on the worksheet, and using the worksheet questions as a guide. Provide paper, pens and overhead transparencies for teachers to report their results. Allow the teachers at least one hour to collate, analyse and interpret the results.

3.2 If you feel your teachers are able to stand up in front of each other and present their results, let them do so. See Section 6.38 for strategies for developing teachers' presentation skills and the characteristics of an effective presentation. (Alternatively, teachers may present their data in the form of a poster for the others to view: see Section 6.39.1.) Allow plenty of time for the presentation of the results, about 5 minutes per sub-group, as well as time for discussing each presentation. Poster presentations will probably take less time than those where teachers use an overhead projector or other aids.

4.1 Following the presentations, elicit any key practical recommendations that the teachers suggest concerning the topic being investigated, using Worksheet 27 on p. 256, for this purpose, if you wish.

4.2 See Task 5.1 for guidelines on how to encourage the teachers to evaluate the effectiveness of Task 4.4. Where appropriate, you may also refer teachers back to the list of questionnaire characteristics on Worksheet 36, adding any new suggestions arising from participants' own experience in conducting questionnaires.

4.3 The momentum of investigating may be maintained by (a) encouraging individual teachers to follow up one of the practical recommendations suggested above in their classes, or (b) directing teachers' attention towards the possible future use of questionnaires: see 'Further action' at the end of Worksheet 35.

FURTHER READING

Consult the literature concerning the use of questionnaires in classroom research, such as:

Youngman, *Designing Questionnaires*, pp. 156–76
Hopkins, *A Teacher's Guide to Classroom Research*, pp. 72–5
Wallace, *Action Research for Language Teachers*, Chapter 7

Task 4.5 Consulting our learners (2): What did you learn today?

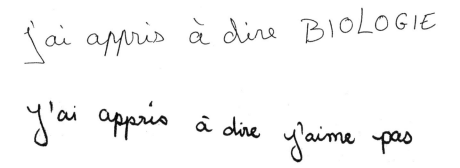

j'ai appris à dire BIOLOGIE

y'ai appris à dire y'aime pas

BACKGROUND FOR THE TRAINER

Task 4.5 includes Worksheet 37 on p. 270, and Options 25, 26 and 27 (see below).

Task 4.5 assumes that the group of teachers has already selected a topic(s) for investigating in class. Finding out what learners think and feel about a particular topic can often be the source of surprising insights for teachers. This task provides a simple way of consulting learners, requiring little preparation and planning by teachers, unlike other methods such as a learner questionnaire (see Task 4.4). At the end of a lesson, learners are asked to reflect briefly about what they have learnt, after which they each write down an answer on a separate slip of paper. The task may also be used to focus teachers' attention on the relationship between what is taught in a lesson and what gets learnt by learners (see in particular Option 27).

TASK AIM

- to encourage teachers to consult their learners as a way of improving the effectiveness of their professional practice

PREPARATION

For each teacher prepare one slip of paper which is large enough to write a sentence or two on.

PROCEDURE

Allow about one hour for this task over two training sessions, between which teachers collect classroom data.

1   Ask the teachers how they know if a group of learners has enjoyed a lesson, or not. For example, teachers might know because of the expressions on learners' faces, the atmosphere in class, the type of questions learners ask, etc. Enquire if teachers also ask their learners for their views on lessons on an informal basis; explain that for this task you wish to encourage the group to do this on a systematic basis.

2   Follow the instructions on Worksheet 37, allowing about 10–15 minutes for Part 1, and about 10 minutes for Part 2. In a brief whole-class discussion, elicit the teachers' responses to worksheet questions 1–3, located at the end of Part 1. In particular, list any responses to question 3 on the blackboard, and discuss these. Some sample answers to worksheet questions 1–3 are provided in Section 6.31.

3   Suggest that the teachers try asking their own learners what they have learnt at the end of a lesson, as shown on Worksheet 37; agree that this should be done by a certain date. If necessary, refer to the benefits of consulting learners in this way, as discussed in answer to the final question in Section 6.31. (It may be that not all the teachers are able, or willing, to ask their learners, but this need not necessarily be a problem.) The teachers could consult their learners in class with reference to a topic being investigated by the group, or by themselves as individuals. Thus, teachers would ask their learners the question 'What did you learn today?' after the learners have been involved in an activity related to the topic selected. Advise teachers to consider carefully which language their learners use to write down their statements, that is to say, their own language or English; this decision will depend on such factors as the learners' age and language competence. Recommend strongly the use of slips of paper for the learners to write their statements on; this makes it much easier for teachers to analyse the data afterwards (e.g. for categorising the statements). Remind the teachers when they should bring their learner statements to a training session.

4   In the agreed training session the teachers bring the slips of paper they have collected from their classes.

4.1 Ask the teachers to analyse their data individually by addressing questions 1 and 2 on Worksheet 37 for about 5 minutes.

4.2 Ask the teachers to compare their results in groups of three or four, using (some of) the questions on Worksheet 42 on p. 276. Allow teachers 15 minutes for this activity.

4.3 In whole-class mode, obtain feedback from the sub-groups' discussions, trying to identify concrete recommendations or aspects related to the topic in question which can be further investigated by the whole group or by individuals.

COMBINING TASKS

Teachers can use the data collected for this task alongside other forms of data, such as photographs, when, for example, giving an informal presentation to other teachers (see Task 5.7).

OPTION 25 WHAT DID YOU LEARN TODAY?

For fun, at the end of the training session in which the group has been focusing on Task 4.5, or indeed another task, give all of the teachers a slip of paper, and ask them to write down something they have learnt in the session. Collect in the slips of paper and read them; you could then start off the next training session by selecting some of the statements to read out to the group.

OPTION 26 OTHER WAYS OF RECORDING CLASSROOM DATA

When investigating a particular topic teachers can be encouraged to do the following, in addition to the forms of classroom data referred to in the tasks in Chapter 4.

1 Keep a *diary*, in which they record their observations, reflections and interpretations in writing (see also Task 2.7 for ways of structuring this).

2 Keep an *audio-diary*. Instead of writing down their observations, reflections and interpretations, teachers audio-record them, preferably following the lesson in question. This alternative avoids some of the potential tedium of writing a diary.

3 *Audio-record* a lesson, or part of a lesson, by placing a cassette recorder on the teacher's desk. This is particularly valuable in that it enables a teacher to focus on aspects of the lesson, after the event, in a way that is quite impossible while actually involved in teaching it. Teachers could record a lesson in which, for example, they were going to experiment with a new teaching idea. Another advantage of this method is that teachers can also listen to the recording as many times as necessary. Learners should be told that they are being recorded, and, if appropriate, why.

OPTION 27 ANALYSING THE PERFORMANCE GAP

1 On completion of Task 4.5, or others like it involving the evaluation of classroom activities, ask teachers to read statement (a) below related to what I call the 'performance gap', and statement (b), an authentic example of a teacher having identified such a gap.

> a A growing body of research suggests, 1. there is often incongruence between a teacher's publicly declared philosophy or beliefs about education and how he or she behaves in the classroom, 2. there is often incongruence between the teacher's declared goals and objectives and the way in which the lesson is actually taught, and 3. there is is often a discrepancy between a teacher's perceptions or account of a lesson, and the perceptions or account of other participants (e.g. pupils or observers) in the classroom (vide, Elbaz, 1983).
>
> (cited in Hopkins, 1985: 48)

> b Investigating in class has helped me to recognise some practice contrary to my principles, for example, my excessive concern about grammatical correctness.
>
> (teacher)

2 Ask the teachers if the above statements reflect their own experience, especially regarding the task(s) they have completed as part of their investigations, and if this experience has helped them to identify a performance gap or incongruence, as described in the statements above. If individual teachers are able to answer this question affirmatively, the gaps identified could provide the focus for further investigation on an individual basis. Even if teachers do not reply affirmatively, the discussion could raise teachers' awareness about such aspects as the relationship between what is taught and what gets learnt, and possibly lead to further profitable reflection about teaching and learning in the future.

Task 4.6 Talking about real people: writing a learner profile

> The experienced lecturer knows how effective it is when he [*sic*] uses a specific instance to illustrate a general principle. The interest of the audience is held when he *talks about real people* or an actual event instead of theoretical principles and abstract ideas. ...Often we understand an idea better if we have an example before us. The specific detail is something which we are familiar with, and the single instance helps us to see how the abstract principles fit together. Quoting cases to illustrate gives the picture a three-dimensional reality.
>
> (Nisbet and Watt, 1984: 72–3; my emphasis)

BACKGROUND FOR THE TRAINER

Task 4.6 includes Worksheet 38 on p. 272, and Option 28 (see below).

This task encourages teachers to write a learner profile, or mini case study, with reference to an individual learner that they teach. A full 'case study', viewed by Hopkins (1985: 81) as being fairly exhaustive and time-consuming, would also in my view be too demanding for busy, practising teachers. See Section 6.32.1 for an extract from a detailed formal case study conducted in mainstream education in the United Kingdom. Nevertheless, I believe that a teacher-friendly *mini case study* can be a useful data collection method for busy, practising teachers. So this task provides a framework for teachers to focus on real people by examining the general characteristics of an individual learner in some detail, as a kind of 'baseline' study, or starting point. Subsequently, teachers may write a second learner profile of the same individual learner, recording, for example, any change, development or progress in the learner, or his or her reaction to a particular teaching activity being investigated by the teacher. This might be summarised as shown in Figure 4.2.

Learner profile 1 (baseline)		Learner profile 2 (written some time later)
general characteristics of learner	➡	identifying change, development and progress in learner, or reaction to a particular teaching activity, etc.

Figure 4.2   A framework for a mini case study

See Section 6.32.2 for an example of a baseline learner profile written by a teacher. Naturally, all the learner profile data may support other types of data collected with regard to the topic being investigated, such as photographs (see for example Task 4.3), in an attempt to give the resulting profile a three-dimensional reality.

TASK AIM

- to provide teachers with practice in investigating what happens in their schools and classrooms from the perspective of an individual learner of their choice (over a period of time)

PROCEDURE

Allow about one hour for this task (as far as stage 3 in the procedure).

1   Suggest to the teachers that they write a learner profile with reference to a learner of their choice; explain in general terms what is required.

Discuss with them briefly the benefits of doing so, referring, where appropriate, to the arguments presented in the quotation at the beginning of this task and/or the background information for the trainer above.

2   Follow the instructions on Worksheet 38, allowing teachers 20 minutes to complete Part 1, and 20 minutes for Part 2. Please note that Part 1 may be completed at home, or in a training session. Some teachers are likely to have difficulty choosing a learner to write about, so the following general guidelines may help. Teachers may choose:

- a learner they know reasonably well
- a 'good'/'weak' learner
- a 'normal' learner (one who is representative of the age group in question)
- a learner who interests or intrigues them for some reason (for example, a learner who experiences a particular learning difficulty)
- a learner who the teacher has identified as a result of another data collection method, for example a questionnaire (in which case the profile may act as a follow-up to the other method)

Where appropriate, refer teachers to the example of a baseline learner profile in Section 6.32.2 before they write their own profiles.

3.1 After teachers have completed Part 2 of Worksheet 38, hold a brief general discussion about the similarities and differences between different learners by inviting different pairs of teachers to comment.

3.2 Use Task 5.1 in order to evaluate this task. In particular, you are encouraged to discuss the usefulness of writing a learner profile: see Worksheet 42.

4   Where appropriate, after several weeks or months have elapsed on the training programme, encourage teachers to write a second, follow-up learner profile of the same individual, especially when they are investigating a particular topic in their classroom, as suggested in the 'Background for the trainer' for this task. Teachers may give you their completed worksheet, for information.

COMBINING TASKS

Individual teachers may refer to their learner profiles, for example in subsequent tutorials with a trainer (see Task 5.6), referring, where appropriate, to any changes they have observed in the learner since the first profile was written.

FURTHER READING

See also Nisbet and Watt, Case Study.

OPTION 28 ILLUSTRATING INSIGHTS BY MEANS OF LEARNER-PRODUCED MATERIALS

When using the learner profile as a way of investigating a topic and presenting the results of one's investigations, a teacher may also include and analyse any work completed by the individual learners in question, as a way of illustrating points raised or insights gained in the case study. This might include copies of texts written by the learner, drawings completed, extracts from workbook exercises completed by the learner, etc.

Task 4.7 An informal interview with a learner

BACKGROUND INFORMATION FOR THE TRAINER

This task includes Worksheet 39 on p. 273.

Interviewing an individual learner informally allows a teacher to gain in-depth information about a specific topic, and may be combined particularly well with learner questionnaires or learner profiles (see Tasks 4.4 and 4.6 respectively). A further benefit is that, as with the learner profile, the information gained from an interview provides a three-dimensional view of reality or of the particular topic being focused on. Hopkins (1985: 68) suggests the following advantages for the teacher/learner interview: the teacher is in direct contact with the learner; the learner is familiar with the teacher, and therefore more at ease; the teacher is able to seek the desired information directly and not through a ream of irrelevant information (such as with a questionnaire); an interview can be held in lesson time or outside the class; problems with the interview can be followed up immediately when they arise. On the other hand, the disadvantages he identifies include that: it is time-consuming; may be carried out with some kind of recording equipment, with the attendant disadvantages, and it is frequently difficult to get younger children to explain their thoughts and feelings. Of course, interviewing effectively is a difficult skill requiring much practice, especially when used as a rigorous research instrument. This task, however, presents the informal interview as an accessible data collection method for busy teachers by helping them to use the interview in combination with other methods. There are practical reasons why I suggest combining methods in this way. Firstly, if interviewing is time-consuming, teachers may use a previously administered questionnaire as a basis for their interviewing schedule. Secondly, many of the technical issues related to interviewing which are important to get right in order for it to be effective are also relevant to questionnaires, including having a clear aim, ethical considerations, the length and layout, the language to be used, the response method, etc. So teachers can transfer their experience of using questionnaires to the new challenge of interviewing (see also Worksheet 36, 'Ten characteristics of an effective questionnaire', for further information).

TASK AIMS

- to help teachers to prepare and evaluate an informal interview (structured or semi-structured) with a learner
- to develop teachers' interviewing skills

PROCEDURE

Allow approximately one hour over two training sessions for this task.

1 Introduce the idea of the informal teacher/learner interview as a way of collecting data about a topic being investigated, especially where the group has already administered a questionnaire on this topic (see Task 4.4).

2 See Worksheet 39.

2.1 Before teachers use the worksheet, help them to decide whether they wish to experiment with a structured interview or a semi-structured interview, using the definitions below to inform the teachers' choice.

Structured interviews are defined by Wallace (1998: 146) as having:

> a very tight structure, and in which the questions will probably be read from a carefully prepared interview schedule, similar to a questionnaire but used orally.

The semi-structured interview, on the other hand, he defines as:

> a prepared interview schedule, but most of the questions will probably be open questions. *The schedule may also contain prompts (i.e. comments, examples or follow-up questions intended to encourage the interviewee to give fuller, more detailed responses.* Semi-structured interviews combine a certain degree of control with a certain amount of freedom to develop the interview.

> (ibid.: 147, my emphasis)

My personal view is that the semi-structured interview is most suited to following up a questionnaire – see the above quotation – but the characteristics of your training situation may lead you to decide otherwise.

2.2 Share with the teachers the following practical advice about interviewing, in addition to other ideas that you yourself may have, or that you find in the literature (write such advice and ideas on the blackboard or on an overhead transparency).

- Be clear about the aim of the interview.
- Keep the interview brief.
- Interview during a class or at other times.
- Try interviewing one learner first. (Then try a second interview if you have time.)
- Interview a learner whose questionnaire provided an insight that you wish to obtain more information on.

- The interview could be conducted in the learner's mother tongue, especially when a learner may experience even more difficulty explaining thoughts and feelings in English than in his or her own language.
- Record the interview if possible.

3   The teachers organise themselves into sub-groups of three or four. Ask the sub-groups to consult the questionnaire(s) that they have previously produced related to the topic being investigated, and to plan their interviews so as to elicit more in-depth information about the focus of the questionnaire. (For practical reasons, it may not necessarily be possible for everyone in a sub-group to conduct an interview, but there should be at least one or two teachers per group who can. Tell the teachers that although there is space on the worksheet for two interviews, they need interview only one learner, reminding them that 'small is beautiful'.) Allow teachers approximately 15 minutes to complete Part 1 of Worksheet 39.

4.1 In another training session, after the teachers have conducted their interviews, ask them to form the same sub-groups as in point 3 above, and process the results of the interviews by completing Part 2 of Worksheet 39. (In addition, teachers could exchange information in pairs about the interviews they have each held, and fill in the relevant information about the other's interview in the second column of the worksheet.) Allow teachers approximately 15 minutes for Part 2 of the worksheet.

4.2 In whole-group mode, use worksheet questions 6, 7 and 8 to elicit learning points resulting from the interviews as regards the topic being investigated, as well as recommendations for improving the teachers' interviewing skills, by writing these on the blackboard or on an overhead transparency. Encourage teachers to copy down any recommendations they feel relevant to them, so that they have something concrete to take away with them and consult at a later date.

COMBINING TASKS

As suggested above, Task 4.7 may be profitably combined with Tasks 4.4 and 4.6.

FURTHER READING

Wallace, *Action Research for Language Teachers*, Chapter 7, 'Questionnaires and interviews'
Hopkins, *A Teacher's Guide to Classroom Research*, Chapter 6, 'Data gathering'

Task 4.8 Experimenting in class

BACKGROUND FOR THE TRAINER

This task is one of the most crucial in *Teachers in Action*, and includes Worksheets 40 and 41 on pp. 274–5.

For most teachers, the experience of experimenting or trying out new teaching ideas in class probably constitutes an important part of professional learning and change: see also Kolb's experiential learning cycle in Task 3.6. However, some people might take a rather dim view of teachers 'experimenting' with learners, comparing this to a scientist experimenting with guinea pigs. Ruddock, however, adds a moral dimension to the present discussion by stating that:

> Not to examine one's own practice is irresponsible; to regard teaching as an experiment and to monitor one's own performance is a responsible professional act.
>
> (cited in Williams and Burden, 1997: 55)

But how specifically can experimenting in class be integrated into a teacher education programme? Trainers can motivate teachers to select, and experiment with, teaching ideas which are compatible with their personality, personal theories and current practice. Possible sources for such ideas might include: colleagues, methodology books or a training programme. For example, in a workshop teachers may have focused on different activities for teaching grammar (see Task 3.6), and, as a result, some teachers wish to try out in their own teaching an activity which fits in with the way they work. Experimenting can, however, produce unforeseen problems and hitches for teachers. Put simply, things can go wrong. So motivating teachers to experiment is more than arousing their initial interest, as it involves helping them to sustain interest and invest time and energy into putting in the necessary effort to achieve certain goals (Williams and Burden 1997: 121). Such help – from the trainer or other teachers – might take the form of support for an individual teacher when there is a problem or hitch with an experiment. Teachers may also find it difficult to evaluate the effectiveness of such experiments systematically, so this task seeks to provide a simple, non-threatening framework for this purpose.

TASK AIMS

- to encourage teachers to experiment with and evaluate the effectiveness of teaching ideas in class
- to encourage teachers to share their experience and ideas

PROCEDURE

Allow at least 75 minutes for this task, over two training sessions.

1. Follow the instructions on Worksheet 40.

1.1 Before completing the questionnaire, the teachers select a teaching idea they would like to try out in class, which they may have identified after having used tasks in previous chapters, or by some other means. In a training session, help the teachers to select an idea. Encourage them either to choose one that appeals to them on an individual basis, or to work in sub-groups in which members try out the same teaching idea and compare the results afterwards. Recommend that teachers experiment with one group of learners only, so that the process remains manageable. Before teachers use the worksheets, agree with them what to do with the texts once they are completed; for example, you may want the teachers to read each other's worksheets (see the Introduction, 'Using the worksheets', point 9). Allow at least 20 minutes for the teachers to try to select a teaching idea to experiment with, and/or ask them to decide outside the training session.

1.2 Ask the teachers to complete the worksheets about their teaching idea at home or in school, and suggest that the group then discusses the completed worksheets in a future training session. Agree on a date for this with the group, leaving plenty of time for teachers to experiment in class. The teachers should allow themselves about 15 minutes to complete the worksheet – after teaching the lesson(s) in which they have experimented. Suggest they fill in the worksheet immediately after the lesson or on the same day, while their memories are still fresh. Encourage teachers to produce a lesson plan for the lesson in question and to bring it to the training session: see Worksheet 41 for an example of a lesson plan sheet. For worksheet question 4, 'What do you think the learners learnt? What evidence do you have?', encourage teachers to use any data collection methods they have practised in other tasks in this book in order to provide evidence, where appropriate. See Section 6.33.1 for a sample worksheet completed by a teacher (it has a similar structure to that of Worksheet 40).

2 In the agreed follow-up training session, in groups of three or four, the teachers evaluate their experiments with teaching ideas by focusing a discussion on Worksheet 40, and in particular question 7:

How worthwhile is/was the teaching idea? Will you use it again? If so, why? If not, Why not?

Ask each sub-group to select one of the teaching ideas which has proved effective in order to tell the whole group about it afterwards. Allow about 20 minutes for this activity.

3.1 In a plenary discussion, the sub-groups report which effective ideas they have selected. Help the group to discuss the merits of these different teaching ideas. Encourage teachers also to articulate the key points/principles underlying those ideas which are judged to be effective (where appropriate, groups can also refer back to other related tasks completed, such as Task 2.2). Ask teachers in particular to describe any changes in their teaching priorities that may have come about as a result of recent experiments. See the example of a completed Worksheet 40 in Section 6.33.1, where, in answer to the question 'What did you learn?' the teacher wrote 'They [learners] feel happy when they can see that the results are positive'. Such a statement could represent a new insight for the teacher in question, reflecting a change in his or her personal theory.

3.2 The teachers' desire to experiment could then be maintained by encouraging teachers to try out a new idea which has been recommended by others in the training session, or by focusing together on the implications of key points or 'changes', such as: 'They [learners] feel happy when they can see that the results are positive'. You may also collect in the completed worksheets and read them, commenting where appropriate in the space provided. The worksheets could also be kept in a file for teachers to use as a source of teaching ideas, allowing them also to write comments in the space provided on their colleagues' worksheets.

COMBINING TASKS

See also Worksheet 22 on p. 250 for another format for recording information about a lesson, which could be used instead of, or as well as, Worksheet 40. A profitable focus for a further workshop might also be to compare various formats for lesson plan sheets that the trainer and group know of, encouraging teachers to select one, and to try it out at school. See Worksheet 41 for one suggestion. As can be seen, this format allows the teacher to plan a lesson in advance and comment on what actually happened in it. See Section 6.33.2 for an example of an example of Worksheet 41 completed by a teacher.

5 Evaluating learning

Introduction

One of the stated aims of *Teachers in Action* – and one which I consider crucial in promoting teacher learning – is 'to help teachers to select relevant goals for, manage the process of, and *evaluate*, their learning and professional development'. The term 'evaluate' means different things to different people, so the following definition highlights the principal purposes that evaluation has in this book: 'to collect information systematically in order to indicate the worth or merit of a programme or project...and to inform decision making' (Weir and Roberts, 1994: 4). Collecting information in

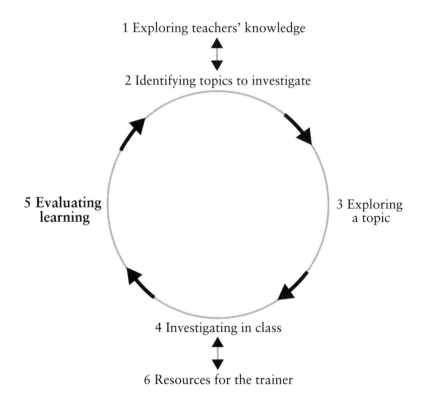

Figure 5.1   The investigating cycle in Teachers in Action

this sense requires trainers to provide time and mental space on a training programme, as well as demanding a great deal of mental effort from the teachers. For this, they will need to step back from what is happening on a busy programme in order to take stock of it or pause to think about all the aspects before deciding what to do next (although naturally this is not all that is involved in making sense). If trainers do not provide teachers with opportunities to evaluate their learning on a programme in the way out-lined above, they run the risk of bombarding them with too much material for them to able to make sense of it, or see connections between its com-ponents. In this respect, from the perspective of a trainer, I would prefer to concentrate on, say, seven topics on a programme rather than squeezing in ten, but consequently be able to include in the timetable plenty of opportu-nities for the teachers to evaluate any learning from the seven topics.

The first six tasks in Chapter 5 provide different ways of helping teachers to evaluate their learning while a programme is in progress, both individu-ally and collectively, while Tasks 5.7 and 5.8 encourage teachers to share their learning with others. All the tasks have their own specific aims and help to indicate to teachers and trainers the merit of a programme, but they also deliberately help to *inform decision-making*, which could take one of the following forms:

(a) Helping teachers and trainers to decide what to do next on a pro-gramme. For example, they may be encouraged to identify a specific topic for further investigation (see Figure 5.1). They may also select specific, relevant, effective learning strategies for the rest of the pro-gramme, or indeed for after it.

(b) While evaluating learning, trainers (and teachers) gain access to partici-pants' detailed, fascinating and sometimes surprising insights regarding a programme, as well as to the idiosyncratic, unique atmosphere sur-rounding it (see, for example, the data for Tasks 5.3 and 5.5, reproduced in Sections 6.34 and 6.36 respectively). Such information also helps trainers to consider and take decisions concerning specific modifications to the content and methodology of future training programmes.

Furthermore, and perhaps most significantly, if teachers themselves are actively involved in evaluating their learning as in the tasks in Chapter 5, there is great general experiential learning potential for them as a result, as asserted by Weir and Roberts (1994: 7–8):

> self-directed formative evaluation is a form of teacher development, arguably one of the most effective forms if done consistently, collaboratively.... The benefits for teachers of involvement in self-directed formative evaluation are considerable, including as they do a deepening and development of teachers' perceptions of classroom events, developments in practice, improved profes-sional dialogue with peers, and improved skills and confidence in exploring and presenting issues of professional concern.

If trainers encourage teachers to take stock in the ways described here, then I believe that they are also, in a sense, setting a good example to the teachers by presenting educating, teaching and learning as an open, flexible, constantly changing process. So one further aim of the tasks in this chapter is to provide teachers with an opportunity to experience the evaluation of learning firsthand and to consider possible applications to their own professional practice in schools.

One final word of warning: trainers should use the evaluation tasks in this book, or others like them, sensitively and judiciously, so participants do not suffer too much from what might be called evaluation-itis!

Task 5.1 Has this task helped me/us to learn?

BACKGROUND FOR THE TRAINER

This task includes Worksheet 42 on p. 276.

This task helps teachers to reflect systematically on the effectiveness of their learning on a training programme. It is designed for use by individuals and groups of teachers after they have been involved in another task or activity in *Teachers in Action*, or indeed another devised by a trainer.

TASK AIMS

- to encourage teachers to evaluate a task by reflecting about whether, how, or what it has helped them to learn
- to help teachers to identify further topics for investigating

PROCEDURE

Allow at least 20 minutes for this task.

1   Explain that you want the teachers to evaluate the task or activity that the group has been involved in. If appropriate, you may briefly refer to a quotation(s) from the Introduction to this chapter on the purpose of evaluation, to explain why you think this is important. For example, the aim of this task is 'to collect information systematically in order to indicate the worth or merit of a programme or project…'.

2   The original aim(s) for the actual task or activity in question will provide a logical starting point for the evaluation. Refer teachers to the aim as stated in the book, and write it on the blackboard.

3   Follow the instructions on Worksheet 42. The teachers complete the worksheet from a personal perspective – either at home or in the training session. Allow approximately 10 minutes for this.

Note: instead of using all the questions on the worksheet, you may wish to select only those relevant to your group, and write them on the blackboard for teachers to focus on. Or you may wish to make up your own questions based on those shown on the worksheet.

4.1 When the teachers have completed their worksheet, ask them to work in pairs to compare their responses, allowing about five minutes for this.

Note: optionally, and depending on the time available, you may ask the teachers to give you the completed worksheets to take away and read, allowing you to respond to them in writing in the space provided on the worksheet. In a subsequent session, return them to the teachers and proceed as suggested below. It is also important to agree on what to do with the worksheets before the teachers complete them.

4.2 With the aim of helping teachers to identify further topics for investigating, in whole-group mode discuss their responses to the worksheet questions – each of which is intended to lead an individual or group on to another cycle of investigating activity. Refer to a worksheet question, for example question 7: 'Is there another topic(s) you wish to investigate now?' Write the question on the blackboard, and elicit responses, also writing these on the blackboard. Where appropriate, try to get the teachers to agree on one or more action points from the resulting responses, thus allowing them to examine their topic in a group or sub-groups, by means of a task from Chapter 3 or 4. Alternatively, and depending on the characteristics of your situation, individual teachers may also be encouraged to follow up particular interests.

Task 5.2 Which learning strategies are helping us?

BACKGROUND FOR THE TRAINER

This task includes Worksheet 43 on p. 278.

Task 5.2 is particularly relevant for groups of teachers who have already completed Task 1.2. Several years ago while reading a book by Wenden and Rubin (1987), I wondered how the following questions they posed regarding language learning strategies[1] might be adapted to teacher education and development:

> What do L2 learners do to learn a second language?
> How do they manage or self-direct these efforts?
> What do they know about which aspects of their L2 learning process?
> How can their learning skills be refined and developed?
>
> (ibid.: 6)

[1]Strategies are defined as:
procedures used in learning, thinking, etc., which serve as a way of reaching a goal. In language learning, learning strategies and communication strategies are those conscious or unconscious processes which language learners make use of in learning and using a language.
(Richards, Platt and Weber, 1985: 274)

128

The original questions once modified provided me with a new, thought-provoking set of questions concerning the strategies employed by teachers in their professional learning:

What do teachers do to learn about teaching?

How do teachers manage or self-direct these efforts?

What do teachers know about different aspects of the process of their professional learning?

How can teachers' learning skills be refined and developed?

It is these questions that form a backdrop to this task, which is designed to be used once a programme has been running for long enough for learning strategies to have established themselves.

TASK AIMS

- to help teachers to analyse and evaluate different strategies which are contributing towards their professional learning
- to help teachers to select effective strategies for their future professional learning

PREPARATION

Make enough copies of Part 3 of Worksheet 43 for each teacher to have one. Then, ideally, cut up each worksheet so that each teacher has a complete set of all the items on separate pieces of paper, which will allow the individual pieces to be easily handled and classified.

PROCEDURE

Allow at least one hour for this task.

1.1 If the group has also completed Task 1.2, refer teachers to any worksheets completed as a result (Worksheets 4 and/or 5), and generate a brief discussion with questions such as:

Which of the learning strategies we discussed originally are in fact helping us to learn?

Are there any that are proving useful which we did not mention in our original discussion?

1.2 If a group of teachers has not completed Task 1.2, you may start the training session by asking the following question:

What is helping you to learn? (e.g. reading, experimenting in class: see Worksheet 43)

2 Follow the instructions on Worksheet 43. Give each teacher a set of strategies, which you have prepared previously. Before they begin Part 1, ensure that the teachers understand both the worksheet questions and the terms used in the items in Part 3. Omit any items on the

worksheet that you feel are not relevant or suitable, and/or add any you feel important for your own training programme. Allow 20 minutes for Part 1 (at home or in the training session), after which you can lead a short whole-group discussion, and 20 minutes for Part 2.

Note: the phrasing of some of the items on Worksheet 43 has been modified for reasons of space. Wherever the word 'teaching' is mentioned, e.g. 'articulating a personal theory of teaching', the full phrase should be 'educating, teaching and learning'.

3.1 On completion of Part 2 of Worksheet 43, ask the sub-groups to present their ideas to the whole group in response to the following worksheet questions:

What are the implications for our future professional learning?

Is there anything that we need to change in the way that we work together?

3.2 Write any resulting suggestions on the blackboard. Discuss these with the group and decide whether to introduce any changes in the way the group will work together on the rest of the training programme as a result. For example, a group might identify 'Consulting learners' as a particularly significant strategy which has really helped them to learn to date. The group could then consider (other) ways of consulting learners, for example by using one of the tasks in Chapter 4, or by repeating another relevant task that worked well before.

Task 5.3 What I/we most like about our training programme is...

I like how well organised the course is; I don't like the fact that we haven't worked on practical ways of teaching.

I'm not sure of my own possibilities of being a good teacher as well as a good educator; I found being in contact with other teachers very useful.

I think the course will help me when I have to design a school syllabus; I've learnt about the importance of working in groups.

BACKGROUND FOR THE TRAINER

This task includes Worksheet 44 on p. 279.

As suggested in the Introduction to Chapter 5, on a busy training programme it is profitable for participating teachers to stand back and try to make sense of the programme while it is still in progress. Expressing views about a programme such as those in the cartoon above, can play an important part in helping teachers to make sense of it from their *personal* perspective. In this way, participants are given time and mental space to reflect on what they like or dislike about the programme, what is helping them to learn, or indeed what is not (of course, what teachers like is not necessarily the same as what they find useful). At the same time, trainers (and teachers) obtain valuable information about teachers' perceptions of what is happening on the programme, which may help to inform decision-making concerning the development of the programme in progress, or indeed future programmes. This task provides a simple, accessible framework for groups of teachers to reflect on a programme and then share their insights with their colleagues. It is suitable for use once a programme has been running for some time.

TASK AIMS

- to help teachers to evaluate a training programme while it is in progress by expressing their views, opinions and feelings about it
- to help teachers to select effective strategies for their future professional learning
- to encourage teachers to consider any implications for their own teaching

PREPARATION

Before the training session, photocopy Worksheet 44 as many times as there are teachers in the group. Cut up each photocopy into nine slips of paper; using separate slips in this way allows the material to be handled easily. Collate the slips so that there is a complete set of the nine different partial sentences for each teacher (unless there are items from the worksheet which you want to omit, or others you want to add). Hold each set together with a paper clip. Alternatively, you could use the worksheet without cutting it up. See Section 6.34 for a set of examples of completed sentences produced by a group of teachers.

PROCEDURE

For this task allow at least 30 minutes over two training sessions.

1.1 Explain to the teachers that you wish to find out their views, opinions and feelings about aspects of the training programme to date. Ask and discuss briefly what the advantages of doing this might be (see 'Background' above and the Introduction to Chapter 5 for some advantages).

1.2 Choose one of the partial sentences from Worksheet 44, write it on the blackboard and invite teachers to respond to it spontaneously, in order to show them what is required for the task.

2 Give each teacher a full set of slips from Worksheet 44. Tell the teachers to use the slips to write individually and anonymously about aspects of the training programme from their personal perspective; they need complete only those slips that they find interesting or about which they have something to say. Explain that the completed sentences will be collected in for you and the other teachers in the group to read (decide exactly what to do with the completed slips before the teachers start writing). Ask teachers to be frank when writing the sentences (to say what they really think and feel), but also to be constructive (e.g. not to focus on aspects that the group or the trainer has no control over, such as the size of the group or the time the session starts). Allow teachers about 10 minutes to complete the sentences.

3.1 Collect in the completed sentences. After the session, collate them into sets of the same sentence; write up all the material in the form of a summary, and photocopy the resulting text for the teachers (see Section 6.34 for an example of such a summary).

3.2 In a subsequent training session, give each teacher a copy of your summary, and ask them to read it.

3.3 Ask teachers to read the sets of sentences again in sub-groups of three or four teachers, considering the questions below as they do so:

Is there anything that we need to change about the way we are working together (because of any comments made by teachers)?

Is there anything we have learnt from this task that is very important for our schools, learners and/or ourselves as teachers?

Allow ten minutes for this activity.

3.4 In whole-group mode, elicit the teachers' responses to the above questions. Then consider:

(a) whether you are willing and able to modify aspects of the programme in the light of the teachers' responses, especially those identified by several teachers (see the first question above)

(b) whether there are implications for the teachers' own classroom practice; for example, teachers may wish to encourage their own learners to evaluate their English classes along the lines indicated in this task, but in an adapted, simplified form (see the second question above and see Task 4.5 for an example of such a means)

Note: part of stage 3.1 could also be completed immediately after the teachers have written their comments, time allowing. Rather than collecting in and then collating the sentences yourself after the session, get the teachers to do so in the session; ask them to collate the sentences and display them on a noticeboard or wall for all to read. Then proceed with stage 3.3, as described above. You could still type up the teachers' sentences as a summary report after the training session, for you or the teachers themselves to consult at a later stage.

Task 5.4 Making sense: reviewing and finding connections

BACKGROUND FOR THE TRAINER

This task includes Worksheet 45 on p. 280.

Sometimes on a busy training programme teachers do not have time to see the potential connections among the different, possibly rather fragmented, programme components (topics, tasks or activities) which have been covered on it. Indeed, teachers may have been so busy that they have forgotten about some of the components altogether! In order to tackle these problems, Task 5.4 provides an opportunity for teachers to make personal sense of a programme by reflecting on it and sharing their perspectives with each other; it is suitable for use during the programme itself, or at, or towards, the end.

TASK AIMS

- to encourage teachers to review the different components (topics, task and activities) of a programme, and to look for connections among these
- to encourage teachers to consider any implications for their own teaching

PREPARATION

Before the training session, make a list of the components (topics, tasks and activities) covered on your training programme to date, for your own reference during the actual session. One by one, copy the programme components on your list on to blank cards. (The number of components and cards will, of course, depend on the nature of your programme, but ideally there should be at least one different component/card for each teacher in the whole group. If there are not enough components for each teacher to have a different card, duplicate some that the group consider especially significant.) See Section 6.35 for a sample list of training pro-gramme components which I covered with a group of teachers on a train-ing programme.

PROCEDURE

Allow approximately 45 minutes for this task.

1   Write the phrase 'Making sense of the programme: reviewing and look-ing for connections' in big letters on the blackboard. Explain to the teachers that you want to help them to review the different components of the training programme and to look for connections among these. Invite them to make a note of how many different programme com-ponents they can remember to date, on an individual basis, where appropriate, without looking at their programme timetable or notes. Allow teachers about 5 minutes to complete this activity.

1.2 Elicit the teachers' suggestions and write them on the blackboard (you may wish to add any items forgotten by the teachers, but which you included in your own list).

2   Follow the instructions on Worksheet 45. Give each sub-group enough cards so that there is one card per teacher. Ideally, the teachers draw the cards at random from a bag or from your hand. While teachers are completing the worksheet, monitor their work, helping out where need be, for example if teachers' memories need jogging about tasks and activities related to a particular programme component. Allow approximately 15 minutes for Part 1, and 10 minutes for Part 2.

   Note: the two worksheet questions in point 4 deliberately encourage teachers to distinguish between any learning which took place around the time when the task was being completed, and any learning that might have taken place since that time.

3.1 Once the teachers have had enough time to complete Worksheet 44, ask the sub-groups to report to the whole group about their response, especially to Part 2; ask them to first state which cards they were given, and then explain the links among their cards. For example, a sub-group might report as follows (with reference to three of the components included in Section 6.35):

> In our sub-group our cards were: 'looking at new coursebooks', 'mixed ability' and 'change and innovation'. We thought that 'change' was linked with 'coursebooks' because we feel that a good coursebook helps teachers to change and develop their own teaching. Also in the session when we looked at new coursebooks which we might wish to use in class next year, some of the books provided the teacher with lots of tips for teaching, including 'mixed ability' classes. And this we thought was very realistic and useful, because it's a big problem in our schools.

3.2 Comment on the teachers' reports, and, where appropriate, add any connections that you may identify among the different combinations of cards.

3.3 Ask the teachers if they have found the task useful as a way of making sense of the programme. You may then wish to encourage them to consider any implications for their own teaching by asking how their own learners review their learning. Ask such questions as:

How do our learners review their learning at present?
In which other ways could they review their learning?
How could we improve…?

Such discussion could lead to a new topic for investigating in class.

COMBINING TASKS

Task 5.4 may be combined with other tasks, such as Task 1.5, for which teachers produce a conceptual framework for educating, teaching and learning, and which would provide a useful backdrop for the task in hand. See also other tasks in Chapter 5, such as 5.1, which is similar to Task 5.4, though narrower in focus, in that it examines only one task. Or you may wish to move forward by linking Task 5.4 with Task 5.5, in some way.

Task 5.5 Applying our learning: looking back and looking ahead

BACKGROUND FOR THE TRAINER

This task includes Worksheets 46 and 47 on pp. 281–2, and Option 29 (see below); it is suitable for use towards the end of a training programme.

It is my experience that teachers' motivation often increases significantly during a training programme. However, before teachers leave behind the support of the group and plunge back into the busy world of school, it is productive to help teachers to look ahead and explicitly anticipate possible changes in their future teaching and discuss potential ways of continuing their professional development. Such reflection and discussion is especially important as my experience suggests that teachers' expectations related to change and professional development are sometimes rather ambitious and unrealistic. The information resulting from the reflection and discussion can be written down by teachers as a kind of bridge between learning on the programme itself and the participants' future professional practice, or as an *aide-mémoire* for future reference. See Tasks 1.8 and 1.9, both of which could be usefully combined with the more classroom-focused task in hand.

TASK AIMS

- to help teachers to reflect on and discuss the relationship between what they have learnt on a programme and their future professional practice

- to encourage teachers to formulate learning points to apply to their future teaching practice, as well as realistic strategies for their future professional development

PREPARATION

Read the extracts from a conversation about professional change which I had with a teacher towards the end of programme in the United Kingdom, reproduced in Sections 6.36.1 and 6.36.2. These extracts are intended to provide a highly detailed backdrop to the task in hand in terms of how an individual teacher perceives the relationship between learning on a training programme and her future teaching practice and development. Prepare enough slips of paper – blank pieces measuring about a fifth of a sheet of A4 – so that there are one or two per teacher.

PROCEDURE

Allow about 90 minutes for this task, preferably over two training sessions (including 30 minutes for the teachers to complete Part 1 of Worksheet 46 at home).

1.1 Draw a bridge on the blackboard. To the left of the bridge write 'training programme', to the right of it 'future teaching practice and professional development', and underneath 'applying our learning'.

1.2 Ask teachers to reflect for a few minutes and comment briefly on what they have learnt, what they will take away with them from the training programme, and what they think they will be able to apply.

2 Follow the instructions on Worksheet 46, asking teachers to complete Part 1 at home, where they can sit down to review their notes and materials quietly, in preparation for a training session. If this is not possible, simply ask the teachers to bring their materials to the training session, and to do Part 1 there and then. Allow 30 minutes for Part 1, and 30 minutes for Part 2. For Part 2, give each sub-group 5–10 slips of paper.

3.1 Following the completion of Part 2, bring the whole group of teachers together again, maybe asking them to sit in a semi-circle or circle.

3.2 Ask teachers from the sub-groups to read out their completed slips one at a time. After all the slips have been read out, you may use Worksheet 47 to summarise and record 5–10 highly significant points – those agreed to by a number of sub-groups – in front of the whole group in the form of a checklist. This can then be photocopied for teachers to take away with them, or ask teachers to complete an individual summary using Worksheet 47. See Section 6.36.3 for an example of a teacher's personal checklist of learning points and strategies. See also Option 29 below for another way of recording teachers' points.

Note: where appropriate, you may also wish to explicitly discuss suitable recommendations with the teachers as to how they can continue to develop professionally after the programme. Ask the teachers what ideas they have regarding suitable strategies, and make your own suggestions. For information, see the list of suggestions below.

STRATEGIES FOR PROFESSIONAL DEVELOPMENT AFTER A PROGRAMME

1 Make small changes in your work; don't try to change everything at once.
2 Keep your programme notes and materials in a safe place; look at them from time to time – and you may find some useful ideas.
3 Select teaching ideas from the programme that you have found interesting and try them out in class, in response perhaps to the following prompt: 'It's time to do something about…'.
4 Before the programme finishes, note down the titles of a few relevant books from the programme bibliography, so that later you can read a professional book, if you have time; share the subscription to a magazine with a colleague(s).
5 Tell colleagues at school who have not attended the programme what you have learnt.
6 Find out about libraries in your area (British Council, university, teachers' centres, etc.) with language teaching materials.
7 Find out about local, national or international teachers' associations and groups, such as TESOL, IATEFL.
8 Make sure that you are on publishers' mailing lists so that you regularly receive information about new teaching materials.
9 Write down the telephone numbers of colleagues on the programme, so that you can stay in touch; agree to meet up with them once in a while.
10 Give a talk at a teachers' conference, or publish an article in a professional magazine, with a colleague(s).

You will probably be able to add other recommendations to this list.

OPTION 29 PRODUCING A MINDMAP SUMMARY OF A GROUP DISCUSSION

This is based on the slips of paper in stage 3.2 of Task 5.5.

One way of summarising a group discussion is by means of a mindmap, a cobweb-like diagram. Section 6.36.4 shows a mindmap called 'Applying learning to our teaching' which I drew with a group of teachers. It was produced as outlined below.

1 While teachers are reading out their slips at stage 3.2 of Task 5.5, encourage them to arrange them one by one to form a visual display, attaching them with reusable adhesive to the blackboard, or pinning

them on a specially prepared part of a noticeboard. If possible, teachers read out their slips in logical sequence, relating their contribution to previous ones, placing closely related slips near each other on the display.

2 There are a number of ways of providing the teachers with a record of the mindmap to keep for future reference:

(a) ask teachers to copy down the display directly from the blackboard or noticeboard

(b) copy the display yourself

(c) ask a teacher to make a copy, drawing it on to a large sheet of paper as it is forming

Where appropriate, for (b) and (c), photocopy the resulting drawing.

Task 5.6 Teacher portfolios

BACKGROUND FOR THE TRAINER

This is a key task in *Teachers in Action* and includes Worksheet 48 on p. 283.

A portfolio is a set of items that represents someone's work, especially an artist's drawings or paintings. In an educational context, the portfolio may be defined as 'a durable file which can act as a method of retaining and recording evidence of a child's learning' (Pollard and Tann, 1993: 270). Its use in schools in the United Kingdom is based on pupil profiles and records of achievement, and helps to contextualise and broaden pupil assessment procedures (ibid.: 271). Task 5.6 adapts the portfolio for use in teacher education and development and is best introduced to participating teachers near the beginning of a training programme. The three-stage process encourages teachers to retain and collect evidence of their learning throughout a programme in the form of an individual portfolio, as in Figure 5.2.

Stage 1	Collect	Teachers collect materials throughout a training programme, such as completed worksheets.
Stage 2	Review	Teachers review such materials regularly and select important items for inclusion in a portfolio.
Stage 3	Report	Teachers report to others, for example to another teacher or to a trainer in a tutorial, using the portfolio.

Figure 5.2   The stages of a portfolio

Portfolios are potentially beneficial in that, among other things, they:

- recognise and give credit for what teachers have achieved
- contribute to teachers' development and progress by improving their motivation, providing encouragement and increased awareness of strengths, weaknesses and opportunities
- help trainers and programme providers to identify the all-round potential of teachers, and to evaluate how well programmes enable teachers to develop

(adapted from Pollard and Tann, 1993: 271)

See also the Introduction, 'Using the worksheets', point 9 (d).

TASK AIMS

- to help teachers to evaluate their professional learning, development and progress by means of portfolios
- to help teachers to identify opportunities for further investigation and development

PROCEDURE

This task is different from others in that its three stages should be spread throughout a training programme: see Figure 5.2.

1 Introduce the idea of portfolios to the group by describing briefly what is involved, and by referring to the potential benefits outlined above in 'Background for the trainer'.

2 Follow the instructions on Worksheet 48.

2.1 *Collect* (see Worksheet 48, stage 1): Ideally, each teacher has a file (ring binder) to organise their portfolio. Encourage teachers to collect and organise as much material as possible on their programme. This might include material from this book such as worksheets produced individually or collectively, lists of priorities, diary extracts, book reviews, key articles or quotations, definitions of key terms, lesson plans, descriptions of teaching ideas, summaries of experiments conducted in class, photographs of learners in action, questionnaire data or learner profiles.

2.2 *Review* (see Worksheet 48, stage 2): The frequency with which teachers review their programme and update their portfolios depends on the nature of the programme in question (its length, the frequency of sessions, etc.). I suggest, however, that the criteria for selection of items for a portfolio be kept rather general; see, for example the suggestions on Worksheet 48. Before starting the portfolios, agree with the teachers on what to do with them once they have been completed.

2.3 *Reporting* (Worksheet 48, stage 3): Reporting to others could take place in one of two ways:

(a) A discussion with another teacher: Ask teachers to show each other and discuss their portfolios in a training session in pairs, possibly using the questions on Worksheet 48, stage 2, as a starting point for their discussion. Try to give the discussions a specific focus by asking pairs of teachers to identify opportunities for development, for example a topic(s) which would be suitable for further investigating (see Worksheet 48, stage 3).

(b) Tutorials between a trainer and an individual teacher: For general recommendations concerning tutorials, see Section 6.37.

COMBINING TASKS

Task 5.6 may be combined with other tasks in *Teachers in Action* since most of them require teachers to collect completed worksheets, which can then be considered for inclusion in their portfolio.

Task 5.7 Sharing our learning (1): giving informal presentations

BACKGROUND FOR THE TRAINER

Task 5.7 includes Worksheets 49 and 50 on pp. 284–5.

This task assumes that teachers have been investigating a topic(s) in class in sub-groups, and that they are ready and willing to present the results of this work to other teachers in the group in a training session(s), on an informal basis. Yet presenting in this way, even informally in a group of teachers who know each other reasonably well, is not without its difficulties. For example:

- it can be threatening to those teachers who have little or no experience of presenting
- teachers may have low self-esteem, perhaps undervaluing their own professional knowledge and practical experience, as well as their own skills to bring about change and promote innovation in their work
- teachers may be very self-critical, and/or critical of others
- teachers may lack confidence in their command of English (if this is the language used for presenting)

Despite these clear difficulties, in my view it is well worth helping teachers to develop presentation skills for the following reasons:

- It underlines the value of teamwork, as teachers learn from and with each other. Teachers often surprise themselves by how much they can learn when working together and presenting in groups (see, for example, Task 3.5, 'Sample of a summary feedback letter', statement 5, 'When I decided to do this course...').

- It promotes a 'bottom-up' approach to change in teaching, as teachers help each other to change, rather than having change imposed on them by others in the educational system.
- Teachers may be able to apply their refined presentation skills and ability to work in teams to other forms of co-operation and development after a training programme (see for example Task 5.8).

However, teachers who are being encouraged to present are likely to need lots of encouragement, guidance and support from the trainer, and indeed from each other (see Section 6.38.1, 'General strategies for developing teachers' presentation skills'). Task 5.7 provides further support by means of a four-stage framework for developing teachers' presentation skills, as shown in Figure 5.3.

Stage 1	Reflecting about presenting (optional, depending on time)
Stage 2	Planning a presentation
Stage 3	Presenting
Stage 4	Evaluating presentations (optional, depending on time)

Figure 5.3   A framework for developing teachers' presentation skills

TASK AIMS

- to encourage teachers to share their learning by means of informal presentations and to learn from each other
- to help teachers to evaluate and develop their presentation skills

PROCEDURE

Allow several training sessions for this task; for further detailed suggestions concerning timing, please see each of the four individual stages below.

1   *Stage 1: Reflecting about presenting* (optional, depending on the time available) Allow about 10 minutes for this activity.

1.1 Explain briefly what you mean by teachers presenting informally, and elicit from the group the characteristics of effective informal presentation by asking:

How can we present the results of our work to each other effectively?

Encourage teachers to consider any previous experience that they may have had presenting, or as members of an audience watching a presentation. For example, someone might suggest: 'We need to plan our presentations carefully'.

1.2 List the suggestions on the blackboard, and encourage teachers to copy them down for future reference. For information, see Section 6.38.2 for some suggestions as to the characteristics of an effective presentation, which you may also show teachers, of course.

2 *Stage 2: Planning a presentation*

Note: exactly how you organise the planning of the presentations before they are given, etc., will depend, of course, on the characteristics of your training situation. However, my experience working with groups of 20 teachers or more suggests that it is worth investing time and effort in getting teachers to plan their presentations systematically and in a focused manner by completing a form such as that reproduced in Worksheet 49. This planning will help to ensure that certain pitfalls are avoided and that as a result the presentations themselves go well, an important factor when considering that the teachers' confidence in presenting could be a little shaky! Here are some further suggestions that might help to structure the planning stage:

(a) Ideally, the planning stage of this task will take up a part of two training sessions, at least 30 minutes in Session 1, and at least one hour in Session 2.

(b) Teachers should plan their presentations in the same sub-groups they have investigated in.

(c) Depending on the situation, teachers may present work related to aspects of the same topic, or they may present work related to different topics.

(d) Consider carefully which language teachers use in their presentation: English, or their mother tongue. Where appropriate, discuss this important issue with the group.

(e) Instead of a standard oral presentation, with the presenters standing in front of their audience, teachers could use a poster to present their work informally to each other, which may prove less inhibiting for some teachers. See Task 5.8, 'Producing a poster', for more detail.

2 Follow the instructions on Worksheet 49. If you have completed Stage 1 of the above procedures, remind teachers to consider the characteristics of an effective presentation in relation to their own! Ideally, organise the planning stage along the following lines:

2.1 In Session 1, sub-groups complete a copy of Worksheet 49 and give it to you before they leave the training session.

2.2 Between Sessions 1 and 2, read the teachers' completed worksheets, respond to any problems and offer advice by making notes in the space provided on the worksheet.

2.3 Return the worksheets to the sub-groups in Session 2, complete with your own notes. Have the resources that teachers require for their presentations ready (paper, glue, card, coloured pens, overhead transparencies, etc.). The sub-groups then continue planning together by collating their material; allow at least one hour for this activity.

3   *Stage 3: Presenting work*
    Allow approximately 5–10 minutes for each presentation, depending on the time available. The sub-groups take it in turns to present their work. Here are some suggestions for organising the actual presentations themselves:

    - Discuss with teachers whether they wish to evaluate a presentation while watching it (see also stage 4 below).
    - Appoint a time-keeper – not someone in the sub-group presenting – to remind the presenters when the time for their presentation is over, or almost over. (Making sure sub-groups have more or less the same amount of time to present is important.)
    - Encourage teachers to applaud before and after each presentation, helping to create a good atmosphere.
    - Invite those teachers who are watching to ask questions.
    - Highlight any points emerging from the presentations that you feel are of particular importance.
    - Where appropriate, make photocopies of any useful materials teachers produce for everyone to take away a copy of

4   *Stage 4: Evaluating presentations* (optional, depending on the time available) Allow approximately 20–30 minutes for this stage.

4.1 Provide a constructive framework for teachers to describe and evaluate each other's presentations, using Worksheet 50. Follow the instructions on the worksheet, making sure that each teacher has a copy.

    Note: ask teachers to complete Worksheet 50 so that every sub-group's presentation is evaluated by (at least) one other teacher from a different sub-group. In this way, an individual teacher only evaluates one other sub-group's presentation. Try to get teachers to agree before the presentations who is going to evaluate which one.

4.2 You may process Worksheet 50 with the whole group by:
    - eliciting responses to the worksheet, especially point 6, and writing these on the blackboard
    - encouraging sub-groups to read the completed worksheet(s) related to their presentation and to learn from the feedback
    - referring back, where appropriate, to the list of characteristics of an effective informal presentation discussed at stage 1, and modifying it accordingly, in the light of the teachers' own experience

When teachers next give a presentation, they can take into consideration all the suggestions made, and present even better as a result!

COMBINING TASKS

Task 5.7 can be combined with many tasks in *Teachers in Action*, especially those requiring the teachers to present to each other, as, for example, in the majority of tasks in Chapter 4.

Task 5.8 Sharing our learning (2): joining forces in the wider educational community

BACKGROUND FOR THE TRAINER

This task includes Worksheets 51 and 52 on pp. 286–8, and Option 30 (see below).

A defining feature of *Teachers in Action* is that teachers share the results of their professional learning with each other: see Task 5.7, where teachers do so by means of informal presentations. This is also an important principle underlying Task 5.8. Teachers' social skills are of vital importance for effective educating, teaching and learning. In this respect, Fullan (1993) states that teachers must actively:

> look for opportunities to *join forces with others*, and must realize that they are part of a larger movement to develop a learning society through their work with students and parents.

> (39, my emphasis)

Fullan goes on to state that organisations that wish to be successful, and I would also argue teachers who wish to be successful, must be: 'actively *plugged into their environments* responding to and contributing to the issues of the day' (ibid.: 39; my emphasis). For language teachers, the educational environment or community reaches beyond the classroom and the school, and consists of inspectors, teachers' centres, ministries, publishers, teachers' associations and international organisations: see Figure 2 in the Introduction. It is my view that trainers are well placed to help teachers to 'plug into' this wider community, to respond to it and, very importantly, to 'contribute to the issues of the day'. But how can busy teachers realistically 'join forces with others' in this way? This task provides one possible means; it encourages teachers to follow up their learning on a training progamme by evaluating and possibly selecting ways of sharing their learning in the community, for example by giving a public talk at a conference.

TASK AIMS

- to encourage teachers to consider and select appropriate and relevant ways of sharing their learning with other participants in the educational community
- to encourage teachers and trainers to explore and exploit professional networks and publications

PROCEDURE

Allow approximately 45 minutes for this task.

1 Suggest to teachers that they share the results of their learning in the wider educational community: see 'Background for the trainer' above.

2 Follow the instructions on Worksheet 51, allowing about 15 minutes for its completion.

3 Encourage teachers to consider the ways of sharing on Worksheet 51 which are appropriate and relevant in your training situation. See Section 6.39.1 for a list of advantages and disadvantages of different ways of sharing. You may draw on parts of this text when discussing with the teachers the advantages and disadvantages of ways of sharing.

4 Elicit the sub-groups' responses to the worksheet questions and lead a discussion about the teachers' preferences. Provide the teachers with any help and encouragement you can to assist them in their endeavours. While being generally positive and supportive in encouraging teachers to select a way of sharing their learning in the wider community, be realistic in that maybe not all of them will wish to take the plunge!

Note: I include below some further advice and information for each of the four ways included on Worksheet 51, which you may wish to draw on when advising and encouraging teachers.

Giving a public talk

See also Task 5.7, as well as the general strategies for developing teachers' presentation skills in Section 6.38.1. You may also refer teachers to the two short articles on effective presentations reproduced in Section 6.39.2. These refer to public talks given at an annual International Association of Teachers of English as a Foreign Language (IATEFL) conference. At this point, you may also like to tell teachers more about IATEFL (or other teachers' associations active in your area or country). IATEFL's own definition of its purpose is: 'Linking, developing and supporting English Language Teaching professionals worldwide'. For more information, contact: IATEFL, 3 Kingsdown Chambers, Whitstable, Kent, CT5 2FL, United Kingdom, or http://www.iatefl.org.

See also Option 30 below, for a further way of encouraging teachers to 'join forces' by developing their skills for a particular kind of public talk or audience, namely, learners' parents.

Producing a poster

In general terms, when working with teachers, seek opportunities to develop their visual presentation skills. For example, see Tasks 4.3 or 4.4 (in particular, reporting results by means of bar graphs, pie charts, etc.), and Task 5.7, which also proposes the use of posters for presenting.

Publishing an article

Encourage teachers to read professional journals and magazines as much as possible. Where appropriate, seek opportunities to develop teachers' academic writing skills, for example, keeping notes related to reading in Task 2.6.

Writing a report

See also 'Publishing an article' above. I have had encouraging experience helping teachers to produce formal written reports in English related to their professional learning. These were officially required as part of the training programme I was working on. (See Roberts, 1998: 258–75, 'Professional development for primary teachers of English in the Basque Country', for further information about this programme.) The finished reports were later made available to other teachers attending subsequent years of the same training programme. I observed that by reading the reports teachers found out about other colleagues' experiences in schools in their own area, and were as a result able to consider experimenting in similar ways in their own school and classrooms. I believe that this system had good face validity for the readers, as the reports featured examples of 'ordinary', local teachers' work in real schools. As a consequence, they were easy for the reader to identify with, and in some cases be inspired by. On a related note, I was also pleased to discover that teachers regularly cited other colleagues' work in the bibliographies of their own reports, an indication perhaps of the potential teachers have to help each other. Where appropriate, consider collecting together teachers' written reports in this same way, especially where teachers are required to produce a piece of academic writing for formal assessment purposes. See also Section 6.39.3 for a set of guidelines for writing a formal report about investigating.

OPTION 30 OUR ENGLISH TEACHER WILL EXPLAIN: ROLE-PLAY

This option focuses on developing teachers' ability to explain aspects of their work to a group of parents assembled at a parents' meeting. The idea for the option stems from a conversation I had with a teacher who told me how she had suddenly been asked to talk to parents at a school meeting about her work as an English teacher, without any preparation! The teacher's description of how she had panicked highlighted for me the importance of teachers being able to explain their work to parents, possibly in the teachers' own language, as well as the fact that teachers could practise this skill in a training session. This could be organised along the following lines:

1 Start a brief, general discussion, asking teachers about parents' meetings at their schools (why?, what?, how?, where?, how often?, strengths, problems, etc.).

2 Teachers work in sub-groups of three (or four); each participant selects one of the three roles on Worksheet 52. Copy the roles on to cards, if you wish, so that there is at least one teacher for each role in each sub-group (if there are any 'extra' teachers without a role, they could take the part of a second parent). Each sub-group should focus the role-play by specifying how old the pupils should be. Allow at least 10 minutes for the participants to prepare, and 5–10 minutes for the actual role-play, which teachers may be realistically asked to do in their own language, if they wish.

3 After the role-play, the observers from each sub-group report to the whole group by answering the questions included in the description of their role. In particular, elicit suggestions for successful strategies for communicating with parents, such as 'don't use jargon', and write these on the blackboard for teachers to copy down for future reference.

4 For some extra fun, one (confident) teacher can volunteer to address the whole group, as if it were a parents' meeting, for a few minutes, and repeat the role-play.

Option 30 might be particularly well combined with Tasks 1.6, 2.2 and 2.3. If teachers have done one of these tasks, this option will enable them to draw on and re-frame the professional priorities they articulated then.

6 Resources for the trainer

Introduction

The materials in Chapter 6 provide trainers with further fully cross-referenced examples and samples of various materials featured in the tasks in *Teachers in Action*. These examples include worksheets completed by groups of teachers or by individual teachers, the purpose of which is to assist trainers when they are reading the book and considering using a certain task in their own training, so they can see clearly how teachers have already responded, and how their own teachers might possibly respond.

1 Exploring teachers' knowledge

2 Identifying topics to investigate

5 Evaluating
learning

3 Exploring
a topic

4 Investigating in class

6 Resources for the trainer

Figure 6.1   The investigating cycle in Teachers in Action

There are also texts for further reading (e.g. curriculum documents, articles, case studies), answer keys and sample responses to questions raised.

A full list of these resources is given below.

List of resources for the trainer

6.1   Some key terms in *Teachers in Action*

6.2   A personal interpretation of 'social constructivism'

6.3   Two case studies of ineffective in-service training

6.4   A case study of a teacher classroom research project

6.5   Sample sequence of tasks, activities and options for investigating 'learner autonomy'

6.6   Example of a completed Worksheet 3, Option 2 (see Task 1.1)

6.7   List of ways of professional learning for teachers (see Task 1.2)

6.8   Stages of investigating: key to Worksheets 6 and 7 (see Task 1.3)

6.9   Exploring teachers' metaphors (see Task 1.4)

6.9.1   Sample discussion of a metaphor

6.9.2   Possible metaphors for aspects of educating, teaching and learning

6.10   Mapping the whole: developing conceptual frameworks for educating, teaching and learning (see Task 1.5)

6.10.1   Sample list of concepts

6.10.2   'Method: approach, design and procedure' model (Richards and Rodgers)

6.10.3   Reflective model for teacher education (Wallace)

6.11   Why teach English? Reflecting on the goals of educating, teaching and learning in the language classroom (see Task 1.6)

6.11.1   Further reading: extract from 'A curriculum for the future'

6.11.2   Example of a school curriculum information leaflet (England)

6.11.3   Extract from an official Spanish curriculum document for Secondary Education

6.12   Key to Worksheet 12 (see Task 1.7)

6.13   Example of a list of factors which will help us to change and/or innovate, Worksheet 15 (see Task 1.8)

6.14   Innovation in our schools: How can we help to promote it? (see Task 1.9)

6.14.1   Example of a completed Worksheet 16 questionnaire

6.14.2   Further reading: 'Students committed to equality project'

6.15   Examining critical incidents (see Task 2.1)

6.15.1   Sample responses to Worksheet 17

6.15.2   Sample critical incident from a teacher

6.16   Sample responses to Worksheet 19 (see Task 2.2)

6.17   Example of a teacher's 'pedagogic manifesto' (see Task 2.3)

6.18   Sample list of topics to investigate (see Task 2.4)

6.19   Further reading 'In her element' (see Task 2.5)

6.20   General reading survey: a class library, bibliography and open forum (see Task 2.6)

6.20.1 Bibliographies for teachers: ten suggestions for trainers

6.20.2 Sample bibliography for teachers

6.20.3 Example of a completed review sheet: Worksheet 23

6.21   Further diary prompts (see Task 2.7)

6.22   Sample of classified diary extracts (see Task 2.8)

6.23   'We can do it!' Self-esteem, us and our learners (see Task 2.9)

6.23.1 Sample response to a prompt on Worksheet 26: 'I have a good day at work when...'

6.23.2 Some practical recommendations for enhancing learners' self-esteem

6.23.3 Further reading: 'It's time we all stood up for teacher' and 'Strategies to help you fight stress' (see Option 16)

6.24   Sample sets of responses for Option 17: 'The correction of learners' oral errors is important because...' and 'Project work in the English classroom is important because...' (see Task 3.1)

6.25   What do we understand by the topic 'x'? (What? Why? Who? etc.) (see Task 3.2)

6.25.1. Summary of a workshop given at a teachers' conference: Using English in Class

6.25.2 Example of a completed Worksheet 28: Using English in class

6.25.3 A sample list of advantages and disadvantages: Using computers with learners (see Option 18)

6.26   Sample Worksheet 29: Helping our learners to work effectively in pairs and groups (see Task 3.3)

6.27   Sample Worksheet 30: Helping our learners to listen to English in class (see Task 3.4)

6.28   Debate: understanding the wider implications of a topic (see Task 3.9)

6.28.1 A sample motion for debate with accompanying roles

6.28.2 Suggestions for other motions for debate

6.29   The benefits of investigating in class: teachers' perspectives (see Task 4.1)

6.29.1 Key to Worksheet 33

6.29.2 Potential difficulties when investigating in class and advice for trainers

6.30   Summary of the advantages and disadvantages of using questionnaires to collect classroom data (see Task 4.4)

6.31   Sample answers to questions on Worksheet 37, Part 1 (see Task 4.5)

6.32   Talking about real people: writing a learner profile (see Task 4.6)

6.32.1 Extract from a detailed formal case study

6.32.2 Example of a baseline learner profile

6.33   Experimenting in class (see Task 4.8)
6.33.1 Example of a completed worksheet
6.33.2 Example of a completed Worksheet 41: lesson plan sheet
6.34   Examples of completed sentences, Worksheet 44 (see Task 5.3)
6.35   Sample list of training programme components: topics, tasks and activities (see Task 5.4)
6.36   Applying our learning: looking back and looking ahead (see Task 5.5)
6.36.1 Extracts from a conversation about professional change
6.36.2 Further extracts from a conversation about professional change
6.36.3 Example of a teacher's personal checklist of learning points and strategies
6.36.4 Example of a mindmap summary of a group discussion
6.37   General recommendations concerning tutorials (see Task 5.6)
6.38   Sharing our learning (1): giving informal presentations (see Task 5.7)
6.38.1 General strategies for developing teachers' presentation skills
6.38.2 What are the characteristics of an effective presentation? Some suggestions
6.39   Sharing our learning (2): joining forces in the wider educational community (see Task 5.8)
6.39.1 Ways of sharing learning: advantages and disadvantages
6.39.2 Further reading: 'Effective presentations'
6.39.3 Guidelines for writing a formal report about investigating

6.1 Some key terms in *Teachers in Action*

(see Introduction, 'Effective in-service teacher education: background issues')

Such terms as 'in-service', 'trainers', 'teacher education', and 'teacher development' have particular and sometimes varying resonances to those professionally involved in the field. I will therefore briefly define how I understand and use these and other key terms in this book.

In-service is usefully defined as:

> those education and training activities engaged in by primary and secondary school teachers..., following their initial professional certification, and intended primarily or exclusively to *improve their professional knowledge, skills and attitudes in order that they can educate children more effectively.*
>
> (R. Bolam, cited in Hopkins, 1986: 18, my emphasis)

The learning needs for *teacher training* are typically defined by a recognisable deficit in the participating teachers' knowledge or skills. The learning aims are often rather short-term and convergent, that is to say, they lead towards a predetermined outcome; in addition, the aims may be specified by the institution which is funding the training. Training in this sense is sometimes referred to as 'top-down'.

In contrast to 'teacher training', *teacher development* often focuses on the extension or development of teachers' existing knowledge or skills. It may be partly or wholly initiated by teachers, and is more individualised and flexible than teacher training with respect to the participating teachers. For example, learning aims and outcomes are more divergent – that is to say, not predetermined. Teacher development in this sense is sometimes referred to as 'bottom-up'.

Teacher education, as I understand and use the term throughout this book, incorporates elements of 'teacher training', and especially 'teacher development', but presents a wider view than both of these. For example, it attempts to cater flexibly for teachers' own learning needs and aims; to develop the whole teacher (knowledge, skills and attitudes); to focus on the teacher's role as an educator and a language teacher of school-aged children in schools; and to help to prepare teachers for career-long learning (see the sections on 'Effective in-service teacher education: background issues' and 'Specific aims' in the Introduction for a fuller description).

A variety of other terms are commonly used for the different participants and elements of teacher education. The teachers themselves are variously referred to as practising or post-experience teachers, while trainers are referred to as teacher educators, tutors or supervisors. Throughout *Teachers in Action*, however, for questions of style and consistency, I will use the following terms: 'teachers', 'trainers', 'learners', 'training programmes', 'training sessions' and the 'training room'.

6.2 A personal interpretation of 'social constructivism'

(see Introduction, 'Teachers' identities')

Over the past few years I have gradually realised that professionally I am and have been a 'social constructivist' for some time, without knowing it! What do I understand by this term? The following interpretation is a very personal one.

Traditionally, for example when I was taught at grammar school as a teenager, the teacher used to come into class already in possession of the 'truth', or the 'knowledge', which he or she wished to impart in the lesson. We, the learners, sat back and 'received' the truth, as it were, as passive receptacles, in the terms of Freire (1972). The truth, in a manner of speaking, already existed before the teacher came into the classroom, and he or she 'simply' passed it on to us.

Of course, this so-called transmission model of learning may also be applied to teacher training but, in my view and experience, not at all effectively. A constructivist model of teacher education and development is different in that teachers explore and experience certain phenomena – in our case, educating, teaching and learning in the language classroom – and as a result construct new knowledge or new meanings *which did not exist before the training session began.*

'Social constructivism' emphasises the importance of knowledge being constructed within and with the help of the group, in our case, with teachers sharing and contrasting ideas, agreeing and disagreeing, etc. The group of teachers in question may also be 'extended' by joining forces with other participants in the educational system, in the form of a wider learning community.

FURTHER READING

Roberts, *Language Teacher Education*, pp 23–30, 'Person as constructivist' Williams and Burden, *Psychology for Language Teachers: A Social Constructivist Approach*

6.3 Two case studies of ineffective in-service training

(see Introduction, 'Change and teacher learning')

The success of teacher education programmes is widely reported (usually by the designers and administrators), and a casual reader of the literature might almost be forgiven for thinking that only successful cases existed. At the risk of appearing negative, however, I want to describe two cases in which the results were not altogether successful.

Teacher 1:

Eva teaches English in a secondary school. She graduated eight years ago and has succeeded in maintaining her passion for English despite the cynicism of many of her colleagues.

On the whole she enjoys teaching. She prepares her lessons meticulously and her students like her and seem to do well in their annual examinations. However, she feels that her English is getting rusty – she has forgotten a lot of vocabulary and seems no longer to be able to think spontaneously in the language. She worries about this so much that at times she feels she should give up teaching. She attributes the decline in her standard of English to the fact of teaching high school students whose own level is so low.

An unprecedented series of seminars for teachers of English was organised in her town on Saturday afternoons and she eagerly agreed to attend them even though this involved a degree of sacrifice and domestic upheaval.

'Visiting experts' demonstrated and explained new classroom techniques. Eva tried out some of these in her classes but felt that many of them were inappropriate to the large classes she taught. She also felt that they failed to take account of the pressure on her to 'get through' the syllabus. Although she welcomed the fact that the medium of instruction initially was English, she was very disappointed to discover that the seminars were not directly designed to help teachers with their spoken skills. Some of the other teachers who attended complained that they could not understand the English of the seminar leaders and eventually the use of English was largely abandoned. At this point Eva stopped attending altogether.

Teacher 2:

Lin has taught in a bilingual primary school for more than twenty years. Until recently she has not thought a lot about her job. The children and their parents respect her and she does more than enough work to justify what she regards as a very meagre salary. She has a large family and a lot of commitments outside her job.

Recently a programme of teacher development has been introduced in schools in her area. Foreign 'experts' have imported what they call 'humanistic' ideas and now the English teachers are required to observe each other and to comment on the lessons in seminars. The 'experts' do not seem to realise the extent to which this inevitably causes loss of 'face'. And yet, since they are both foreigners and experts, even greater loss of face would be involved in explaining this and convincing them of it. Even the local officials are keeping quiet and tacitly supporting this programme. New materials have also been introduced to replace the old ones. These contain very few texts to analyse and are written entirely in English. Lin gets the children to repeat the dialogues but worries that they are not really learning the grammar.

Lin has just learned that a foreigner will be coming to one of the her classes to watch. Lin has to choose the time, invite the foreigner and talk about the lesson. The foreigners have not been explicit about how the teachers should teach but it is rumoured that that they seem to like the children working in groups even though this makes a lot of noise and makes discipline difficult. For the first time since she began teaching, Lin is anxious about her work and unable to enjoy it. ...

The experience of these...teachers is not necessarily typical. However, it is sufficiently common to cause concern and to require that we look at how people in similar situations can be helped more constructively through programmes of teacher education.

(adapted from Parrott, 1991: 37–41)

6.4 A case study of a teacher classroom research project

(see Introduction, 'Investigating')

A CASE STUDY BY SANDRA MEISTER, A FIRST YEAR TEACHER WHO WAS TAKING AN IN-SERVICE COURSE

This text provides an example of a 'strong' form of classroom research, which many busy teachers probably do not have enough time for.

The purpose of this research project is to become familiar with educational research within the classroom, to analyse and improve one aspect of my teaching style. But I have had some difficulty in pinpointing which aspect of my teaching I wished to focus on. As a harried first year teacher, I really had not given much time to actually thinking about the way I taught, rather I tended to worry about keeping things peaceful until the three o'clock bell rang. I decided, however, to look at the types of questions I asked, the order in which I asked them, and to whom the questions were directed. This sequence appears to be the key to training a child to think independently. In order to become aware of my own teaching style, I decided to obtain data from myself as teacher, from my class, and from an outside observer who was previously known to myself and my students.

Social studies was an area I find particularly dull at this level. The entire primary curriculum centres around 'myself and my family in our community', 'components of our community', and finally 'the interaction of communities'. The lessons I had taught were scattered and poorly sequenced. As a final unit, I decided to divide the class into three groups and have one group research communities of the past, one look at Prince George as it is today, and one group design a community for the future. Most of the knowledge came from group lessons and discussions where, through various questions and brainstorming techniques, I hoped to direct the student to some logical conclusions as to the necessary requirements for community life.

The lesson used as the basis for the research was on different modes of communication. I taught the lesson while the observer recorded the types of questions asked (i.e. fact, critical thinking, explanation, yes/no, etc.), which students responded and the teacher reaction to the response. The data was gathered by the observer using a checklist. The lesson was audio-taped which enabled both the teacher and the observer to review data afterwards.

The results were really quite an eye-opener. The majority of my questions required critical thinking or an opinion while the remainder were questions for the purpose of gathering facts. Most of the questions required one or two answers. The following is an analysis of my questioning techniques.

Types of questions asked: on the positive side, most of the questions required critical thinking, i.e. 'How would you feel...?' 'What would you do if....?' Many questions required students to express an opinion, I avoided Yes/No questions which is something I was pleased to note. On the negative side, I seemed to avoid asking any questions which required any type of explanation. This is an important area which I have overlooked.

Sequence of questions: the order in which the questions were asked seemed logical and new information built on previous answers. The weakest area here seemed to be in moving from one topic to the next. I'll need to work on having a few key questions as pivot points for my lesson.

To whom questions were directed: on the positive side, I would often ask one question such as, 'Who do you talk to on the phone?' and randomly choose many students for a one word answer which keeps them all involved and interested. On the negative side, whenever I asked an open question I seemed to respond to one of three students regardless of who may have had their hands up. These particular students are those with whom I try to avoid confrontations.

Teacher responses to answers: this is the area which I feel this project has identified as something for me to question. As I looked at the data, I realized that I rarely praised the students verbally. The majority of teacher responses were repeating what the child said and nodding to affirm their stance. The next frequent teacher response was no reaction. The observer noted that the students seemed satisfied with the way that their opinions were accepted without much comment and didn't appear to act differently when verbal praise was given. I also appeared to accept an answer regardless of whether hands were up or not.

There are three areas where the observer and I saw possibilities for improvement. The first is to accept answers and request answers from all students rather than a select few. An obvious way to improve this is to limit the size of the group to whom the lesson is being taught. Perhaps using a phrase such as 'let's let someone else have a turn' would help. The changes need not be large and I'm glad this was brought to my attention – imagine some poor child spending a year in my class and never being asked a question!

The second area for change is in making a smooth transition from one topic to the next within a lesson. I feel this can be accomplished by noting beforehand a comparison phrase or question and recording differences or similarities between the two topics.

Finally, I must learn to allow the children an opportunity to give detailed explanations. This is an ideal opportunity for improving verbal lucidity and compositional skills.

After some reflection on the research project, I feel that it was a valuable exercise. Having another individual working on the project immediately reduced the feelings of isolation I had from the staff.

The other area that was most valuable was the opportunity to go through a research project under guidance from an experienced researcher.

Now that contacts have been established, the feasibility of classroom research in Prince George has expanded. Having completed the process once makes a world of difference for considering future research projects.

The next time I conduct or participate in a research project, I will use the 'triangulation approach'. The insight of an outside observer is invaluable and also allows the students to offer some feedback. I would also like to participate in a project where the observer would be the director (adviser) and have more than one classroom involved. By playing a small role in a larger scale project, I feel I would gain more first-hand knowledge and become confident in being a teacher researcher.

(Hopkins, 1985: 6–8)

6.5 Sample sequence of tasks, activities and options for investigating 'learner autonomy'

(see Introduction, 'Investigating')

Section 6.5 shows in detail how different tasks, activities and options in *Teachers in Action* might be applied to a specific topic, that of 'learner autonomy'. (Each task, activity or option taken from the book for this sequence may also be found by means of the references given below.) I hope that providing an example of a sequence in this way will help trainers to create their own sequences.

INVESTIGATING LEARNER AUTONOMY

Aim

- to provide teachers with an opportunity to consider the principles, appropriateness and possible application of learner autonomy in their own teaching situations

TASKS AND ACTIVITIES

The numbered stages that follow refer to the chapters of this book.

2 *Identifying a topic*

I am assuming that the topic of learner autonomy has already been identified, perhaps as a result of the teachers completing Task 2.2, which had helped them to establish that promoting learner autonomy was a high priority in their schools and classrooms.

3 *Exploring the topic*

3.1 Introduction: lead a brief general discussion based on the factory caricature, using (some of) the following questions:

Does the drawing express realistically what happens in schools in general today in your region or country, or in your own school? Or is the drawing an unrealistic caricature? Does this drawing show what used to happen in schools? Do we want this to happen in our schools? If not, what should replace it?

List on the blackboard any points emerging from the discussion for future reference. Further suggestions for exploring the topic include: 'Learner autonomy is important because...' (see Option 17 on p. 79); 'What do we understand by learner autonomy?' (see Task 3.2); producing a working definition: 'Learner autonomy' means...' (see Task 3.2).

3.2 Refer teachers to the following annotated bibliography on the topic of learner autonomy (a section of a longer training programme bibliography), which is also linked to the extracts in Task 3.8, and encourage them to follow up any interests they might have by reading the relevant texts.

Learner Autonomy, Bibliography

The following texts can be found in the box in the training room, or in the Resource Centre. If you have problems locating a particular text, ask a trainer.

Allwright, D. (1988). Autonomy and Individualisation in Whole-Class Instruction. In A. Brookes and P. Grundy (eds.), *Individualisation and Antonomy in Language Learning*, *ELT Documents* 131. Modern English Publications in association with The British Council. (a realistic view of learner autonomy in the context of state sector schools)

Dam, L. (1991). Mimeo extract from a paper given at a teachers' conference in Zaragoza, Spain.

Dickinson, L. (1993). Talking Shop: Aspects of Autonomous Learning. in *ELT Journal*, 47, 4. (a very readable, accessible interview)

Dickinson, L. and Carver, D. (1980). Learning How to Learn: Steps towards Self-Direction in Foreign Language learning in Schools. *ELT Journal*, **35**, 1. (a 'classic', yet still very useful)

Ellis, G. and Sinclair, B. (1989). *Learning to Learn English.* Cambridge: Cambridge University Press. (coursebook focusing on practical activities)

Freire, P. (1972). *Pedagogy of the Oppressed.* London: Penguin. (by the great Brazilian humanist thinker, who believed in the liberating power of education)

For further information about bibliographies, see Section 6.20.

3.3 Workshop: Demonstrate a number of teaching ideas to the teachers with regard to a more specific topic such as 'learner autonomy and developing learners' writing skills' by focusing on (some of) the following activities or stages:

1 Share your aims with the teachers for the writing lesson (you are going to write a text in pairs, etc.).

2 Give the teachers instructions which will enable them to write a text on an agreed topic, and ask them to brainstorm ideas and language related to the topic.

3 The teachers write a text in pairs.

4 The teachers display their texts on the wall and read them.

5 The teachers comment on each other's texts (which do we like best? why? what are our criteria?); self-correct and/or peer-correct their texts. The trainer collects in the texts.

6 The teachers reflect on the writing process (stages 1–5).

Ask the teachers to evaluate the above activities by using the questions in Task 3.6, which are designed for this purpose, for example, 'What did the activities have in common?' Instead of, or as well as, demonstrating some activities, give teachers a list of relevant teaching activities, asking them to select/rank those which are priority in their teaching situation. For example, for the topic of learner autonomy: encourage learners to explore; share aims with learners and/or learners formulate their own aims; demonstrate different learning strategies; the learners self-correct, self-assess, reflect on the learning process; encourage learners to take risks with new language; encourage learners to ask questions about language; use reference materials, such as dictionaries, in class; learners work in groups or pairs.

Teachers produce a list of practical recommendations for promoting learner autonomy, using Worksheet 27.

4 *Investigating in class*

See Task 4.8, whereby teachers try out in their classes over an agreed period of time ideas recommended in the above workshop. They may use Worksheet 40 to report on the effectiveness of their experiments in a subsequent training session, and/or Tasks 4.4 or 4.5, in which teachers ask their learners for feedback during the period of experimentation with an aspect(s) of learner autonomy. Teachers may also keep a classroom diary during the period of experimentation (see Task 2.7).

5 *Evaluating learning*
See Task 5.1, in which the teachers have an opportunity to take stock of the tasks and activities they have completed in relation to their work on the topic of learner autonomy. Or…

See Task 5.7, in which teachers use Worksheet 49 to plan informal presentations. Teachers then present their work related to the topic of learner autonomy. Or …

See Option 29 (on p. 137), for which the group produces a mindmap summary of their work, with each teacher taking home a copy.

6.6 Example of a completed Worksheet 3, Option 2
(see Task 1.1)

This text was written by a teacher.

1 I am a teacher because: *at the time I wanted to start working the best I could do was teaching English and I enjoyed it.*
2 The things I enjoy about being a teacher are: *working with a lot of different people in a creative way.*
3 The things I don't enjoy about being a teacher are: *correcting exams, handling students who don't care about learning, or are impolite.*
4 My main qualities as a teacher are: *being creative, patient, funny (sometimes).*
5 I think the main role of a teacher is to: *make their classes interesting enough; assure that people improve.*
6 I like learners who: *participate in my classes, who are open to communication.*
7 My learners think I am: *good but not as hard as I should be.*
8 At the end of a class I usually feel: *sometimes satisfied, or I have to change or improve.*
9 I think teaching is a/an *demanding* profession.
10 If weren't a teacher, I would like to be a/an: *(I haven't found the ideal job for me).*
11 My feelings and expectations about doing this training programme are: *I want to find out about new teaching ideas and also brush up my English.*

Note: in the interests of authenticity, teachers' statements here and elsewhere have been edited only to clarify meaning.

6.7 List of ways of professional learning for teachers

(see Task 1.2)

Teachers may learn in many ways, only some of which are offered by formal training programmes. Here are some examples.

Through teaching:
- development of skills through experience; following the guidelines from coursebooks and/or accompanying teacher's books
- experimenting with the curriculum, or taking on a new role at work
- developing a specialism; placement in another institution / job swapping

Through collaboration:
- joint work with a skilled collaborator, with other professionals; joint curriculum development: formative evaluation; team teaching
- 'shadowing', watching someone else at work
- discussion of practice with colleagues; access to their specialist knowledge
- peer supervision or support; being a member of an interest group / working party

Through innovation and research:
- writing and presenting a paper at a conference; working on a policy statement
- developing materials; doing action research

Through helping others learn:
- providing a course / skills work for others; giving talks/workshops
- helping prepare training materials
- presenting an aspect of one's practice to peers
- collating and disseminating information to others
- supervising trainees or novice teachers

Through courses:
- attending a course, conference, workshop or seminar
- distance learning; feedback on performance on courses

Through self-study:
- time to reflect on current practice, knowledge or skill; study leave; reading

Through language learning:
- learning a new language at the level of one's learners; on-going language development and awareness of learner perspectives

(adapted from Cline *et al.*, cited in Roberts, 1998: 224–5)

6.8 Stages of investigating: key to Worksheets 6 and 7

(see Task 1.3)

This is one possible sequence for the stages of investigating on Worksheets 6 and 7; there is no fixed order, particularly in the first five stages, although some stages logically precede others: A, E, D, G, B, F, C and H.

1 *Select a topic for investigating*
   For example, try to think what you would like to improve in your work.
2 *Find a colleague(s) to work with*
   Working together helps you to share ideas and the workload, when feeling fed up or stuck!
3 *Preliminary exploration*
   Read as much as you can find on the topic you select, and about investigating, keeping notes about your reading. Ask other colleagues for advice.
4 *Set aims and 'start small'*
   Do not try to do too much, too quickly; set modest aims for investigating, for example by focusing on one class you teach for a limited period of time.
5 *Decide which data to collect*
   For example, you can take photos, keep a classroom diary, collect lesson plans, or write a simple questionnaire. Ask other colleagues for advice.
6 *Teach, and collect data*
   Actually teach for the period in question. Make sure that collecting data does not interfere too much with your teaching
7 *Evaluate your work*
   For example, ask: What did my/our pupils learn? What did I/we learn? Where is my/our 'evidence'? What recommendations can I/we give colleagues interested in the same topic?
8 *Share the results with colleagues*
   Tell the colleagues in your group or at a school staff meeting about your recommendations by making a poster about your work. Or you could write a brief report or an article, or give a talk at a conference.

6.9 Exploring teachers' metaphors

(see Task 1.4)

6.9.1 SAMPLE DISCUSSION OF A METAPHOR

The following text is an extract from the transcription of a discussion related to the drawing of the classroom as a garden (see Task 1.4). A teacher representing his sub-group is addressing the other teachers, as described in the procedures for Task 1.4.

TEACHER 1: It's quite obvious that the gardener's a teacher, so it's a teacher-centred sort of approach. As you can see, the…teacher is quite puzzled, because a lot is going on in his head. He's got…sometimes he's got a brilliant idea. He's puzzled and so on.…The idea is that in a teacher's brain a lot is going on, it's really another world. He's got obvious tools which are obviously rake, spade, bucket, etc.…And then he's got special tools like fertiliser, weedkiller, pure soil, and so on. He's got also a little library here, so we just gave the idea of the different approaches and the different, PPP.…We didn't give too much importance to all the books because they are in a way a sort of library, they're there. You know they're there, but you don't go round surrounded by books. They form your background. You can go back to them, you can take one book instead of another. It depends what's going on in the classroom and what you need.

TRAINER: The interesting thing is all the children are there immediately with pressing needs. That comes across very strongly, doesn't it?

TEACHER 1: …shelves in the background are, I hope that it's clear enough. There's a classroom…and every plant is a child. And they're growing differently. At different speeds. They succeed in different ways. They don't succeed. At the back…you've got the lazy ones. (laughter) This one for instance is not, is reading comics. And then you've got the two – the boy and girl who fell in love. And then you've got in the front row, obviously, you've got the very smart ones. They're always ready to learn. They're powerful. They get a lot of fertiliser. (laughter) This one, you've always got one of those. Very nasty one. (laughter) And you can go on, too. He's in the front row, because he's disturbing all the time. He's there. You try…but…you can physically put him in the back, but he's never in the back. We thought it was a good idea because you can add and add and read and read. For instance, we put here a weedkiller. Now weed is a sort of dust which is very difficult to kill and you can think of it as something the child has learnt which is wrong, and it is difficult to kill this information, and put another one, the right one in its place. So very often a teacher is really aggressive and uses lots of weedkiller. The results of this …

TRAINER: Overcorrecting?

TEACHER 1: Overcorrecting, so you can really…I've finished now but obviously there's a lot to say. It's quite obvious, like the theatre. You can come along with…

TEACHER 2: I would say that this is the role of the teacher. The students are just the result of what the teacher does. I don't think this is the real situation. I mean, it's very nice, the analysis of the teacher's role, but I don't think that a class works on only what a teacher thinks.

TEACHER 1: It's only a metaphor.

TEACHER 2: Yes, that's just what I wanted to say about the limit, maybe, of your metaphor. In the sense that the plants are a result of what the teacher does, which is not true. I don't think so. I don't think this is the situation…

6.9.2 POSSIBLE METAPHORS FOR ASPECTS OF EDUCATING, TEACHING AND LEARNING

Examples of metaphors suggested by teachers I have worked with, or that I have read about, include:

1 *The classroom as:*
   courtroom, bullring, factory, hairdressing salon, jungle, ship, church, the sea, football stadium, beehive, prison, maze, kitchen, opera house, pizzeria, 'at the chalkface', a conversation
2 *The teacher as:*
   judge, juggler, wearing different hats, feeding chickens, a doctor, football manager, a preacher, saint-teacher, moral martyr, reformer, film director
3 *The learners as:*
   butterflies hatching, chickens being fed, defendants in a courtroom, empty vessels, resisters, receptacles, raw material, clients, partners, individual or democratic explorers
4 *Learning as:*
   climbing a mountain, travelling through a long tunnel
5 *Teacher education and development as:*
   creative turbulence, going on a journey, walking down a corridor and opening doors
6 *Beginning school / a course as:*
   opening a door, jumping into cold water, turning on a light, planting a seed, signing a contract, joining a club, sitting down to a meal (Ur and Wright, 1992: 51)

6.10 Mapping the whole: developing conceptual frameworks for educating, teaching and learning
(see Task 1.5)

6.10.1 SAMPLE LIST OF CONCEPTS

This list shows concepts referring to a training programme taught by the author, presented here in alphabetical order:

attitudes; change; classroom; communication; curriculum; goals and aims for learning; knowledge; learners; learners' needs; materials for learning (e.g. coursebooks); parents; professional magazines and journals; publishers; research; school; self-esteem; skills; society; syllabus; tasks and activities for learning; teachers; teaching aids; teaching principles (personal theory); teaching techniques; the English language; using games and songs

6.10.2 'METHOD: APPROACH, DESIGN AND PROCEDURE' MODEL

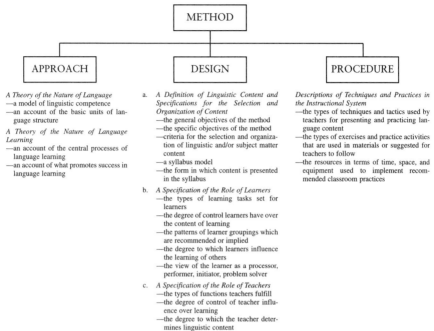

a. *A Theory of the Nature of Language*
 —a model of linguistic competence
 —an account of the basic units of language structure
b. *A Theory of the Nature of Language Learning*
 —an account of the central processes of language learning
 —an account of what promotes success in language learning

a. *A Definition of Linguistic Content and Specifications for the Selection and Organization of Content*
 —the general objectives of the method
 —the specific objectives of the method
 —criteria for the selection and organization of linguistic and/or subject matter content
 —a syllabus model
 —the form in which content is presented in the syllabus
b. *A Specification of the Role of Learners*
 —the types of learning tasks set for learners
 —the degree of control learners have over the content of learning
 —the patterns of learner groupings which are recommended or implied
 —the degree to which learners influence the learning of others
 —the view of the learner as a processor, performer, initiator, problem solver
c. *A Specification of the Role of Teachers*
 —the types of functions teachers fulfill
 —the degree of control of teacher influence over learning
 —the degree to which the teacher determines linguistic content
 —the types of interaction between teachers and learners
d. *A Specification of the Role of Materials*
 —the primary goal of materials
 —the form materials take (e.g., textbook, audiovisual format, etc.)
 —the relation materials have to other sources of input
 —the assumptions the materials make about teachers and learners

Descriptions of Techniques and Practices in the Instructional System
 —the types of techniques and tactics used by teachers for presenting and practicing language content
 —the types of exercises and practice activities that are used in materials or suggested for teachers to follow
 —the resources in terms of time, space, and equipment used to implement recommended classroom practices

(Richards and Rodgers, 1982: 165)

6.10.3 REFLECTIVE MODEL FOR TEACHER EDUCATION

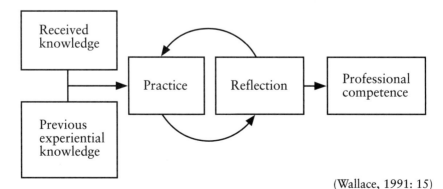

(Wallace, 1991: 15)

6.11 Why teach English? Reflecting on the goals of educating, teaching and learning in the language classroom

(see Task 1.6)

6.11.1 FURTHER READING

Extract from 'A curriculum for the future':

…If many of the children now in school have to retrain several times during their working lives, and if most of them can look forward to many years of good health in their Third age, then their appetite for learning must stretch way beyond the years of compulsory schooling. In order to flourish over what could be a very long lifetime, they will need a firm foundation of knowledge, skills, attitudes and forms of behaviour, alongside positive personal characteristics, such as determination, flexibility, imagination. They will also require the social intelligence and will to pool their strengths with those of their fellows, as well as independence of mind to act autonomously. This strong combination of personal and intellectual qualities is particularly important, given the explosion of knowledge, which continues to gather pace. The many forms of new interactive technology available require vision and tenacity from those wishing to benefit from them, if they are to be used to their full potential.

In the circumstances, a single dimension view of the curriculum would be inadequate. It is simply not enough to conceive of a school or college curriculum as nothing more than a flat, unidimensional list of subjects or topics. In order to develop the range of talents needed for a prosperous future, children must learn over a wide range and variety of ways. That is why a multi-dimensional view of the curriculum makes good sense. The most significant and exciting challenge facing the whole of society, not just those who work professionally in education, is how to devise and provide a coherent programme for young people that recognises the many forces at work, anticipating successfully some of the needs of an uncertain future, synthesising the distilled wisdom of hundreds of generations, while at the same time sponsoring both autonomy and teamwork.

If this can be done successfully, then teachers can actually help their pupils to shape the future, rather than find themselves the unwitting and impotent victims of it.

(Wragg, 1997: 22)

6.11.2 EXAMPLE OF A SCHOOL CURRICULUM INFORMATION LEAFLET (ENGLAND)

This document is suitable for learners' parents. The text has been slightly adapted for reasons of space. (Although there have been changes since 1995, when this document was published, it can still be used effectively.)

The School Curriculum. A Brief Guide

Schools should give all pupils the opportunity to achieve their best, within a broad and balanced curriculum. The National Curriculum, including assessment, plays an important part in providing this opportunity. The Office for Standards in Education (OFSTED) inspects schools, and they have confirmed that the National Curriculum is raising standards. This leaflet explains the school curriculum in England.

Which subjects do pupils have to study?

Pupils aged 5 to 16 in state schools must be taught the National Curriculum, which is made up of the following subjects: English, mathematics, science, design and technology, information technology, history, geography, music, art, physical education (PE) and a modern foreign language. The National Curriculum sets out, in broad terms, what schools must teach for each subject.

The National Curriculum is divided into four stages. These are called key stages and depend on pupils' ages. The table below shows when the pupils study each subject.

KEY STAGES AND PUPILS' AGES

	Key Stage 1 Aged 5 to 7	Key Stage 2 Aged 7 to 11	Key Stage 3 Aged 11 to 14	Key Stage 4 Aged 14 to 16
English				
Mathematics				
Science				
Physical education				
Design and technology				
Modern foreign language				
History				
Geography				
Music				
Art				

Pupils going into Key Stage 4 before September 1996 do not have to be taught design and technology, information technology and a modern foreign language. Pupils must also study religious education (RE), and secondary schools must provide sex education. The content of these two subjects is decided locally but must remain within the law. The Government also plans to make all secondary schools responsible for providing careers education. Schools organise their own timetable, and can decide what else to teach their pupils.

How does the National Curriculum work?

Every school has National Curriculum documents for each subject. These documents describe what teachers must teach at each key stage. Most National Curriculum subjects are divided into different areas of learning. For example, English is divided into three areas: speaking and listening, reading, and writing. The National Curriculum does not include detailed lesson plans for teachers. Schools and teachers draw up their own lesson plans based on the National Curriculum. Teachers will plan these lessons, taking into account their pupils' needs. Schools decide for themselves which text books and other teaching materials to use.

How is each pupil's progress assessed?

The National Curriculum sets standards of achievement in each subject for pupils aged 5 to 14. For most subjects these standards range from levels 1 to 8. Pupils climb the levels as they get older and learn more.

- *The standards at level 2 should challenge typical 7-year-olds*
- *The standards at level 4 should challenge typical 11-year-olds*
- *The standards at levels 5 and 6 should challenge typical 14-year-olds*

More able pupils will reach the standards above these levels, and exceptionally able 14-year-olds may reach the standards above level 8. The National Curriculum for music, art, and physical education does not use levels 1 to 8. Instead, there is a single description of the standards that most pupils can expect to reach at the end of a key stage for each area of learning. All teachers check their pupils' progress in each subject as a normal part of their teaching. They must also assess pupils' progress in English, mathematics, and science against the National Curriculum standards when pupils reach ages 7, 11 and 14. The teacher decides which level best describes a pupil's performance in each area of learning in the subject.

Do pupils have to sit national tests and examinations?

There are national tests for 7-, 11- and 14-year-olds in English and mathematics. Pupils aged 11 and 14 are also tested in science. The tests give an independent measure of how pupils and school are doing compared with the national standards in these subjects. Most 16-year-olds take GCSEs or similar qualifications.

How can parents find out how their children are doing?

At least once a year schools must give parents a written report on how children are doing in all subjects. This report will also explain how parents can arrange to discuss comments in their report with teachers.

What choices are available for 14- to 16-year-olds?

At Key Stage 4 the National Curriculum gives schools the opportunity to offer pupils aged 14 to 16 a wider choice of subjects. This includes a range of GCSE and vocational courses. The diagram (above) shows which National Curriculum subjects pupils aged 14 to 16 must continue to study. English, mathematics and science remain a central part of the curriculum and most pupils will take a GCSE course in these subjects. Pupils must also continue to study RE and PE. From September 1996, schools must also teach design and technology and a modern foreign language to pupils starting Key Stage 4. They must teach at least a short course in these subjects, which will be roughly the same as doing half a GCSE, but many schools will offer full courses. Pupils must also study information technology from September 1996.

Can parents withdraw their children from some subjects?

Parents can withdraw their children from some or all RE and sex education lessons. They cannot withdraw them from any other part of the National Curriculum. There are some pupils, however, who do not have to follow the National Curriculum. Usually, this only happens if all or part of the National Curriculum is not suitable for a pupil because he or she has certain special educational needs.

How can I find out more?

Each school has a prospectus and this must explain the school's curriculum, how the curriculum is organised for different year groups, and how it is taught. Parents can ask to see copies of the National Curriculum documents, the RE syllabus the school is using and the school's sex education policy. You may also find copies of the National Curriculum documents in public libraries, and you can buy them from bookshops that sell HMSO publications.

(Department for Education and Employment, 1995)

6.11.3 EXTRACT FROM AN OFFICIAL SPANISH CURRICULUM DOCUMENT FOR SECONDARY EDUCATION

This document defines the general objectives of foreign language teaching in Spanish secondary schools.

General objectives for foreign language teaching

1 To understand the global and specific information of spoken and written messages in the foreign language....

2 To produce oral and written messages in the foreign language…demonstrating an attitude of respect and interest towards understanding and being understood.

3 To read written texts…related to the communicative situations both within and outside the school context….

4 To use the reading of texts for different purposes, valuing their importance as a source of information, enjoyment and leisure, and as a means of access to other cultures and ways of life different to their own.

5 To reflect about the functioning of the linguistic system in communication….

6 To value the support provided by the knowledge of foreign languages for communicating with people from cultures different to our own and for participating in international relations….

7 To value the richness of different languages and cultures….

8 To maintain a receptive, critical attitude towards information from the culture of the foreign language…and use such information to reflect on one's own culture.

9. To use strategies of autonomous learning of the foreign language constructed on the basis of experience with other languages and the reflection on the learning processes themselves.

(adapted from Spanish Ministry of Education and Science, 1995: 32–33)

6.12 Key to Worksheet 12

(see Task 1.7)

1	educational goals	very general, broad targets to be aimed at (White, 1988: 27)
2	fluency	speaking or writing with ease and without excessive hesitation
3	syllabus	a way of specifying, selecting and organising the content of teaching for a particular subject
4	utterance	something that is said/spoken
5	accuracy	the production of instances of correct language
6	curriculum	'the totality of content to be taught and aims to be realized within one school or educational system' (White, 1988: 4)

6.13 Example of a list of factors which will help us to change and/or innovate, Worksheet 15

(see Task 1.8)

The list below shows how a group of teachers responded to Worksheet 15.

Factors which will help us to change and/or innovate:
- the teachers' acceptance of the new idea
- the teachers' readiness for the new idea
- the teachers' willingness to change
- the 'change agents' (if there are any) must make it clear from the beginning what the change consists of, so that later there are no misunderstandings, so that all, or most, people involved are working in the same direction
- to have or to get the material/resources (for example, computers, if teachers want to learn to use them at school)
- to realise or to be conscious of the fact that something is not working or can be improved
- having realistic objectives
- everybody must feel involved in it
- teamwork
- the staff, pupils' and parents' agreement and involvement
- pupil and teacher motivation
- the co-ordination between teachers and students is very important
- being ready to do extra work
- there must be some benefits for the teachers who are carrying out the innovation

6.14 Innovation in our schools: How can we help to promote it?

(see Task 1.9)

16.14.1 EXAMPLE OF A COMPLETED WORKSHEET 16 QUESTIONNAIRE

(written by a teacher)

1 What was the innovation? In materials, technology, organisation, curriculum, etc.?

A course about the use of computers in school.

2 Why was the innovation introduced?

Because teachers saw the importance of the use of computers in our school.

3 Who first suggested the innovation?
Some teachers at school.

4 How was the innovation first introduced?
Some teachers thought about the idea and told a teacher at school specialised in computers. They proposed it in a teachers' meeting.

5 What factors promoted or inhibited the innovation?
There was in the school a computer centre, but only two teachers could use it. So they really welcomed the proposal.

6 What was the effect of the innovation on yourself or others involved?
All the people involved in the innovation were very enthusiastic about it.

7 If you could implement the innovation again, what improvements would you make to the way it was implemented?
Now it wouldn't be an innovation because they now do these courses from our local teachers' centre. So the improvements have already been made.

8 What factors are important in the implementation of an innovation?
- to have or to get the material/resources (in this case, the computers)
- the teachers' acceptance of the innovation
- the teachers' readiness for it

6.14.2 FURTHER READING: 'STUDENTS COMMITTED TO EQUALITY PROJECT'

This is an article from *Comunidad Escolar*, a Spanish weekly newspaper about educational issues

Students committed to equality project.

The Dolores Ibárruri High School, of Gallarta (Vizcaya), celebrates International Working Woman's Day. Bilbao. MARISA GUTIERREZ

Plays, films, talks, debates, and games were some of the activities that students of the Dolores Ibárruri High School, in the Province of Vizcaya, were involved in, in order to celebrate International Working Woman's Day. In a festive atmosphere, the day helped students and teachers to reflect on the situation of women in our society, and enabled everyone, both boys and girls, to question their own acts and attitudes.

Not so many years ago, at the beginning of the 90s, no high school in the province of Vizcaya was named after a woman, except for those named after the Virgin Mary. This high school in Gallarta was the first to do so, by officially adopting the name of Dolores Ibárruri in 1991 (popularly known as 'La Pasionaria'), in the year of the centenary of her birth. As part of a co-education project, the adoption of this name sought to remember a woman in the town of her birth, a woman who, in addition to her particular political affiliation, was ahead of her time, and who participated actively in the society in which she lived.

The project mentioned above is more ambitious, as at the time of writing the teachers at the school are involved in drawing up a School Educational Plan with a specifically co-educational focus. Their reflection and teaching practice over the past years has made them aware that simply putting boys and girls together in the same schools and the same classrooms, is not in itself enough to achieve co-education. On the contrary, often mixed education in the same physical space only serves to familiarise girls with masculine values, so as to participate in a world 'of men', to which they can now gain access.

Sexist values

These teachers were also aware of the blatantly sexist values which are still conveyed by some textbooks and by some school material. They saw that most subjects are still presented from an exclusively male point of view, and that, in contrast, female values are ignored, or are simply presented as being secondary. They were even aware that they themselves, sometimes almost without noticing, accepted boys' greater spontaneity and participation – speaking more in class, or asking more questions – as being natural.

These are the issues which are being worked on in the School Educational Plan. Two of the teachers are more intensively involved with the topic of comprehensive education, participating in a seminar which meets in the nearby Teachers' Centre in Ortuella. They have started revising the books and materials used in class, as well as the adminstrative stationery and school signs and notices, in order to avoid the unique and omnipresent linguistic masculine forms used previously. Marisa Otaduy, the School Director, explains that now not one single piece of paper leaves the school, if someone can help it, where only the masculine form is used. She illustrates this with one small yet significant example. That same morning she had changed – with a pen, until the mistake can be fully rectified – an 'o' for an 'a' in a document that a female student had to fill in.

Otaduy also explains that the teaching staff involved in this co-education project are determined, for example, to rescue the memory of women writers and scientists who are not mentioned in textbooks. They are also determined to formulate the questions asked in class differently, so as to include information from the female world. They would also like to talk about the past differently, so as not to systematically forget women.

This is why 8 March is such an important day in the school. For the past seven years International Working Woman's Day has been celebrated, enabling everyone, both boys and girls, teachers and students alike, to reflect on their role in school and in society. This year, an important day in the school plan for the year, everyone's participated and the day was celebrated at different age levels without having to change the school timetable.

Congratulations

The day had a distinctively festive flavour, and started off with everyone in the school receiving a special message of congratulations. This message was similar in format and partly shared the same texts (such as a fragment of the lecture given by Emila Pardo Bazán in 1892 at the Second Pedagogic Conference: 'The education of women today cannot strictly be called education; rather it is 'taming'…I hope, gentlemen, that you will recognise that woman has her own destiny, that her first natural duties are to herself, that her happiness and dignity have to be the essential purpose of culture'); the messages presented were varied, depending on the recipient.

The female students were congratulated, among other reasons, 'because you do not give up the right to study and learn' and 'because you struggle to have your own voice'. To adult women – teachers, mothers and non-teaching staff – 'because you do not give up the right to be yourself, despite having a double working day' and 'because you work so that male and female students can be educated in a non-sexist way'. To the men 'because you question the role that society has given you' and 'because you respect and value your female companions'. And to everyone 'because you work every day for your own happiness and personal liberty'.

The activities which took place throughout the day were many and varied, and organised at different age levels. The students, with their requests, suggestions, ideas and co-operation, worked on the preparation. The Dolores Ibárurri High School in Gallarta showed two films, 'Who did Gilbert Grappe love?', and 'The Piano'; as well as a video produced by the United Nations about the situation and power of women in the world; a talk by the sexologist Marisa López Ibarraondo, requested by the students; two plays performed by groups from within the school; various debates; readings of and commentaries on comics and texts. The game 'alter ego' was also played, in which the participants discuss values and attitudes, and, among other things, posters referring to the date were designed and made.

These were objectives established in 1991 by 'Emakunde', the Basque Institute for Women, and which are still very relevant in 1996: 'The sexist stereotypes in teaching materials and in curricula will be fought against. Teachers will be encouraged to change their attitudes, by means of awarenessraising activities and the provision of in-service training. Equal opportunities will be guaranteed for girls and boys for all types of schooling and all types of training, in order that they may develop their aptitudes as fully as possible, without conditioning careers advice by the different expectations that we have of girls and boys, as a result of the social role that they are assigned.'

(Gutierrez, 1996; my translation)

6.15 Examining critical incidents
(see Task 2.1)

6.15.1 SAMPLE RESPONSES TO WORKSHEET 17

A colleague used Worksheet 17 to interview me about one of my critical incidents.

Q: What happened?

A: Several years ago I joined a group to learn Basque, which met twice a week at lunchtime at work.

Q: Who was involved?

A: My colleagues, nine or ten of us. We had a Basque teacher, a dynamic, enthusiastic native speaker.

Q: What/who made it happen?

A: Colleagues had asked for opportunities to learn Basque.

Q: What did it feel like? For whom?

A: I felt very curious about Basque, and enjoyed the classes, in general. We were involved in communicative activities, and the teacher spoke Basque all the time, not using Spanish or English. But I realised that I had a number of quite specific doubts or questions about language, as things cropped up in class. Things like: 'I wonder if you can say "x",' or 'What happens if you put this verb…'. There were no opportunities in class for me to ask about these points.

Q: What does it mean? To whom?

A: It meant to me that I missed out on some learning opportunities. The teacher was unaware of my questions.

Q: Why did it happen?

A: Because we weren't expected to ask questions of this sort, or, at least, I assumed so. I didn't ask the teacher if I could, or we hadn't discussed what we could do or not do in class.

Q: Did I like it?

A: It was not a major problem, but I did feel slightly frustrated.

Q: Was it a good thing?

A: Well, it helped me to think about the implications for my own teaching.

Q: Why?

A: Because I wondered if my own students experienced anything like what I had experienced.

Q: What is it an example of?

A: A discrepancy between teacher and student expectations?

Q: What do I do as a result/should I do as a result?

A: I now encourage my own students to ask me questions about language, if they have them, although at designated times, as otherwise students' problems 'interrupt' the flow of a class, at least if I assume that the agenda is already set, and that students should not ask individual questions.

Q: How?

A: I explain in a text of guidelines which I give students at the beginning of a course, the ways in which I think we can work together profitably. During the course we discuss the text, and make any necessary modifications to the guidelines. Perhaps the Basque class incident has reinforced my understanding that discussing with students openly about teaching and learning is very important.

Q: When? Where?

A: In my current teaching.

6.15.2 SAMPLE CRITICAL INCIDENT FROM A TEACHER

The following text, describing a critical incident, was written by a teacher living in the bilingual community of the Basque Country in Spain, where both Castilian/Spanish and Basque are spoken. It was written after the teacher heard me describe my Basque language class, as in the text in Section 6.15.1:

> This happened four years ago. I wanted to learn German so I joined a beginners' group in G. Our teacher was a native-speaking German girl, very tolerant I must say and with a very good command of the language – that is what it seemed at least. Well, we were about fourteen students in that group, and none of us knew a single word of German. From the very beginning, the teacher started to speak to us only in German. At the beginning it was very funny and we all seemed to enjoy it, but as time went by I realised that I often felt insecure and somehow frustrated in the classroom. There were many occasions in which we wanted to know the exact meaning of a word (its equivalent in Spanish); or for example a grammar rule, we wanted her to explain it again in Spanish/Basque so that we were sure that we had got it right. We often asked her for that, but she couldn't. She said that was a German class and that we had to forget that our mother tongue existed. I know that her intentions were good, but I often felt strange in that class, very insecure and I was not the only one as we, the students, talked it over more than once and we all agreed. So now…what did I learn from this critical incident? Well, I came to realise that I behaved with my students, the same way as my German teacher. I spoke to my pupils every single word in English, giving them no chance to use their mother tongue. If they didn't understand something, or wanted the Spanish word, I wouldn't tell them. I just explained the item in a different way. From my German experience, I came to see now how my pupils themselves often felt. I knew they were right to use their mother tongue when they were not sure if they had understood something. From that moment onwards, I have let my students use their own language when necessary, and I even get them to explain some important grammar points in their mother tongue, too.

6.16 Sample responses to Worksheet 19
(see Task 2.2)

These responses to Worksheet 19 were made by a group of teachers.

Learners should:

- be encouraged to self-evaluate
- be encouraged to take risks
- be able to contribute their own experience, knowledge and skills to the learning process

- work together in pairs or groups
- learn about the world through English

The teacher should:
- be able to work in teams (with other teachers)
- encourage learners to investigate
- try to motivate learners by involving them in the learning process (even physically)
- be interested in improving themselves
- have a good relationship with learners' families

The curriculum/syllabus/materials/tasks should:
- be up-to-date and meaningful to the learners
- have clear aims, and provide a clear structure for teachers and learners
- help the learners develop knowledge, skills and attitudes
- include varied approaches
- be at least in part flexible to learners' needs and interests and determined by these

6.17 Example of a teacher's 'pedagogic manifesto'
(see Task 2.3)

This text is an extract from a teacher's pedagogic manifesto:

> It is generally accepted that certain things improve with age. I have heard more than once that teachers do. Having been a teacher for some years now I cannot agree with this point of view thoroughly. Only those teachers who are able to reflect on their teaching principles improve. Although this reflection can teach you what a bad teacher you are, I firmly believe that doing it is of benefit both to you and your work.
>
> When we use the expression 'teaching principles', we are referring to a broad number of features or elements which take an important role in the classroom; the students, the teachers, the syllabus and some external elements such as parents or educational authorities. These 'principles' have suffered an important change in recent years due to a new, modern way of considering the learning process. The students' role has turned into an active one, that is to say, our students are more involved in the activity of learning than we were. The teacher is not the centre of the world – considering the classroom as the world – any longer. From my point of view, it is worthwhile considering that most of us teachers weren't taught in this way and that a broad reflection has been made and must still be made among us to change both teaching beliefs and attitudes.
>
> Taking this striking change into account, I find a new global view of the different features of the teaching world necessary. I have already mentioned that nowadays the teaching/learning approach is student-centred. It must be

clearly understood that this change implies a variation of roles in the class-room. Teachers were instructors only. The job of a modern teacher, as far as I am concerned, is more varied and complex. Besides I don't think we should speak about 'role', but 'roles'.

There is a tendency to speak about the lack of motivation as the biggest problem teachers must face, so being a motivator seems to be one of the roles all teachers, not just English teachers, have to take. Bored students will not pay attention, that is to say, they will not learn and will probably prevent classmates from learning. I firmly believe that as a teacher I am bound to provide my students with a wide range of exercises, varied and appropriate in topics and in language points. Besides, teachers must show certain characteristics, such as being open-minded, flexible, receptive to students' needs and worries, to be able to create the correct learning atmosphere. The learning experience, as I see it, should be cooperative, rewarding, rich and stress-free. But teachers shouldn't forget that they are dealing with visions, ideals, necessities and worries.

Besides being a motivator, the teacher possesses the information the students need and is the conductor of the lesson. He/she must give rules, check under-standing, provide models and, of course, correct. Deciding what, how much, or when to correct is, as far as I am concerned, one of the biggest problems I have to face. From my point of view, over-correcting can be as harmful as not correcting enough, that is why it is so difficult. Doing it wrongly can destroy the students' confidence or create a confidence they don't deserve. However, it would also be a terribly big mistake not to correct 'what is said' because students must communicate something coherent and intelligent.

Learners have changed because of global change. First, they were just pas-sive students. Now, we expect them to take part in organising their work, negotiating the syllabus and in suggesting any change they find suitable for the future. They are asked to be collaborative in school activities, as well as cooperative with others/peers, in order to develop their autonomy.

Despite being the most important elements in the learning process, neither teachers nor students are alone in the education business. Parents should take an important role in the children's learning process, being behind them, help-ing teachers to make the process a successful one. Unfortunately, many par-ents see themselves as the teachers' controllers rather than the teachers' helpers.This creates an atmosphere of conflict which pollutes the learning process, making it unsuccessful.

The most disturbing element I have realised in the last few years, and the most difficult to handle, is the classroom itself. I think that I should be able to get the most out of it, but I have to state that, in fact, it is not the classroom, but classrooms. I mean that I spend most of the time travelling along corridors feeling as if I'm in no-man's-land, carrying books, pencils, or dictionaries. After the trip, sometimes long and difficult, you are forced to face an in-rows seating arrangement which is difficult to change because the rest of your colleagues reject any change. Actors, singers, and zoo-keepers prepare their stage. Teachers are given the stage as it is and sometimes cannot change it at all. Probably asking the students about the 'refurnishing' of the class so that a more comfortable atmosphere could be achieved could be a good way of improving the students' motivation. The same can be said about the school. I've seen exhibitions made by students in their Art lessons, the work on Ethics is known by all school members because posters are shown to everybody. What happens with the work students do in their English classes? At best it is seen by two or three of the people in the classroom. I feel it's time to start publishing (wall-publishing) the work students do and for them to feel proud of the work they do.

As a matter of fact everything I have written above is an idyllic view of the teaching world. Unfortunately, reality is absolutely different. Classes are full of students; some of them highly motivated, and many of them, not only hating English, but also hating learning in general. Despite the efforts teachers make, if the students reject the idea of learning, they won't learn. So what can be done? Probably if we worked more on the affective side of the teacher–student relationship, our lessons would improve. But, I am afraid, doing that would mean turning into the mother of 200 students and forgetting the role as a teacher of English. Besides all this, help from outside should realise its role in the whole drama of the teaching–learning process. Only when everybody takes part in this drama, starts considering their work and their part in the learning process, will education start being really successful.

6.18 Sample list of topics to investigate
(see Task 2.4)

This list shows the topics I used on a training programme.

 1 assessment and testing (including self-assessment)
 2 cross-curricular (interdisclipinary approach)
 3 discipline in class
 4 games in class
 5 information technology (computers, Internet, etc.)
 6 (teaching) mixed ability groups
 7 planning teaching: schemes of work, units of work, lessons
 8 (teaching) skills: speaking, listening, reading and writing
 9 (using) stories in the classroom
10 teaching materials (coursebooks, textbooks, etc.)
11 the teachers' own ideas for topics

See also the sample list of programme components in Section 6.35.

6.19 Further reading: 'In her element'
(see Task 2.5)

Julie Fleetwood and Pauline Edwards share the award for secondary teachers. **Reva Klein** and **Victoria Neumark** sit in on two lessons

In her element

A science teacher once told me that the problem with science teachers is that they think of themselves first and foremost as scientists who teach as a bit of a sideline. My own schooling bore this theory out. I always had science teachers who couldn't communicate their way out of a petri dish. They mumbled, they fiddled with test-tubes and bunsen burners, they occasionally threatened. They were in a world of their own that they didn't seem to want to share with us.

So it was with some trepidation that I met Julie Fleetwood of Ralph Allen School in Bath, joint winner of the secondary science teacher award. Would I drift off into one of my 45-minute comas the minute she opened her mouth as I had done throughout my school years? I not only stayed awake but was stimulated and captivated by her energy and, incredibly, her communication skills. As her head of department, Jane Kerr, puts it: "Julie is a natural teacher who happens to be a scientist. She has a unique combination of scientific mind and tremendous creativity."

© Christopher Jones

Julie Fleetwood: 'a natural teacher who happens to be a scientist'

Libby Steel of the Association of the British Pharmaceutical Industry and one of the judges for the award, agrees. "In the lesson I observed, she not only gave her pupils fun and exciting things to do that were relevant to everyday life, but was incredibly rigorous in terms of content."

Making things relevant to her students, who range from low ability and special needs children to A-level, seems to be a driving force. "It's so important to pitch it right in the first year of secondary school," she says. "They need to see that science is applicable to so many things in their lives. I say to them at all levels: 'go home and tell the folks at home what you've learned today.' And then I'll get parents coming in at parents' evening telling me that the kids come home and say 'Mum, do you know what you have in your stomach?'"

This is 28-year-old Julie's third year of teaching at Ralph Allen, the only non-denominational, co-educational state comprehensive in Bath. An Oxford chemistry graduate, she did her PGCE at York before going to India to teach chemistry at a private school for missionaries' children. Her inspiration for teaching came from an English science teacher at this school — she returned there last summer to recharge her batteries.

She seems to be an inspiration to her own students, too. Of the eight A-level students she taught last year, five got As and two went to university to read chemistry. This year, of the four applying for chemistry, three hope to go to Oxford. While motivating high-achieving students may be one of the perks of the job, Julie is clear about the need to have high expectations of all the children she teaches. "I adopt the same attitude for all ages and abilities," she insists. She works closely with the special needs co-ordinator and has developed worksheets which make it easier for pupils to record and recall experiments. Libby Steel, who observed her in a special needs class, says: "I admired how she ensured that special needs pupils could still achieve. She knows that their low achievement is not necessarily about science — it could be their reading and writing."

The pace of her lessons is best described as whirlwind. But it works. Acknowledging children's short attention spans, she has them moving briskly from one related activity to another. In her lesson on the digestive system, the Year 8 mixed-ability class of 24 worked through half a dozen activities all designed to stimulate and to help retain the information through graphics and role play — if that's what you call getting up in front of the class in groups and putting your hand on the next person's shoulder to illustrate how enzymes break down foods. "Fats, come to the front of the class," she calls out to the next group of food chemicals, who were asked to break down into fatty acids. Then they were told to draw the process before going through a verbal review, backed up by a model of a boy who gets stripped down to his innards.

A measure of the pupils' stimulation came in between tasks, when they were positively bursting with questions. "Miss," asks one boy, "what happens when you're sick?" "Miss," asks a girl, who had obviously been kept awake with this one, "why do boys have Adam's apples?" "Miss," asks another boy from across the room, in all seriousness, struggling to fill in his worksheet, "what does your anus do?" She answers each in turn calmly, thoroughly, as she sees to collecting up all the anatomical flash cards and making sure that a glue pot reaches its destination. Julie Fleetwood is in her element.

REVA KLEIN

(Klein and Neumark, 1997)

6.20 General reading survey: a class library, bibliography and open forum
(see Task 2.6)

6.20.1 BIBLIOGRAPHIES FOR TEACHERS: TEN SUGGESTIONS FOR TRAINERS

Bibliographies are strange creatures. As a student, I remember receiving lengthy lists of books and references to articles at the beginning of a term, which I found very demotivating and uninspiring. All the things I knew that I would not have time to read! But on training programmes there are ways of making bibliographies more reader-friendly, so that they are a valuable learning tool. Perhaps even more importantly, bibliographies are a potential tool to enable teachers to follow up interests they develop, and to sustain learning after the completion of a programme.

Ten suggestions:

1 Consider the length of the document carefully: if it is very long, it might be overwhelming and rather demotivating for teachers.
2 Divide it up into different sections, e.g. general and specific, for different topics, e.g. coursebooks, using games, learner autonomy, mixed ability, etc.
3 Next to each entry, give a brief explanation of the usefulness of the book. Recommend key sections.
4 Where appropriate, include books from your own local context, in the teachers' own language, not just in English, especially official curriculum documents.
5 Encourage reluctant readers of English to select their first book in their own language.
6 Decide on a format for the bibliography (e.g. which conventions such as bold type, italics, etc. to use for recording the names of authors, dates, etc.). Encourage teachers to use the same conventions when recording information about publications.
7 Give teachers a copy of the bibliography as soon as the programme begins.
8 Welcome teachers' own suggestions for additions to the bibliography.
9 Give teachers an idea of how many books you expect them to read from the bibliography during the course of the programme.
10 Try to include in the bibliography as many coursebooks used locally as possible.

See also sample bibliography below.

6.20.2 SAMPLE BIBLIOGRAPHY FOR TEACHERS

This is an extract from a bibliography I used on a training programme for primary teachers in Spain.

Bibliography

As you may know, there are a great many books published on the subject of English Language Teaching. Below we give information on a selection of general titles for you to use both during and after the course. Perhaps you will be able to add others. The books can be found in the box kept in the training room, or in the Resource Centre. If you have problems locating a particular book, please ask a tutor.

General titles

Gobierno Vasco. (1992). *Diseño Curricular Base de la Comunidad Autónoma Vasca*. (long, official document well worth looking at)

Halliwell, S. (1992). *Teaching English in the Primary Classroom*. Longman. (excellent general introduction but packed with practical ideas)

Hopkins, D. (1985). *A Teacher's Guide to Classroom Research*. Open University Press. (this will be very useful later in the course; when you need to select a focus for your action research see especially Chapter 5, 'Problem formation')

Littlewood, W. (1981). *Communicative Language Teaching*. Cambridge University Press. (a still popular, accessible introduction to theory and practice)

Scott, W. A. and Ytreberg, L. H. (1990). *Teaching English to Children*. Longman. (down to earth and easy to read)

If you want a book on a particular subject ask a colleague or a tutor to recommend one.

6.20.3 EXAMPLE OF A COMPLETED REVIEW SHEET

Worksheet 23 (completed by a teacher)

Title of book/magazine/ article	An article 'Songs and rhymes', in JET Magazine
Author/date/publisher	Annie Hughes
Subject (main, useful ideas, key quotations or terms, etc. with page references)	• songs must be suitable for the learners' age group • they must reflect the learners' interests • they must match my learners' level of English • the melody must not be too difficult • don't introduce too many new items of vocabulary • the recorded song must be clear for the learners
Your opinion (Would you recommend it to a colleague? Why? Why not?)	I recommend it to teachers who are interested in working with songs in class. There are not only several songs but some ideas and activities to practise with each one.

What do you want to *know*, if anything, about the topic of this book now?

- *I want to know how I can do different activities with 8-9-year-old children who have just started learning English and don't know some of the verbs or expressions that appear in many songs.*
- *I want to know what Annie means when she says: 'Don't teach one line at a time but let the children join in as they want to.'*
- *I want to listen to many different songs which Annie names in the magazine like 'Tommy Thumb' or 'London's burning'.*

What do you want to *do*, if anything, about the topic of this book now?

- *I think it's easier to work on songs with older children than with young learners, or, at least, I think I can find more appropriate activities for older learners, so I'll try to find songs and activities to work with 8–9-year-old children.*

6.21 FURTHER DIARY PROMPTS
(see Task 2.7)

Select judiciously and sparingly from the diary prompts below – arranged in alphabetical order – in order to help teachers to start describing and evaluating in their diary what happens in a class or training session. Be careful not to overwhelm teachers, or restrict the nature of their reflection, by using too many of the prompts. Instead, use those that relate to the needs of your own particular training situation, or recent developments on your training programme. You may, of course, wish to create your own prompts, in which case those below may provide some starting points.

Aims and purposes	What I want to achieve is…; My school wants to…; The educational system wants…; My learners need to…; My learners will need to…
Assumptions	I used to think that…, but now…
Beliefs	I believe that…; Educating/teaching/learning is about…
Change	Am I changing as a teacher? What do I need to change?
Classroom	At the moment my/our classroom is…, but I would like to…
Concepts	I find the idea of…very interesting/stimulating/…; What does…mean in my situation?
Consequences	If my learners…, they will…; If my trainer…, he or she will…; If I…, I will…; If my school…, it will…, etc.
Critical incidents	Something really unusual / surprising / puzzling happened today…
Experimenting	Today I tried…for the first time and…

Feelings	I feel that…; My learners feel that…
Language	I didn't know how to say…in English today in class.
Learners	Today in class my learners…; I noticed that…
Principles	Education / the curriculum / the syllabus / schools / teachers / learners / materials should…
Priorities	The most important thing for my school / my learners / my development is…
Questions/problems	I don't understand…; How can I…? Should I…? Why does/do…?
Skills	I can…; I cannot…; My learners can…; My learners cannot…; I want to be able to…; My learners want to be able to…
Specific aspects	For example: using songs, using video, reading, discipline, homework, learner autonomy, the course-book.
Successes/failures	Something that worked well today was…Why? Something that didn't work well today was…Why not?

6.22 Sample of classified diary extracts
(see Task 2.8)

This is a sample of classified diary extracts completed by a group of 20 teachers who had kept a confidential diary in the first ten days of an intensive training programme devoted to language development, in which they recorded their perceptions related to the programme itself. The subsequent discussions in a training session were held in four sub-groups, three of which produced a category of diary extracts related to their 'feelings'. These extracts are reproduced below in their entirety.

First feelings:

- At the beginning I felt a little bit nervous, but happy because I'm going to be a student again.
- A student again! I was nervous and expectant.
- Being back in class as a student has been great, away from children and away from school.

Personal feelings:

- It has been a hard week for me because I have been changing my mind from day to day.
- Feeling better and better each day.
- I feel a bit afraid of not being able to go with the rhythm of the class, because of my lack of fluency and experience in teaching English.

- good atmosphere in the classroom
- I've found a group that has the same interests as me.
- I don't feel like doing any work in groups.

Feelings:
- Sometimes I feel rather nervous.
- The first time I joined a course like this I was quite stressed, but now I feel really comfortable here and I enjoy learning English.
- Sometimes I feel a bit stressed because they give us many activities to do for a short period of time. But if you think about it, that makes you make an effort and, as a consequence, learn.
- I think that reading in English is a very good idea, although I don't enjoy myself reading in English as much as my own language.
- We are very worried about methodology and we carry on looking for a 'super-teacher'.
- I realize that my mind is working in English without stopping to think. That's good though I'm not able to translate my thoughts into words.
- I hope to improve my English as well as learn the best ways of teaching it.
- To be a student again is very relaxing.
- I wanted to come to the course and forget the school, but there is always something that reminds me.
- I feel more comfortable speaking in a little group (or with a partner) than in a big one.
- My partners here are very nice people. I don't mind if I make mistakes, so I don't mind speaking in English.
- As I said before in this diary, I must speak less to allow other people shyer than me to do so.

6.23 'We can do it!' Self-esteem, us and our learners
(see Task 2.9)

6.23.1 SAMPLE RESPONSE TO A PROMPT ON WORKSHEET 26: 'I HAVE A GOOD DAY AT WORK WHEN...'
(written by a teacher)

I have a good day at work when I feel that all or many of my efforts have been worth it, when my motivation was good and when I feel that the kids were willing and ready to go with me through the jungle of language or when my enthusiasm came across and maybe motivated them. A good day doesn't necessarily depend on a perfect preparation although I feel it is good and necessary to be well-prepared and to have routine in what you are doing. What is very important, however, is one's attitude, one's personal state of being that day, one's enthusiasm and will, as well as the kids' feelings and attitudes for the day. The best is when even though they might be in a bad mood or are tired, you are able to pull them along and when they (not openly – it's not 'cool') somehow enjoyed your lesson, and also learnt something, be it a study technique, some grammar or something relevant for life. It's difficult to be happy with all your lessons when you have 6, 7 or 8 a day. Chances that something goes wrong are obvious. I have a good day when I see that after some struggle with e.g. the passive, they are finally getting it and when they get the feeling that they are able to do it, that they know it, when they are aware of that success. You can't always have a good day. A normal good day is probably a little less successful than a perfect day which I described above. Many things influence me on having a good day at work: the weather, my general personal feelings for the day, atmosphere in class, the kids' attitudes, the circumstances, etc. Most important is the open or hidden will to work together!

6.23.2 SOME PRACTICAL RECOMMENDATIONS FOR ENHANCING LEARNERS' SELF-ESTEEM

1 Learners self-evaluate	Encourage learners to self-evaluate, for example by reviewing their learning achievements at the end of coursebook units.
2 Listen to learners	Ask learners and get them to talk about their feelings, problems, etc. by completing these sentences: 'I enjoy English classes when…', 'Now I can…', 'I don't understand…', in their own language or, where appropriate, in English. (See 'Combining tasks' below.)
3 Learners take risks	Learners try out new language without being corrected by the teacher, increasing their confidence.
4 Projects	Producing tangible results, which all can take pride in and display.
5 Consider attitudes when planning	When planning lessons, teachers think explicitly how these will contribute towards learners' self-esteem, confidence, etc.
6 Praise learners	Reward good performance by saying 'Well done!' See the Kahn article below for further practical recommendations for enhancing learners' self-esteem.

Combining tasks

See Task 4.5 for a more detailed procedure for this idea.

6.23.3 FURTHER READING: 'IT'S TIME WE ALL STOOD UP FOR TEACHER' AND 'STRATEGIES TO HELP YOU FIGHT STRESS' (SEE OPTION 16)

It's time we all stood

Tim Kahn joins stressed educators taking a course in confidence-boosting so they can pass on the benefit to their classes

MURRAY put another definition of 'teacher' on the overhead projector. 'A teacher is like a candle which lights others while consuming itself.' There was an audible ripple of discontent from the group.

It was composed of 14 educators working in a wide range of settings — from primary school through further education to teacher training. All had given up a Saturday to attend a workshop for teachers on enhancing their self-esteem — some travelling from as far as Manchester and East Anglia to Regent's College in London.

The workshop was presented by former headteacher Murray White, who is a founder member of the Self-Esteem Network that sponsored the event.

What had brought everybody together was the belief that teachers need to nurture themselves to be able to nurture the self-esteem of the children in their classes. Although it is difficult to measure self-esteem, there is evidence that the way children feel about themselves affects their academic performance and determines the kind of adults they will become.

The overhead projector now presented advice given to air travellers: 'In the event of oxygen failure, those of you travelling with children should place an oxygen mask on your own face and then — *and only then* — place a mask on your children's faces.' The was a stunned silence as participants thought through the implications for themselves as teachers.

They did not want to be consumed like candles, but how could they put their own needs first when there hardly seems to be time in the school day to look after children's emotional needs?

Then participants took three-minute turns in pairs to answer the question: 'I have a good day at work...' Ruth, from an east London Primary school, found the exercise refreshing, while Karen found that the negatives kept creeping in.

Murray summed up most people's feelings with his comment, 'When you talk about your positive qualities there always seems to be a "Yes, but" on their tail.'

The focus on the positive was relentless. Everyone took pen and paper and was given three more minutes to list answers to the question: 'I am very good at...' This was followed by a round of: 'One of my greatest strengths as an educator is ...', and after lunch: 'What I would like one of my colleagues to say to me is...'

By this time they all found it easier to talk positively about themselves. It was as if the group had created a new culture, very different from the one outside. That culture requires people to keep quiet about their successes, to reject compliments in the name of modesty and to talk about problems, not successes.

The importance of praise came next. We had all experienced empty words of praise and realised that praise needed to be thoughtful and specific to be meaningful.

Dean said: 'When I organised the school play I received lots of compliments. One mum's words stick in my mind: "You really encouraged my daughter to take part when she

up for teacher

is normally so shy. And you brought out the best of other children, too." I was on a high for days because she had noticed.'

There were comments throughout the day about the culture of the staff room. 'We seem to spend so much time moaning about problems and difficulties — and they are very real difficulties — that it can be hard to keep your spirits up.' Murray reminded us of the domino effect. 'If one person says something negative, then it can lead to negativity all round, but if one person is positive...'

There is a small but growing number of schools that have adopted a 'self-esteem

"Well it's better to have wasted my youth than have done NOTHING with it."

brian bagnall

approach' to education. Valerie Al-Jawad, the special needs co-ordinator at Latchmere Junior in Kingston, described the process her school went through: 'We were already working to improve the school ethos when Murray led a staff-training day on children's self-esteem. The training finished at 3.30pm but the whole staff stayed voluntarily until 6.30pm, discussing implications for the school.

'We introduced many strategies aimed at raising children's self-esteem and we developed our work to support teachers' self-esteem. We praise each other, we have lots of staff meetings, which has led to good communication, and we have found a way of talking about problems in the classroom without teachers feeling criticised. Most important of all, everybody is involved in decision-making and planning.

'We have "bubble time" throughout the school. Children have bubble time with their teacher, which is a time for the children to talk about anything that is on their mind, without interruption. Parents have a similar bubble time with their children's teachers, and staff have bubble time with the head. As a staff team we socialise in and out of school — teaching and non-teaching staff alike.

'It is a living policy that we constantly work at, it's not just filed away in a drawer. And it has definitely improved the atmosphere of the school.'

Teachers are under great stress. They feel the external pressure from government, the National Curriculum, the interminable paperwork, the media's oversimplified views of teaching, parents' concerns, league tables — and more. And they put themselves under pressure from their own self-critical voices and perfectionism. In the current climate, it takes a bold teacher and a bold school to find time to devote to enhancing self-esteem.

The overhead projector went on for the last time. The education guru John Holt was quoted: 'A good teacher makes the children glad it's Monday.' Everyone agreed you can only do that for the children if you are glad it is Monday too.

(Kahn, 1993)

Strategies to help you fight stress

Anne Cockburn finds there are some simple measures that enable teachers to counter that familiar overloaded feeling

Teaching under pressure seems to be unavoidable as class sizes grow, pupils become more disruptive, the paper mountain increases and money seems to be in ever shorter supply. As a teacher said to me the other day: "We all seem to do too much in too little time for too little recognition." It is not hard to point fingers and assign blame but — while we are all waiting for a miracle to happen — what can primary teachers do to ease their burden?

Judging by my survey of 335 Norfolk teachers, and other interviews I have conducted, part of the answer lies in predicting and avoiding potential pressure points and overload whenever possible. In so doing, teachers feel more in control and are less likely to collapse in a heap at the end of every term with 'flu and a chronic sore throat.

Several teachers I interviewed used a similar strategy as an extension of daily planning. "Before I leave work every night, I map out the next day, ensure that everything is available, that there will not be constant demands on my time, and that there will be time both for high-quality teaching and a bit of a breather," was one fairly typical comment.

A variation of this technique is to reduce the possibility of overload when your brain is whizzing away with numerous ideas and chores to be tackled. Try keeping a notebook handy, and whenever inspiration strikes or yet another job to be done comes into your head, jot it down to stop it distracting you from the task in hand. At the end of the day, review the list, throw out any unnecessary tasks (do you really need to do X *and* Y?) and arrange the remainder in priority. (Incidentally, it can often save time to group jobs which can usefully be done together.) Then give yourself time to mull over the ideas you noted, for they may be the catalyst for some really interesting and effective teaching.

Given that teaching is often unpredictable, however, one cannot always rely on such precise organisation. A complementary strategy is to extend the flexible approach that primary teachers are so well-known for and not feel bad about it (that's the hard part!) Thus, when attacked by "time bandits" who are saying, "We want your time now",

you can postpone what you are doing if the bandit merits your attention, or you can carry on as you were, thus refuting a Year 6 teacher's claim that "as a profession we are incredibly bad at saying 'No'".

Sometimes such flexibility is called for when — quite simply — you have had enough and P has just been sick and Q and R are being pains. Why not stop the session at this point and do something completely different with the children — songs, a story or some exercise for the more energetic. You can then return to the original work as and when appropriate. When stressed, Brenda, a Year 1 teacher, resorts to whole-class lessons. She feels guilty and apologetic about it, but recognises that, although the quality may not be great, "at least each child has produced a piece of work" and, more importantly, her sanity has remained intact.

Taking a step back, it is important to remember that there is more to life than teaching so that, in the years to come, you never have to say: "My family deserves better" and "I have missed my children growing up." It is a

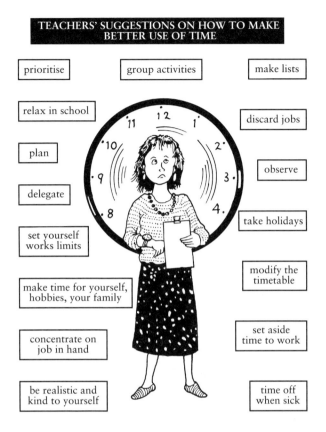

TEACHERS' SUGGESTIONS ON HOW TO MAKE BETTER USE OF TIME

prioritise

group activities

make lists

relax in school

discard jobs

plan

observe

delegate

take holidays

set yourself works limits

modify the timetable

make time for yourself, hobbies, your family

set aside time to work

concentrate on job in hand

be realistic and kind to yourself

time off when sick

question of priorities: why do schoolwork half the night when you are exhausted, not to say, ineffective? I appreciate that much of the planning and paperwork has to be done, but perhaps you need to compromise and recognise that it may be unrealistic to work to the very highest standard both in and out of the classroom.

Marianne, an experienced teacher, said: "I think many teachers are like me, and have this sort of professional perfectionism. You're always trying to do your best ... and there is just too much to do and never enough time to do it."

Rather than settling for being exhausted, mediocre teachers who have no personal life, some people recognise the importance of setting clearly defined limits, "I rarely work after I've eaten at night. So if I have something to do, I'll do it and then eat so that I can switch off with a clear conscience." That does not mean stopping schoolwork only to start on the housework. Obviously the chores need to be done but, rather than feeling guilty if any of them is neglected, why not find a cleaner, gardener or whatever to share the load?"

If all else fails, stand back and take some credit, for, as one Year 2 teacher said: "I think many teachers find it incredibly hard to stop and take stock of their achievements, but it is about time we leaned to celebrate our successes."

■ **Anne Cockburn** lectures in primary education at the University of East Anglia. Her book, Teaching Under Pressure: looking at primary teachers' stress, was published last month by Falmer Press.

(Cockburn, 1996)

191

6.24 Sample sets of responses for Option 17

(see Task 3.1)

The following sets of responses to Option 17, presented in random order, were collected from two groups of teachers:

THE CORRECTION OF LEARNERS' ORAL ERRORS IS IMPORTANT BECAUSE...

- otherwise we don't understand what they want to say
- they will make the same errors again
- learners will repeat other learners' mistakes
- errors can sometimes lead to misunderstandings (but what is an error?)
- because the errors mustn't be repeated (you remember what you hear)
- I'm at a loss to answer because correction is useful. However, if you spend your time correcting, you take the risk of discouraging learners.
- the teacher should only correct errors that prevent intelligibility, otherwise the learner could be frustrated
- it makes learners notice their mistakes. That's the only way to improve...
- we are teachers and we KNOW!
- mispronunciation often leads to misunderstanding (but at the same time learners sometimes understand each other, even if they make mistakes)
- the task of the teacher is to put the learners on the right path while learning English. Learners should have a critical eye on the process of learning a foreign language.
- the next time they won't make the same mistakes and that helps them to improve (I feel very happy myself when a native speaker corrects me);
- it makes the learner improve communication provided that the teacher does it 'at the right time', i.e. without interrupting (fluency should come first); some errors are acceptable in oral language, but not in written English
- otherwise the learners tend to make more and more mistakes, and very quickly become unintelligible for the rest of the class
- it may be a means for the starting point of a lesson of grammar (if a lot of learners make the same errors), so it is useful for everybody
- learners should be made aware of their mistakes, so as to correct them in the future.... This can be done with the help of the other learners.
- the learners know they make mistakes, but, of course, they don't know where the mistakes are, they don't know the importance of their mistakes, and even when this is explained, they repeat them. So they expect us to correct them (at least the learners who care and are interested do!).

PROJECT WORK IN THE ENGLISH CLASSROOM IS IMPORTANT BECAUSE…

- each learner is allowed to become involved in the part of the project that especially interests, attracts and fascinates him or her, and thus, he or she learns with 'brains, heart and hand'
- learners are responsible for their work and the results which have been achieved independently
- learners learn to work in groups, learn by doing, are very busy all the time, and are proud of their results
- many skills are required
- learners have more room to be creative than in 'normal' lessons
- learners (probably) have fun
- everyone has a say in the group
- learners learn to organise themselves
- learners learn something about group behaviour
- the learners work on a topic *they* are interested in
- learners probably feel satisfied afterwards
- it adds extra challenge and motivation to opt out of the daily routine of teacher-centred lessons and helps learners to develop skills that aren't addressed often enough
- learners learn to work within time limits, to use different sources of information and to think about various ways of presenting their work
- learners listen to each other and work together in groups
- it's not only transmitting knowledge but active, creative teamwork
- because they fit in with a cross-curricular approach
- learners can create something new

6.25 What do we understand by the topic 'x'? (What? Why? Who? etc.)

(see Task 3.2)

6.25.1 SUMMARY OF A WORKSHOP GIVEN AT A TEACHERS' CONFERENCE: USING ENGLISH IN CLASS

(practical recommendations and advice)

'Sorry, I don't understand!'

This active workshop demonstrated simple ideas for gradually getting pupils accustomed to and confident in using English naturally and socially in class. The session began actively with the Instructions Game. I asked the group to stand, and then gave them instructions to respond to physically, such as: 'Touch your nose', 'Whisper "We're having a good time"', 'Sit down slowly'. This was done with no little hilarity! Then, in pairs, the audience got their revenge by thinking up other instructions which I then had to enact in front of the whole group.

Following this, we discussed some of the theoretical assumptions underpinning this kind of classroom technique. If teachers and pupils use English in class in such ways (and this *is* difficult for teachers), we can assume that non-native-speaker teachers feel reasonably confident about their level of English, and that they believe that pupils should be involved actively in the process of teaching and learning. I went on to suggest that if English is used naturally in class, such as in the request 'Please, may I go to the toilet?', then this is truly communicative, in a way that many other classroom activities are artificial. Similarly, if pupils were surrounded by English in class, this would give them practice in perhaps the most important skill, that is to say, listening, or receiving messages successfully in English. In this way we might also be stimulating the 'acquisition' of English, or the unconscious learning of the language. I also suggested that pupils understand much more than they can produce, but that they should concentrate on producing a limited set of expressions in class, which did not need to be analysed grammatically, and which could be extended step by step with the teacher's help.

To demonstrate more clearly what I meant, I showed an example of a set of expressions that a primary teacher in the Basque Country got her pupils to use:

Greetings (hello, good morning, etc.)
Can I go to the toilet? Can I clean the board?
I've finished. Have you got a…?
Can I borrow your…? Yes, here you are.
Do you like…? Yes, I do. / No, I don't.
How do you say…in English? How do you spell…?

I also showed a set of ten marvellous posters of different classroom expressions, each complete with a colourful drawing made by pupils to illustrate the expression. A suggested procedure to produce such posters is:

1 Ask pupils what they wish to say in class in English (ask them in their mother tongue).
2 Select, say, ten example expressions from the suggestions and translate them into English.
3 In groups, pupils select one of the expressions, for example 'Sorry, I don't understand', and illustrate it on an A3 sheet of card/paper.
4 Display the finished posters around the classroom. When pupils wish to use an expression but have forgotten it, they can look at their posters to remind themselves.

The session concluded with some general suggestions for teachers wishing to work in the manner referred to in this workshop.

- Start small – get the pupils to use a limited set of expressions, as in the example above, and gradually add new ones, if appropriate, by means of new posters.
- Play games such as the Instructions Game.

- Note down systematically any linguistic problems you might have saying things in English in class as a non-native speaker, and ask a colleague or friend to help you.

By way of conclusion, if in the future our pupils say to us, for example, 'Sorry, I don't understand' in English, I believe that this is but one small example of their becoming more confident and more actively involved in the process of learning. If this happens, I think we are on the right track. Good luck!

6.25.2 EXAMPLE OF A COMPLETED WORKSHEET 28

Topic: *Using English in class*

1 *What* I think it means or is	*I think it means using English as a social language in class. For example: 'How do you say "x" in English? What does "x" mean? Shall I begin? I don't know/remember', etc.*
2 *What* I think it does not mean	*I don't think it means that everything said in class should be in English; we have to be realistic.*
3 *Why* is this topic important?	*If learners use English in class, this is truly communicative; it also gives learners practice in receiving and understanding messages in English; it stimulates language 'acquisition', and develops learners' confidence to use English.*
4 *Who* is involved?	*Me, the teacher! I try to use as much English as I can…and the learners, of course (all different levels and ages of learners).*
5 *Where* and *when* does this take place?	*This all happens in class. I do this from the very beginning of the school year, especially where learners are not used to using English.*
6 *What* I do in school or in class	*I explain to my learners why we need to speak English in class, if necessary in their language!! I ask learners to select ten everyday phrases that they could use in class; they produce posters illustrating classroom phrases. We play the Instructions Game.*
7 *What* I like about this topic in school or class	*Sometimes my learners greet me in English outside the classroom, for example in the school playground. When this happens, I feel that my efforts are bearing fruit!*
8 *What* I find difficult about this topic	*My learners lack confidence in using English… Sometimes, quite often, actually, I don't know how to say something in English, especially when I'm giving instructions…*
9 Other comments	

6.25.3 A SAMPLE LIST OF ADVANTAGES AND DISADVANTAGES: USING COMPUTERS WITH LEARNERS
(see Option 18)

The following information was collected from a group of teachers.

Advantages:
- ☺ the learners are motivated
- ☺ the learners know a lot about computers
- ☺ English is used a lot in the world of computers so learners see it in real use
- ☺ I am developing learners' real-life skills
- ☺ it is viewed very positively by parents

Disadvantages:
- ☹ I am not sure what material there is
- ☹ it's very expensive for my school
- ☹ I have to move all the learners to the computer room
- ☹ if something goes wrong, I look silly in the learners' eyes, and have to call on someone else for help
- ☹ it is very time-consuming

6.26 Sample Worksheet 29
(see Task 3.3)

Topic: *Helping our learners to work effectively in pairs and groups*

Find someone who...

(Teacher's name)	(Partially completed sentences)
1 *Brigitte*	*uses groupwork and pairwork regularly in class*
2	*has a practical recommendation for getting learners to work together*
3	*feels that helping learners to co-operate by working together in groups or pairs is one of the most important aims of education*
4	*has identified problems with groupwork and pairwork*
5	*has used groupwork or pairwork in class today/this week/this term/this year*

6.27 Sample Worksheet 30
(see Task 3.4)

Topic: *Helping our learners to listen to English in class*

PART 1

Statement 1 Some people are good listeners in real life, and some people aren't; it's not something that you can learn. ☐
(Write ✓✓, ✓, ✗✗, ✗ or ? in the boxes provided.)

Statement 2 We help learners listen to English in class in order to…(choose more than one of the following responses if you wish):
1 be able to present examples of language (grammar, vocabulary, etc.) in context. ☐
2 provide input for other activities, e.g. watch a video before a discussion. ☐
3 give them practice in listening, develop their listening skills. ☐
4 help them learn to communicate orally. ☐
5 expose them to language, and promote unconscious learning, or acquisition. ☐
6 (something else? please specify) ☐

Statement 3: Listening to English in class is the most difficult, but the most important of the four skills (listening, speaking, reading and writing) for my/our learners. ☐

Author's comments

Statement 1 This item can be combined with Option 19, 'Reflective listening' (see Task 3.4). Relate teachers' responses to statement 1 to their own experience of reflective listening. My own view is that if teachers want to help change schools and their own practice, etc., they have to do so with other teachers. So sitting down and listening to each other is an important step in this process.

Statement 2 Most teachers will probably feel happy with selecting a few of these alternatives, although it is my experience that teachers often overlook item 5, the potential of listening for promoting language acquisition, in the technical sense. Item 1 represents a somewhat traditional view, although one which is real for many teachers, including myself.

Statement 3 It has been suggested that in real life / our own language(s) we generally spend more time listening than speaking, and relatively little time reading / writing. Whether this also reflects, or should reflect, priorities in the foreign language classroom is a matter of opinion; when teachers consider the issue of communicating orally in English, they often give priority to speaking, perhaps unjustifiably, as listening is very much part of the communication process. So learners need listening practice in class.

PART 2

Ten practical ways of (or recommendations for) helping learners to listen to English in class

The following recommendations were made by a group of teachers:

1 learners reflect on and discuss the process of listening (where appropriate in the learners' language or in English)
2 provide the learners with a reason for listening, e.g. a task such as listening for gist, or for specific information
3 encourage involvement: learners anticipate what they will listen to, before listening, by exploiting their knowledge of the topic, etc.
4 build up learners' confidence, e.g. Teacher: 'OK, listen, but don't panic! You won't understand everything!'
5 repeat listening activities as often as learners think necessary
6 stage learners' response after listening: individual, check in pairs, and then check in whole-class mode
7 don't overload learners' short-term memories – use worksheets
8 use information/opinion gap activities, but *do* something with the information obtained afterwards
9 develop the learners' communication strategies (in preparation for) when they encounter problems listening, e.g. the use of phrases such as 'Sorry, I don't understand'
10 encourage the natural social use of English in class: learners listen to the teacher / each other

6.28 Debate: understanding the wider implications of a topic
(see Task 3.9)

6.28.1 A SAMPLE MOTION FOR DEBATE WITH ACCOMPANYING ROLES

Motion

Significant innovation is necessary in English language teaching in our country in order to prepare learners for the challenges of a rapidly changing world.

Teachers choose one of the following roles in order to debate this motion.

Debating teams

1 a member of the *for the motion* debating team (maximum of four teachers), or
2 a member of the *against the motion* debating team (maximum of four teachers), or

Members of the public (one per teacher)

3 a demotivated student about to leave a local school for the workplace who feels that it is impossible to find a job in your community
4 an enthusiastic, highly motivated, practising teacher who has just finished an in-service teacher training programme just like yours
5 a rather sceptical, disillusioned, practising teacher who has just finished an in-service teacher training course just like yours
6 an anxious parent who is confused about what exactly their son or daughter is required to do to pass his or her English examination at a school in your community
7 an optimistic teacher trainer who has just finished working with a group of practising teachers just like yours
8 an overworked, yet optimistic, government adviser or inspector working in your area
9 a personnel manager from a multinational company with a factory in your area or country who is rather frustrated by the disappointing level of school-leavers' foreign language skills (give examples)
10 a newly appointed representative of the Ministry of Education in your area or country with a special interest in foreign language teaching
11 a researcher at a university in your area who has just completed a doctoral thesis investigating aspects of innovation in primary and/or secondary education in your country
12 an enthusiastic publisher's representative (choose which publisher) who is very keen about the foreign language coursebooks and materials of his or her company, which have been especially developed for use in your context (you can say in what way)
13 another role of your choice

6.28.2 SUGGESTIONS FOR OTHER MOTIONS FOR DEBATE

You may wish to prepare a motion for debate and roles for the specific topic that you are investigating with teachers. However, here are some further suggestions for thought-provoking, polemical and productive topics:

1 Coursebooks: for or against?
2 Testing: for or against?
3 Are we educators, teachers, or both?
4 Language teaching – for purpose 'x' or for purpose 'y'?

5 Homework: for or against?

6 Information technology in language teaching: friend or foe?

6.29 The benefits of investigating in class: teachers' perspectives

(see Task 4.1)

6.29.1 KEY TO WORKSHEET 33

A (6); B (3); C (5); D (4); E (2); F (1)

6.29.2 POTENTIAL DIFFICULTIES WHEN INVESTIGATING IN CLASS AND ADVICE FOR TRAINERS

Below I outline five areas of difficulty I have encountered as a trainer when helping teachers to investigate in class, and suggest ways of addressing these difficulties:

1 Teachers' unfamiliarity with the idea of investigating in class:
   - explain and discuss what is involved in investigating in class (see, for example, Task 1.3 or Task 4.1)
   - encourage teachers to read about teacher-directed classroom research
   - show teachers examples of completed reports of teachers' work investigating in class, where appropriate, and/or invite teachers who are experienced in investigating to talk to the group in a training session

2 Teachers' difficulty in identifying a topic for investigating in class:
   - the topic identified should be important to the teacher's school, and the learners, as well as to the teacher(s) in question (see, for example, Option 17 on p. 79 and item 3 on Worksheet 28)
   - provide teachers with individual help when they are trying to identify a topic, where appropriate and possible (see Task 5.6)
   - encourage wide reading of the professional literature (see Task 2.6)
   See other relevant tasks in Chapters 1 and 2.

3 Teachers' lack of data collection skills:
   - seek opportunities to develop teachers' data collection skills collaboratively and collectively (see, for example, Tasks 4.4 and 4.5)
   - don't be too ambitious or demanding regarding the rigour of the data collection methods and analysis: teachers are busy people!
   - limit the period in which teachers are investigating in class (for example, where appropriate, over a period of 3–5 weeks)
   See other relevant tasks in Chapter 4.

4 Teachers' attitudes towards theory and practice:

Teachers often express a limited interest in so-called theory, and are more interested in practical ideas.

- attempt a balance by helping teachers to find out about 'public' theories related to language teaching and learning, to develop their own personal theories, as well as to focus on practical issues
- provide plenty of opportunities on a programme for teachers to find out about and/or experience practical teaching ideas (see, for example, Task 3.6)
- provide plenty of opportunities to reflect on, analyse and evaluate teaching ideas and activities, as well as teachers' current professional practice, if possible from the beginning of a programme (see, for example, Task 2.4)
- develop teachers' ability to theorise (see, for example, Tasks 2.2 and 2.3)

5 Getting teachers to write a formal report regarding their work investigating in class:

In some situations teachers may have to write a report about their work in class, as part of the official requirements of a training programme, particularly when it is funded by an official institution such as a ministry.

- don't be too demanding or meticulous about the conventions of academic discourse of a report (for example, allow teachers to write in the first person)
- allow teachers to write their reports in their own language, where their level of English is low
- give teachers a clear framework with guidelines for structuring their written report, but also allow teachers to adapt this framework to suit their own needs (see Section 6.39.3 for further information)

See also Task 5.8 for more on writing a report.

6.30 Summary of the advantages and disadvantages of using questionnaires to collect classroom data
(see Task 4.4)

This is a summary of the advantages and disadvantages of using questionnaires to collect classroom data, adapted from Hopkins (1985: 74). In square brackets after each disadvantage are my suggestions for solving the problem.

Advantages

- easy to administer
- easy to follow up
- provides direct comparison of groups and individuals
- provides feedback on whatever teachers want to ask about, for example: attitudes, adequacy of resources, adequacy of teacher help, preparation for next session, conclusions at end of term
- the data is quantifiable

Disadvantages and solutions

- The analysis is time-consuming, though less so than other methods [so help teachers to decide how to report the data before conducting the questionnaire; restrict each teacher's work to one group of learners].
- Extensive preparation is necessary to formulate clear and relevant questions [so *Teachers in Action* provides teachers with means to identify topics to investigate; the trainer can help teachers formulate precise areas within broad topic areas].
- It is difficult to formulate questions that explore in depth [but teachers could follow up a questionnaire by means of a learner profile or interview: see Tasks 4.6 and 4.7 respectively, for example].
- The effectiveness of a questionnaire depends much on the reading ability and comprehension of the learner [so take all reasonable measures to make the text clear, such as showing it to a colleague for proof-reading or piloting it; see also Worksheet 36, 'Ten characteristics of an effective questionnaire'].
- Learners may be fearful of answering a questionnaire candidly [so respondents complete questionnaire anonymously].
- Learners will try to produce the 'right' answers [so ask learners to respond frankly].

6.31 Sample answers to questions on Worksheet 37, Part 1
(see Task 4.5)

Here are some of my suggestions for possible answers to questions 1–3 on Worksheet 37, with reference to the learner statements on the worksheet.

1 What do the statements have in common, and how are they different?

I think that the statements show that the learners focused on for me surprisingly quite different aspects of the lesson: some on language itself, e.g. vocabulary (no. 1), or structure (no. 3), some functional (no. 2), others with a very general focus (no. 8). Looking at the statements, I also realised that perhaps the learners had learnt more than what I had intended that they learn and had included in the lesson aims. In other words, what I taught was not necessarily what the learners learnt.

2 In your opinion, how typical are the statements for 12- to 13-year-olds, in terms of how they reflect the learners' cognitive development?

My reaction was that I think that the statements show a high degree of insight by young learners into the learning process; this was a real discovery for me. I also wonder whether in general we teachers sometimes underestimate our learners, and in this case, our learners' perceptions of what happens in the classroom.

3 Would you consider asking your learners the same question at the end of a lesson? Why? Why not? If you do this, what might the long-term benefits be to you as teachers and to your learners?

It certainly helped me, and possibly the learners, to gain a greater aware-ness of what is involved in the language teaching/learning process, as well as an awareness of learners' learning preferences. Perhaps consulting learners regularly like this would help teachers to value more the insights that their learners can provide about classroom practice, as well as providing a way of helping learners influence what happens in class.

6.32 Talking about real people: writing a learner profile
(see Task 4.6)

6.32.1 EXTRACT FROM A DETAILED FORMAL CASE STUDY

The data below is part of a formal study tracing the home, playground and classroom experiences of a small group of children through their primary school careers. It shows an extract from a table entitled, 'Factors and processes in a boy's approach to learning from 5 to 7 years old', charting the development of one boy, Neill, from reception class to Year 1 class.

	Reception class	Year 1 class
Home relationships	One younger sister. Both are 'strong characters' – sparks. Confidence unpredictable; she can back off or respond with frustration to Neill's pace. Their parents resist putting on pressure.	He shows increased determination/persistence. His home writing for his own needs contrasts with school writing. His mother is pleased with school. Has changeable relationships with his sister. Volatile. Some jealousy? Mother explains and discusses moods of children.
Peer group relationships	Jointly most popular child in the class. A close but volatile relationship with Richard. Neill's group of friends acknowledge their friendship with girls.	Peer group not as astute as Neill, so he cannot extricate himself from trouble. Neill and his group are very scathing and dismissive of girls.
Teacher relationships	He is one of the oldest in the class, but is achieving well below chronological age. 'Total confidence'. Likes to 'play' not 'work'. He is able but has a minimalist approach to academic tasks. 'Strong willed'. 'Doesn't like being told what to do.'	He is of average age for the class, but is working at or above this level. 'Boisterous', 'a leader', 'assured', 'noisy', 'a bit devious', 'potentially a deviant', 'works slowly as a tactic'. Likes the 'fun' and stages of maths and reading. Hates 'boring' writing. Becomes product-oriented.
Identity	Very popular, confident, strong-willed. Difficult to discipline, and has volatile relationships at school.	Moderately popular. A leader. Confident and likes a bit of a laugh. A bit devious. Socially astute.
Learning	Minimalist approach to school. Sometimes has a tendency to angry frustration at home. He withdraws from challenges.	Motivated by extrinsic rewards at school – product, parental approval. Engages in learning selectively at school. Differentiates activities. Initiates the creative/practical at home. (...)

(adapted from Pollard, with Filer, cited in Pollard and Tann, 1993: 71)

6.32.2 EXAMPLE OF A BASELINE LEARNER PROFILE

This learner profile was written by an English teacher about a student, following the format provided by Worksheet 38.

1 *Personal information* (age, sex, personality, family background, interests outside class, etc.)	*T. is 16, female, friendly, open and good-humoured; comes from a family with 5 children; plays basketball and is interested in politics.*
2 *Relationships* (with you, with other learners)	*Friendly to teachers and fellow students, has good friends in the class. Always tries to create a good atmosphere with difficult students in her class.*
3 *Attitudes* (e.g. to school, other school subjects, English)	*Attitude to school is good. She knows it's good to study hard because she wants to study journalism; she is a reliable learner, not always achieving very good results, though; likes English, and is ambitious to improve.*
4 *Learning* (behaviour in class, likes/ dislikes, strengths/weaknesses, etc.)	*Never tired of trying; brave enough to ask; likes projects; is good at structure (she knows Latin); has problems with idioms.*
5 *Development* (progress achieved, future progress, etc.)	*So far she has done OK; she is now going to the States for a year; she will do well in her exam.*
6 *Other comments*	*Pleasant nature, with strengths and weaknesses; has sense of humour, as well as the necessary ambition to do well in life.*

6.33 Experimenting in class
(see Task 4.8)

6.33.1 EXAMPLE OF A COMPLETED WORKSHEET

This worksheet, similar to Worksheet 40, was completed by a teacher.

1 Which teaching idea did you try out? Please describe it briefly.
   An activity focusing on the present simple for habitual actions.

2 Why did you select it?
   Because we're revising this tense (questions and answers).

3 What did the learners do?
   They had to listen to a conversation between two friends. Then they had to fill in a table with true and false answers.

4 What do you think the learners learnt?
They concluded that they could understand a real conversation and get the information they needed to fill in the table.

5 What did you do?
I explained the aim of the task. I wrote some verbs that the learners could easily confuse (walk/talk), or the meaning of sleep/dream. Then I played the cassette twice. The first time to have a general idea and the second to let them choose the appropriate answers.

6 What did you learn?
1 *They could do it even when they have some difficulties because the characters spoke quite quickly.*
2 *They feel happy when they can see that the results are positive.*

6.33.2 EXAMPLE OF A COMPLETED WORKSHEET 41, LESSON PLAN SHEET

This is an example of a lesson plan sheet completed by a teacher, for information (see 'Combining tasks', Task 4.8).

Worksheet 41 Lesson plan sheet
(see Task 4.8)

This worksheet will help you to plan a lesson and to record what happened in it.

Class/group: *YEAR 7, UNIT 6A: A TOUR OF SCOTLAND*

Date: *March 7th*

Remember to: *Overhead transparency: a Scotsman's wallet*

Stages	What I plan to do	What happened/comments
1	Brainstorming, talking, vocab. 'Scotland'	Pupils' answers: rainy, green, hilly, Gaelic, Loch Ness, Nessie, Aberdeen, kilt, stingy people,...
2	Overhead transparency: A Scotsman wears a kilt and a sporran (wallet). What's inside? Have you ever seen a Scotsman in a kilt/been to Scotland?	→ description of content of sporran: coins, bills in a mouse trap, spider, whisky, mice, cheese → own experience
3	Book p. 63 + 64/ 1, 2, 3 Text 1: presentation, vocab? read Text 2 : Text 3	
4	Discussion of map, pictures and photos	→ many pupils are interested in Loch Ness & Nessie → some boys would like to see the Highland Games
5	Questions on the text + pictures (books closed)	Answers mainly from texts in the book and from information today's lesson

New vocabulary/grammar to review in next lesson:

to discuss sth, possibility, whether, nearly, a diver, down there, to cycle, YHA membership card, to take place, tossing the caber, a tree trunk, to dance, a kilt

Homework:

vocabulary, text

6–8 sentences: which of the three possibilities would you choose? Why?

6.34 Examples of completed sentences, Worksheet 44

(see Task 5.3)

A group of teachers was asked to evaluate their learning on a training programme by individually completing a choice of nine different partial sentences. The summary below shows a selection of the completed sentences.

What I most like about the programme...:
- the balance between theory and practical activities
- I like listening to English
- how well organised it is...I think it's going to give me a lot of ideas for my work
- the atmosphere in the class...
- the variety and the different activities
- I have the opportunity of being with other colleagues
- the course has made me think about things that I haven't even thought about as a teacher

What I least like about the programme is...:
- that we haven't worked on practical ways of teaching the English language to our students
- that it is too rigid with the schedule
- Frankly I'm very interested in the course. It's quite useful (...) I'm quite involved in the sessions.
- homework
- coming in the afternoons
- As we are in a group, and every one of us must co-operate, it takes a bit long to go straight to the point...I must say that some of these are worth listening to
- the unit of work

I'm not quite sure about...:
- the life or the future of the curriculum plan in spite of the fast changes that we are seeing in teaching and learning
- cross-curricular (3 teachers)
- if the pupils are going to learn in the curriculum plan, or if the teacher can manage to teach with 30 pupils, etc.
- my own possibilities of being a good teacher as well as a good educator
- if the atmosphere in my new school *will let me* develop all the new points of view
- if I will finish the course
- how much innovation there will be in the English lessons from this school year to the next one

I found the following very useful...:
- sharing experiences

- being in contact with other teachers
- warmers
- because now I know a little bit more about the Curriculum Reform, but in a realistic way
- I think it is very useful to revise and compare the new textbooks
- to make teaching and learning more active
- we are learning to build up a unit of work

I think the programme will...:

- help us to change, reflect
- improve me as a teacher
- provide us with a reasonable amount of knowledge in order to deal with the terrible teaching units (especially by having practised them)
- be too short for such deep and dense contact
- Help me when we teachers have to design our school syllabus plan.... I'm proud of feeling like a 'pioneer'.
- give us an opportunity to change into educators

So far one of the things I've learned is...:

- we have to change our minds and be positive with our work and pupils
- something about units of work
- there is always something to learn
- teachers want to be ready and do their best
- to exchange my opinions about the Curriculum Reform
- the importance of working groups...in order to solve problems

I found the following surprising...:

- to meet people from secondary schools – I thought the course was only for primary teachers
- hearing about what I've been hearing about the last 3–4 years
- I thought it was going to be more theoretical
- meeting you two again [the trainers]
- the level is very high
- how you persuade us to do the 'hard' activities

I've been reading about...:

- the official curriculum document
- the latest methodology 'items' on which innovation is based on
- assessment
- planning classwork, English in the new plan
- Madame Doubtfire

I'd like to ask if...:

- don't you think it's very hard work to do a unit of work?
- they or you or someone is/are planning some follow-up of future group-work for teachers

6.35 Sample list of training programme components: topics, tasks and activities
(see Task 5.4)

This list includes the components I covered with a group of teachers on a training programme, presented in alphabetical order.

Change and innovation
Course evaluation by you
Critical incidents
Cross-curricular approach
Drawing my school
Effective teaching and learning in our schools
Learner training and learner autonomy
Looking at new coursebooks
Mixed ability
Peer teaching
Planning a unit of work together
Practical activities and warmers
Reading the official curriculum document
Role of teacher and/or educator
Selecting and reading methodology books
Testing

See also the sample list of topics to investigate in Section 6.18.

6.36 Applying our learning: looking back and looking ahead
(see Task 5.5)

The following extracts are taken from a conversation I (P) had with a teacher (T) at the end of a three-week training programme in the United Kingdom.

6.36.1 EXTRACTS FROM A CONVERSATION ABOUT PROFESSIONAL CHANGE

P: Has your training programme helped you to change as a teacher? If so, how? If not, why not?

T: Yes, it makes me think, and I realise that we have to be more tolerant with students because when we ourselves become learners, we have reactions that we can see on our learners' faces sometimes. And so I realise that sometimes the way I give them homework to do must have been boring. But very often when I feel bored myself, they are bored as well, and I say, well, it's time to do something about it. ...

P: If you are changing, what exactly is it that is changing? Your knowledge about educating, teaching and learning? Your professional skills? Your attitudes to educating, teaching and learning? Something else?

T: I think it's skills for me. The approach to different ways, because my behaviour as a teacher has never changed really, concerning the pupils. I've always been very strict, very demanding, I give a lot of work, I mark a lot of essays, but after all, I'm free to do it or not. Nothing is compulsory, but it's my habit, and this I think I will not try to change.

P: So those are the deep…

T: My deep, ingrained belief is that you must be a demanding teacher. …

P: How would you describe the process of professional change for teachers (e.g. slow/fast, sudden/gradual, etc.)?

T: No. It won't be slow. The feeling I have of a need to change comes slowly, possibly. But then when I decide, it's very fast. And then I change everything. And then, of course, I get used to it for a while, possibly start repeating…

P: So what about this idea about making little changes, taking little steps?

T: I suppose I'll have to, because life will compel me to, I mean everyday life. …

P: Do you anticipate that your training programme will help you in your professional future? If so, how? If not, why not?

T: I'm going back with ideas. … So now I'll have to go back and select, and tell my other colleagues what I've done here, because some of them were interested. And try to start a kind of team…

P: With other English teachers?

T: Yes, other English teachers. [I will try to] create something new in the school, with some other teachers, and establish something in common, first.

6.36.2 FURTHER EXTRACTS FROM A CONVERSATION ABOUT PROFESSIONAL CHANGE

Extract 1 Restlessness as a cause of change

P: Let's start. Talk about something quite general and deep and difficult. Changing as a teacher. Do you need to change?

T: Well, I *think* I am changing…and I think I feel a need of change. …I become very restless. I think I just get fed up with a certain type of exercise. I think I've done them too often. …And especially in my country where we are fairly constricted. So after a while, I really feel I must do something else, or at least I must do it differently.

Extract 2 *Some teachers don't want to change, but learners are creative*

T: But each time you change, anyway, it's far more work.

P: Maybe that's why some people don't want to change.

T: I suppose so.

P: They're happy in their…

T: I suppose some people need this security of repeating for ever and ever, the same thing, but…

P: There comes a point when presumably not changing, you lose touch.

T: Well, you become bored. In my school, for instance, some teachers have been in this same school since they started as teachers …, and they criticise the children.

P: When we walk into the staffroom, we start complaining about the…

T: Yes, and I don't see the point. The kids are really great, actually. I even think kids are usually more amazing than teachers. Because of their imagination. Each time I correct things, I complain about their level of English, sometimes. But sometimes the way they create things…their imagination is usually much higher than mine. Very often I give an essay and I would have never thought of all the things they say. So I am really amazed at what they can produce.

Extract 3 *I realise that working with other teachers…*

T: We made fun of the word synergy, but I think this is something that we felt here in this group particularly.

P: You can do a lot by working together.

T: Exactly. Teamwork.…I knew that it was very interesting, but I never realised, I was never aware or conscious of how *much* we got from each other.… You know, we are all in our little pigeon holes, I would say. We go back home, and we have our homework to do, and we have so much to do that we never have time for teamwork, and actually, we all have our personalities, and we get into a rut.

Extract 4 *Change involves more work, but I want to…*

P: Doesn't change involve more work for busy teachers?

T: Oh yes. Of course. Far more. I know that it's going to be even worse than before.

P: What, when you go back now, thinking…?

T: Yes, because I'll have to change lots of things in my teaching…

P: You don't have to…

T: Well [hesitates], I'll have to, I'll have…to get rid of this habit of testing, instead of teaching.

P: Is that a big idea you're taking from the course?

T: Yes. Well, I felt that I shouldn't test as much as I do, and I would like to teach children how to learn…

Extract 5 I want to reflect more…

T: I think I'm going to think more about the way I teach, about my own method, you see, and to question it again.

P: So reflecting…

T: Reflecting on the way I teach, and applying a certain number of principles that we have seen here.

P: It's quite difficult, extrapolating principles. I mean, one is functioning at a different level; you're experiencing something, and then…

T: Yes, you have to think about it and analyse it. I'm not always very good at that.

P: Difficult!

T: Yes, I think it's certainly the most difficult part. It's certainly the most abstract thing, and I usually like concrete things.

Extract 6 I want to read…

P: What about books, do you think you will have time to read methodology books?

T: No, I would say for me, time is the main problem. I'm always short of time.

P: Are there any books that you might like to…?

T: I think I'll go to the British Council Library again, because years and years ago I enrolled there, and I would borrow books, and I will do that again this year,…I didn't want to buy too many books, because I know the habit of buying books, and never reading them. So I've just put a few asterisks on the course bibliography, and I'll go and check if they have them.

Extract 7 I want to ask learners what they think

P: Teaching and learning as a shared experience?

T: Yes, and asking the learners what they think about it. And what they learnt today, how their minds work, and this is something that possibly I've never done.

P: That might be an area to explore.

T: Yes, certainly. Certainly, I think it is necessary for them to understand the procedures, and why they like them or not, for instance. Why did they appreciate them, or not?

P: Also good feedback for you.

T: Yes,…

6.36.3 EXAMPLE OF A TEACHER'S PERSONAL CHECKLIST OF LEARNING POINTS AND STRATEGIES
(see Worksheet 47)

These are examples of a teacher's learning points and strategies which she wished to apply when returning to school after a training programme. The teacher in question was able to formulate these ideas while taking stock of the training programme at its end. (I have compiled the examples by selecting relevant extracts from a conversation I held with the teacher, reproduced in detail above).

- I think I'll go to the British Council library again. I've put a few asterisks on the course bibliography, and I'll go and check if they have them.
- I'll have to get rid of this habit of 'testing' instead of 'teaching'. I felt that I shouldn't test as much as I do, and I would like to teach children to learn how to learn.
- I'm going to think more about the way I teach and question it again.
- I'll have to go back and tell my other colleagues what I've done here, because some of them were interested. And try to start a kind of team with some others and establish things in common.

6.36.4 EXAMPLE OF A MINDMAP SUMMARY OF A GROUP DISCUSSION

This mindmap, produced with a group of teachers and drawn by me, summarises the learning points they articulated during a group discussion entitled, 'Applying our learning to our teaching'. The discussion was held at the end of a training programme (see Option 29, at the end of Task 5.5):

6.37 General recommendations concerning tutorials
(see Task 5.6)

Tutorials are perhaps a rather labour-intensive way of using precious time with teachers, and may therefore be inappropriate in some training contexts. However, where trainer:teacher ratios permit, a tutorial between a trainer and an individual teacher can be an efficient way of monitoring a teacher's progress, promoting learning and development in general, and/or helping a teacher to set learning aims. I feel that a tutorial is particularly valuable when teachers are investigating a topic individually – see any of the tasks described in this book – and/or when training programmes set formal demands on teachers in terms of assessment (see, for example, Task 5.8, especially the guidelines for writing a report about investigating in Section 6.39.3).

Alternatively, a tutorial may be more informal and more developmentally focused. Using such questions as those on Worksheet 48 (point 4 in the 'Review' stage) will help teachers to prepare for the more informal tutorial. I include below further recommendations for making the most of the time available for tutorials:

- Decide how much time is available for a tutorial; a minimum of 20–30 minutes is recommended. (Consider the possibility of tutorials with two teachers, where time is short.)
- Explain clearly to teachers the purpose of the tutorial, for example to review the training programme so far and set new learning aims by means of a teacher's portfolio.
- Help teachers to plan for the tutorial, for example by asking them to submit a portfolio to you in advance, so that you are better prepared, and able to use the time more effectively.

6.38 Sharing our learning (1): giving informal presentations
(see Task 5.7)

6.38.1 GENERAL STRATEGIES FOR DEVELOPING TEACHERS' PRESENTATION SKILLS
(see Task 5.7, 'Background for the trainer'):

Here are some suggestions for general ways of developing teachers' presentation skills throughout a training programme:

- Emphasise how much teachers can learn from each other (the value of synergy)!
- Explain the long-term benefit of developing presentation skills. For example, it promotes confidence in teachers' own ideas and their ability to change things.

- Encourage teachers to practise presenting in pairs and/or small groups, as proposed in the tasks and worksheets in this book; ideally start doing this from the very first training session.
- Build teachers' confidence slowly and gradually, for example by praising their efforts, or by encouraging them to share their own successful teaching ideas in general in training sessions.
- Provide a clear framework for what is required for a presentation (aims, resources, timing, aids, etc.). See Worksheet 49, for example.
- Where appropriate, allow teachers to use their own language when presenting, if they feel too self-conscious or reluctant to use English.
- Encourage teachers to use posters when presenting in order to provide visual support to their work: a large sheet of card on which they may display handouts, photographs and other relevant materials. The posters should be informative, clear, memorable and attractive; they are particularly suitable for teachers who lack confidence when speaking in front of others (see Task 5.8).
- Other strategies that you can add...

6.38.2 WHAT ARE THE CHARACTERISTICS OF AN EFFECTIVE PRESENTATION? SOME SUGGESTIONS
(see Task 5.7, Procedure, stage 1, 'Reflecting about presenting')

- Plan carefully; check any equipment before you begin.
- State at the beginning of your presentation what you are going to do, and also think of a way of summing up at the end.
- Speak slowly, using notes if you wish, but don't just read from them.
- Use visual aids such as the blackboard, the overhead projector, photographs, posters, etc., which will help you to bring your work to life.
- When using the overhead projector, print clearly in large letters, and don't stand in front of it.
- Don't try to do too much in the time you have available. Instead, select a small number of points, perhaps five, which you wish to explain, and focus on these.
- Don't just speak to your audience, try to involve them actively in other ways, for example, by giving them something to do during the presentation (e.g. trying out a task).
- Decide what to do about questions from the audience, and tell the audience about your policy at the beginning of your presentation. For example, do you want to leave time at the end of your presentation for questions, or is it acceptable for the audience to interrupt you with questions?
- Decide if you wish to give out handouts, bibliographies, etc.
- Practise beforehand, checking your timing in particular.
- Other ideas that you can add...

6.39 Sharing our learning (2): joining forces in the wider educational community

(see Task 5.8)

6.39.1 WAYS OF SHARING LEARNING: ADVANTAGES AND DISDVANTAGES:

Giving a public talk

Advantages:

- A talk is likely to be relevant to a local audience, from a teacher's region or country.
- A talk is viewed as positive for a teacher's CV, if this is a consideration in the local context.
- Sometimes teachers receive financial support to attend a conference if they give a talk.

Disadvantages:

- Teachers lack confidence, thinking, often wrongly, that other teachers will not be interested in their work.
- Teachers will probably only reach a small audience, although maybe this is an advantage!
- Giving a talk is a difficult skill in its own right. Facing an unknown public audience (often for the first time), is a daunting experience for everyone! But the members of the audience will be on the teacher's side. Teachers may give a talk in their own language rather than in English, and/or together with other colleagues.
- Often teachers do not know about conferences, and/or are not able to find the time or money to attend; help teachers to find out about such events.

Producing a poster

Advantages:

- A poster is teacher-friendly in that it can be produced in groups, and is less threatening than giving a talk.
- Little writing is involved, and it allows teachers to exploit visual presentation skills.
- Teachers can stand by their poster at a conference and chat to interested teachers as they pass by, thus targeting their audience precisely.
- Posters can also be displayed in different places, for example at a teachers' centre, or in a school staffroom.

Disadvantages:

- A poster in some people's views perhaps lacks the academic seriousness of a talk or an article.
- Teachers often undervalue their visual presentation skills.

Publishing an article

Advantages:

- Teachers can write an article with others.
- An article may reach a larger audience than a talk, beyond the local community. Therefore, potentially more colleagues will be able to read and benefit from teachers' work.
- An article can be more in-depth than a talk or poster, and may be positive for a teacher's CV, if this is a consideration in the local context.
- Sometimes publishers pay a fee for articles!

Disadvantages:

- Writing is a difficult skill, but teachers can write in their own language;
- Teachers lack confidence. An article may seem threatening, time-consuming, or too academic.
- Teachers often do not know about professional publications, or cannot find the time to read professionally; help teachers to find out about publications which are available.

Writing a report

Advantages:

- Reports can be made available to other teachers in the local area, for example in teachers' centres, and may prove very relevant to them. The other teachers can read and benefit from the reports, and possibly follow up recommendations included in them.
- Reports are more in-depth than a talk or a poster.
- Reports have more academic respectability for some people, and develop academic skills such as writing.

Disadvantages:

- Writing is a difficult skill, but teachers may write in their own language.
- Teachers lack confidence, and writing a report may prove time-consuming, or threatening, as teachers may be unfamiliar with academic discourse.
- A report is usually written individually.
- Other teachers may not know about the reports, or be able to find the time to read them. Tell other teachers about them!

6.39.2 FURTHER READING: 'EFFECTIVE PRESENTATIONS'

Effective presentations
Two of the York participants offer their tips

"It does get easier…"

There was a wide choice of talks and workshops to go to at the York conference, most of them very interesting. While I admire anyone who has the guts to stand up and talk about their ideas, I couldn't help noticing that the standard of presentation skills was, to put it politely, variable.

Nerves

Many of the problems stemmed, I felt, from nerves: often speakers took a long time to 'warm up' and had no time to finish their talks, let alone take questions, just when it was getting interesting. A few tips:

– Relaxation exercises can help.

– Use cards as prompts in case you forget your lines.

– Practise in front of a mirror and tape-record yourself.

IATEFL audiences are kindly; they don't heckle or bite. They want to hear what you have to say. Look at them and smile!

Planning and timing

As teachers we are aware of the need to plan lessons, to pace them, and not to try to squeeze too much in. Keep it relevant, and leave time for questions at the end – if you have an interesting idea, people are bound to want to know how to do it!

Don't talk non-stop for 90 minutes – nobody can concentrate for that long. Activities can illustrate your points far better than half an hour of talking.

If you're on first thing in the morning or after lunch, keep it lively!

OHTs

Even experienced speakers tried to show overhead transparencies crammed with tiny text. Your audience can't take it all in, especially if you talk about something else.

OHTs are a visual aid, not a thesis. They should be

– brief; they are good for showing illustrations, diagrams, etc.

– readable from the back of the room: as a rough guide, the letters should be 2 cm high.

Leave the transparency up long enough for people to copy it, especially if you don't have a hand-out. And turn the projector off while you're not using it!

Finally

Don't let this put anyone off – it *does* get easier with experience.

Julia Sallabank

"Just love your audience..."

Attending a conference always brings about mixed feelings.

Meeting many people who are all interested in the same issue is wonderful! But not always wonderful is the level of the presentations. As the May newsletter put it: "Some sessions were uniformly excellent and others were...less so". Even if a speaker has a lot of interesting things to say, then it is difficult to listen continuously for one hour to a speech that is not alternated with any overhead sheets or just a few simple lines on the blackboard. We know that the attention span of most people has grown rather short in recent years.

Are there any useful tips for a successful presentation? Yes, I think there are. I discovered these tips to be very useful when I had to do a presentation myself:

1. Start with a (funny?) introduction: thus you draw the attention of your audience.

2. First tell your audience what you are going to tell them.

3. Keep your audience informed about their role. Are they just listeners or...whatever?

4. Keep eye-contact.

5. Vary the sound of your voice, the position of your body. Don't look into one direction all the time. In short: mind your body-language!

6. If possible: insert an activity in which your audience can take part.

There are many more tips – far too many for a short article in a newsletter.

I was once told:

"Just love your audience; the most important thing is not what you tell them but how you do it"

Ineke Brussaards –
Bureau Volwasseneneducatie
The Netherlands

(Sallabank and Brussaards, 1995)

6.39.3 GUIDELINES FOR WRITING A FORMAL REPORT ABOUT INVESTIGATING

These guidelines are taken from a document used on a training programme, which was photocopied and given to teachers. The original document is several pages long, but here I include only key advice, which you may also be able to use with teachers.

Writing a formal report about investigating

Please read the following text carefully; if you have any questions, ask a trainer. If possible, type or word-process your report, although this is not obligatory (if you cannot word-process, why not learn now?). Include on the front page of the report your name and the address of your school, so other teachers can contact you. Unless you are a genius, you will need to write a draft for your finished report! Show your draft to other teachers, so that they can check it for clarity, and any gross syntactic mistakes: don't worry, though, we don't expect your English to be 100% accurate!

The structure of your report should be as follows:

- the title page (should be concise and eye-catching; check the grammar with a trainer)
- abstract/summary (leave this until last)
- list of contents (number these please)
  1 introduction, including learner setting, methodology, and general focus of the investigation
  2 action plan, description of procedure
  3 analysis of results, conclusions and recommendations (select significant data)
  4 appendices (don't include everything – select significant material)
  5 bibliography (use the format we have used during the training programme)

Learner setting (see 1 above):
Include such personal information about yourself as how long you have been teaching (English), other subjects you teach, type of school, etc.

Methodology (see 1 above):
Give a brief general description of the priorities in your work as a teacher (personal theory, syllabus, coursebook, typical activities in class, etc.).

General focus of the investigation (see 1 above):
Why did you choose the topic? How does it fit in with the school curriculum? Review of the literature.

Action plan (see 2 above):
Include the aims of your work; don't be too ambitious here! Include a description of procedure (what you actually did, which data collection methods you used, etc.) by means of a diagram or chart showing a timetable. Did you change the focus of the work during the time you were investigating?

Analysis of results, conclusions and recommendations (see 3 above):
This section is perhaps the most important and the most difficult. Consider this question: What actually happened in the classroom as a result of your action plan? Select significant data and explicitly analyse and evaluate these in terms of the aims that you set at the beginning, considering the following:

- What did your pupils learn?
- What did you learn about the topic selected?
- What recommendations would you make for teachers who may wish to introduce the topic of your report in their own situations (mention any special difficulties encountered)?
- Do you wish to modify your personal theory of educating, teaching and learning as a result of your work?
- What are the implications of your work for your future teaching practice and professional development?

Finally, when writing your report, imagine that a teacher from a different city or country who is not familiar with your school, etc. will read it. Include information that would enable another teacher to read about your work and to try your ideas out, without being able to speak to you!

Good luck! We hope that you find writing the report an interesting and rewarding learning experience.

Worksheets

List of worksheets

1 Getting to know each other: questionnaire (Task 1.1)   225
2 Getting to know each other: something about us… (Task 1.1)   227
3 Getting to know each other: focus on me as a teacher (Task 1.1)   228
4 How do I learn? (Task 1.2)   229
5 Ways in which we can learn together (Task 1.2)   230
6 Possible stages of investigating (1) (Task 1.3)   231
7 Possible stages of investigating (2) (Task 1.3)   233
8 'It's quite obvious the teacher's a gardener': exploring teachers' metaphors (Task 1.4)   234
9 Producing maps of key concepts related to our training programme (Task 1.5)   235
10 Why teach English? (Task 1.6)   236
11 What we agree about and what we disagree about… (Task 1.6)   237
12 Are we speaking the same language? Understanding general terms related to educating, teaching and learning (Task 1.7)   238
13 A personal glossary of key terms related to educating, teaching and learning (Task 1.7)   239
14 Reflecting on the nature of change in education: What helps us to change? (Task 1.8)   240
15 Reflecting on the nature of change in education: factors which will help us to change and/or innovate (Tasks 1.8 and 1.9)   242
16 Innovation in our schools: How can we help to promote it? Questionnaire (Task 1.9)   243
17 Examining critical incidents: questions (Task 2.1)   244
18 High-priority topics for the group to investigate (Task 2.1)   245
19 Effective educating, teaching and learning in the language classroom (1): What are our priorities? (Task 2.2)   246
20 Effective educating, teaching and learning in the language classroom (2): my priorities (Task 2.3)   247
21 Our current professional practice: strengths, weaknesses, opportunities and benefits (Task 2.4)   248
22 My best lesson / teaching idea (Task 2.5)   250
23 Reading survey: review sheet (Tasks 2.6 and 3.8)   251
24 Reading survey: alternative review sheet (Task 2.6)   252
25 Keeping a diary (Tasks 2.7 and 2.8)   253

26 'We can do it!' Self-esteem, us and our learners (Task 2.9)   254
27 'We can do it!' Practical recommendations for... (Task 2.9)   256
28 What do I understand by the topic 'x'? (What? Why?
   Who?, etc.) (Task 3.2)   257
29 What do we already do in school or class regarding the
   topic 'x'? Find someone who... (Task 3.3)   258
30 Do we agree that...? (Task 3.4)   259
31 Understanding key terms related to a specific topic (Task 3.7)   260
32 Preparing a debate: instructions (Task 3.9)   261
33 The benefits of investigating in class: teachers' perspectives
   (Task 4.1)   262
34 Which data collection method? (Task 4.2)   264
35 Consulting learners (1): planning, administering and evaluating
   a simple questionnaire (Task 4.4)   266
36 Ten characteristics of an effective questionnaire (Task 4.4)   268
37 Consulting our learners (2): What did you learn today?
   Sample data (Task 4.5)   270
38 Writing a learner profile (Task 4.6)   272
39 An informal interview with a learner (Task 4.7)   273
40 Experimenting in class (Task 4.8)   274
41 Lesson plan sheet (Task 4.8.)   275
42 Has this task helped me/us to learn? (Task 5.1)   276
43 Which learning strategies are helping us? (Task 5.2)   277
44 What I most like about our training programme is... (Task 5.3)   279
45 Making sense: reviewing and finding connections (Task 5.4.)   280
46 Applying our learning: looking back and looking ahead
   (Task 5.5)   281
47 Applying our learning: a checklist (Task 5.5)   282
48 Teacher portfolios (Task 5.6)   283
49 Planning an informal presentation (Task 5.7)   284
50 Evaluating informal presentations (Task 5.7)   285
51 Some ways of sharing our learning in the wider educational
   community (Task 5.8)   286
52 Our English teacher will explain: role-play (Task 5.8)   288

Worksheet 1 Getting to know each other: questionnaire

(see Task 1.1)

This worksheet will help you to get to know each other.

PART 1

Consider the following questions, and write your replies in the spaces provided in the first column. Answer questions only if you have something to write; if a question does not apply to your situation, leave it blank. Spend about 20 minutes on Part 1.

	You (your name ....)	Another teacher (name ....)
1 What do you teach (English, etc.)?		
2 How long have you been teaching (English, other subjects)?		
3 Where do you teach (district, town, city, country, etc.)?		
4 Describe your present school (type, history, size, staff, physical characteristics, strong points, etc.).		
5 Describe the learners you teach in general terms: age(s), motivation, what they (dis-)like doing, attitudes to English, etc.		

© Cambridge University Press 2001 Photocopiable   225

(Worksheet 1 continued)

	You (your name ....)	Another teacher (name ....)
6 Do you use a coursebook? If so, please describe it, explain why you use it. If not, why not?		
7 What are your feelings about the training programme? Why did you come on it? What do you expect from it?		

PART 2

In pairs, interview another teacher using this worksheet, noting down your partner's responses in the second column; you will have 20 minutes for this activity. Make sure that you both get a chance to speak about yourselves. Be ready to tell the whole group afterwards about each of the following: (a) something you have in common; (b) something that you do not have in common; (c) something that surprised you, or (d) what you expect from this training programme.

 © Cambridge University Press 2001 Photocopiable

Worksheet 2 Getting to know each other: something about us...
(see Task 1.1)

This worksheet will help you to summarise aspects of the discussion that you have in pairs. After your discussion, make notes in the spaces provided below. Try to find at least one item for each of the 4 points. You will have 20 minutes to complete this worksheet. Be ready to show it to the whole group.

1 Things we have discovered that we have in common:

2 Things we have discovered that we do not have in common:

3 Something that surprised us in our discussion:

4 Our expectations and feelings regarding the training programme we are beginning:

Names:

Date:

Worksheet 3 Getting to know each other: focus on me as a teacher

(see Task 1.1)

This worksheet will help you to describe aspects of your work so that you can share this information with others.

Complete the following sentences about yourself; write something only where you have something to say, otherwise leave the space blank. Be ready to show the completed worksheet to your trainer and/or colleagues. Spend a maximum of 15 minutes on this worksheet.

1 I am a teacher because:

2 The things I enjoy about being a teacher are:

3 The things I don't enjoy about being a teacher are:

4 My main qualities as a teacher are:

5 I think the main role of a teacher is to:

6 I like learners who:

7 My learners think I am:

8 At the end of a class I usually feel:

9 I think teaching is a/an .... profession.

10 If I weren't a teacher, I would like to be a/an:

11 My feelings and expectations about doing this training programme are:

Name: Date:

Comment (from trainer or a colleague):

 © Cambridge University Press 2001 Photocopiable

Worksheet 4 How do I learn?

(see Task 1.2)

This worksheet will help you to reflect about what helps you to learn, or what has helped you to learn, about teaching, in order to select ways of learning which are relevant for your group and training programme.

PART 1 PAST AND PRESENT LEARNING

Read this list of ways that might help you to learn; decide how effective they have been for your own learning and circle the appropriate number. Spend a maximum of 10 minutes on this worksheet. Be ready to discuss your response with the others, giving examples from your own experience.

		Not effective				Very effective	
1	The act of teaching itself (e.g. trying out new teaching ideas)	1	2	3	4	5	☐
2	Being involved in action/classroom research	1	2	3	4	5	☐
3	Helping inexperienced teachers	1	2	3	4	5	☐
4	Self-study, (e.g., reading professional magazines/ books)	1	2	3	4	5	☐
5	Attending a teachers' course, or conference	1	2	3	4	5	☐
6	Using a new coursebook	1	2	3	4	5	☐
7	Taking on a new responsibility in school	1	2	3	4	5	☐
8	Sharing ideas with colleagues informally	1	2	3	4	5	☐
9	Observing others teach	1	2	3	4	5	☐
10	Being observed teach by others	1	2	3	4	5	☐
11	Initial training	1	2	3	4	5	☐
12	Other ways (please specify)	1	2	3	4	5	☐

PART 2 FUTURE LEARNING

Choose three ways from this list that you feel will be most useful for you. Tick the corresponding numbers in the boxes provided in the right-hand column. Reflect on why you have chosen these ways.

Would they be effective for your training programme?

Name: Date:

© Cambridge University Press 2001 Photocopiable

Worksheet 5 Ways in which we can learn together
(see Task 1.2)

This worksheet will help you to agree on the main ways of learning together.

In small groups, produce a list of up to three suggestions of ways in which you all think the whole group can work together in order to learn effectively on the programme, ranking them in order of importance, with the most important item first. Use the spaces provided below. Spend 20–30 minutes on this activity. Be ready to show your completed worksheet to another group of teachers.

•

•

•

Names:

Date:

© Cambridge University Press 2001 Photocopiable

Worksheet 6 Possible stages of investigating (1)
(see Task 1.3)

This worksheet will help you to obtain an overview of the stages of 'investigating' your professional practice.

PART 1

The eight stages of investigating are presented below in random or arbitrary order (except for A and H). Individually, read stages B–G, and try to find a logical sequence for the stages, writing down the letters in order. Which stage comes after A, etc.? Note that there may be more than one possible sequence. Spend 10 minutes on Part 1, and be ready to share your ideas with the others.

A *Select a topic for investigating*
For example, try to think what you would like to improve in your work.

B *Decide which data to collect*
For example, you can take photos, keep a classroom diary, collect lesson plans, or write a simple questionnaire. Ask other colleagues for advice.

C *Evaluate your work*
For example, ask: What did my/our pupils learn? What did I/we learn? Where is my/our 'evidence'? What recommendations can I/we give colleagues interested in the same topic?

D *Preliminary exploration*
Read as much as you can find on the topic you select, and about investigating, keeping notes about your reading. Ask other colleagues for advice.

E *Find a colleague(s) to work with*
Working together helps you to share ideas and the workload, when feeling fed up or stuck!

F *Teach, and collect data*
Actually teach for the period in question. Make sure that collecting data does not interfere too much with your teaching.

G *Set aims and 'start small'*
Do not try to do too much, too quickly; set modest aims for investigating, for example by focusing on one class you teach for a limited period of time.

H *Share the results with colleagues*
Tell colleagues in your group or at a school staff meeting about your recommendations by making a poster about your work. Or write a report or article, or give a talk at a conference.

© Cambridge University Press 2001 Photocopiable

(Worksheet 6 continued)

PART 2

Compare your ideas related to Part 1 with another teacher, and try to agree on one sequence. Also consider the following questions:

Which of the eight stages do you think would be the easiest / most difficult? Why?

You will have 10 minutes for Part 2. Make notes if you wish.

 © Cambridge University Press 2001 Photocopiable

Worksheet 7 Possible stages of investigating (2)
(see Task 1.3)

This worksheet will help you to obtain an overview of the stages of 'investigating' your professional practice.

Look at the following sequences of the stages of investigating. Your trainer will give you the names of the missing headings; please write the headings in their corresponding places on the worksheet (the first one has already been done for you). Spend 10 minutes on this worksheet:

1 *Select a topic for investigating*

   For example, try to think what you would like to improve in your work.

2 ....

   Working together helps you to share ideas and the workload, when feeling fed up or stuck!

3 ....

   Read as much as you can find on the topic you select, and about investigating, keeping notes about your reading. Ask other colleagues for advice.

4 ....

   Do not try to do too much, too quickly; set modest aims for investigating, for example by focusing on one class you teach for a limited period of time.

5 ....

   For example, you can take photos, keep a classroom diary, collect lesson plans, or write a simple questionnaire. Ask other colleagues for advice.

6 ....

   Actually teach for the period in question. Make sure that collecting data does not interfere too much with your teaching!

7 ....

   For example, ask: What did my/our pupils learn? What did I/we learn? Where is my /our 'evidence'? What recommendations can I/we give colleagues interested in the same topic?

8 ....

   Tell colleagues in your group or at a school staff meeting about your recommendations by making a poster about your work. Write a report or an article, or give a talk at a conference.

Worksheet 8 'It's quite obvious that the teacher's a gardener': exploring teachers' metaphors
(see Task 1.4)

This worksheet will help you to record and analyse different metaphors for aspects of educating, teaching and learning:

Classroom	Teacher	Learners	Miscellaneous/ typical features
Example 1 garden	gardener	plants	growth is very slow, organic, not visible, requiring sun, water, fertiliser and care
Example 2			
Example 3			
Example 4			

 © Cambridge University Press 2001 Photocopiable

Worksheet 9 Producing maps of key concepts related to our training programme
(see Task 1.5)

This worksheet will help you to anticipate, organise and use key concepts related to your training programme.

PART 1

1 Form small groups of three or four teachers.
2 Look at the set of cards your group is given, each of which contains a key concept related to educating, teaching and learning in the language classroom.
3 Put a large piece of paper on to a table and write the title 'Educating, teaching and learning in the language classroom', in large letters in the middle of your sheet. Place all the cards face up on the paper, and arrange them around the central title in an order which you feel is logical, making a kind of map or framework. You may place those cards which you feel are closely related near each other, and indicate connections between concepts by means of arrows, or show emphasis by underlining items.
4 Blank cards: you also have five blank cards on which you can write the names of concepts which you feel are important, but which are missing from the cards you were given. You may also use any concept more than once for your map, by simply copying the concept on to one of the blank cards.
5 When you are satisfied with your framework, attach the cards to the paper with reusable adhesive, sticky tape, etc., so that later it can also be displayed on the training room wall. Copy your own framework down on to a sheet of paper, writing your name and date on it, for future reference.

You will have at least 30 minutes to complete Part 1.

PART 2

Look at the maps produced by the other sub-groups, and compare them with your own:

What similarities or differences are there between your own map and the others?

© Cambridge University Press 2001 Photocopiable

Worksheet 10 Why teach English?

(see Task 1.6)

This worksheet will help you to clarify the goals of educating, teaching and learning in the language classroom.

Why teach English in your situation?

In sub-groups of three or four teachers, consider the list below of reasons why learners should be taught English or another foreign language.

1 Select and rank in order of importance five reasons which are valid or the most important in your own teaching situation, with the most important items coming first.

2 Decide which reasons you can eliminate as not valid for your situation, and say why.

If you wish, you can modify the statements to match your views, or combine different statements in the list. Be ready to report your choices to the whole group in terms of what you agree about, and what you disagree about. Be as specific as possible in justifying your choices. Choose someone to represent your sub-group. You will have approximately 30 minutes before sharing your ideas with the whole group.

We teach English in order to...:

1 make a difference in learners' lives (how?)

2 prepare learners for their future lives after they leave school (which aspects?)

3 contribute towards learners' general education (which aspects?)

4 encourage learners to understand and respect other ways of thinking and acting, other cultures and languages (for example?)

5 contribute towards learners' general cognitive development (which aspects?)

6 enable learners to communicate with English-speaking people in the future (who exactly?)

7 help learners to learn the language (which aspects?)

8 help learners to learn about the language (which aspects?)

9 help learners to understand their own language(s) and culture better (why?)

10 help learners to gain access to information in English in the future (how?)

11 act as a foundation for future, more specialised, learning of the language (what? when?)

12 something else (you may, of course, choose other reasons which are not included here)

 © Cambridge University Press 2001 Photocopiable

Worksheet 11 What we agree about and what we disagree about...

(see Task 1.6)

This worksheet will help you to record your decisions about the following topic:

.... (write name of topic in this space)

After your discussion, record what you agree about and what you disagree about in the spaces provided below. Rank your choices in order of importance, with the most important coming first. You will have about 15 minutes for this worksheet.

We agree that:

1

2

3

4

5

We disagree that:

1

2

3

4

5

We are not sure about...

Names:

Date:

© Cambridge University Press 2001 Photocopiable   237

Worksheet 12 Are we speaking the same language? Understanding general terms related to educating, teaching and learning

(see Task 1.7)

Sometimes the terminology used in discussing education, teaching and learning is confusing and difficult to understand. This worksheet will help your group to agree on some key terms.

Work in pairs.

PART 1

Match the terms (a)–(f) with the definitions 1–6 by writing the correct word in the appropriate space. You will have 5–10 minutes.

(a) syllabus   (b) utterance   (c) accuracy   (d) fluency   (e) curriculum
(f) educational goals

1 .... very general, broad targets to be aimed at (White, 1988: 27)

2 .... speaking or writing with ease and without excessive hesitation

3 .... a way of specifying, selecting and organising the content of teaching for a particular subject

4 .... something that is said/spoken

5 .... the production of instances of correct language

6 .... 'the totality of content to be taught and aims to be realized within one school or educational system' (White, 1988: 4)

PART 2

Can you use these terms to talk about yourselves as teachers or language learners?

EXTRA ACTIVITY

What other terms do you know related to education, teaching and learning which are important? Write them in the space below.

          © Cambridge University Press 2001 Photocopiable

Worksheet 13 A personal glossary of key terms related to educating, teaching and learning
(see Task 1.7)

This worksheet will help you to record key terms that you encounter in your reading or from other sources, and which are important for schools, teachers and learners. Why are these terms important in your opinion?

Term	Definition	Source
curriculum	'the totality of content to be taught and aims to be realized within one school or educational system'	White, R.V. (1988). 'The ELT Curriculum: Design, Innovation and Management'. Blackwell. Page 4.

Name: Date:

© Cambridge University Press 2001 Photocopiable

Worksheet 14 Reflecting on the nature of change in education: What helps us to change?

(see Task 1.8)

This worksheet will help you to make sense of aspects of the theory and practice of change in education.

PART 1

On your own, read the following statements related to the phenomenon of change in education. For each statement, decide if:

(a) it reflects your own experience and views
(b) it does not reflect your own experience and views
(c) you are not sure / do not understand

Then circle the corresponding letter (a), (b), or (c). Try also to think about the reasons for your responses, and give examples from your experience; make notes on another sheet of paper. Spend about 30 minutes on Part 1.

1 *Dynamic or static schools*

There needs to be a collective will to do things things better, and this is often the mark of a successful school, that it changes…judiciously. If teachers can work together to refine one another's professional skills, to reflect on the curriculum and modify what is done as is necessary, then the school can be said to be 'dynamic', as opposed to 'static'.

(adapted from Wragg, 1997: 111–12)

(a)   (b)   (c)   Why?

2 *Helping learners to learn about change*

Teachers' capacities to deal with change, learn from it, and help students learn from it will be critical for the future development of societies.

(Fullan, 1993: ix)

(a)   (b)   (c)   Why?

3 *'Top-down' or 'bottom-up' change?*

you can change systems, you impose this or that from on high – but the impact in the classroom, the difference, is small…. That is because cash nor systems teach children. Teachers – human beings alone in their rooms – do that.

(*Guardian*, Comment, 25 July 1994)

(a)   (b)   (c)   Why?

   © Cambridge University Press 2001 Photocopiable

(Worksheet 14 continued)

4 *Why all this talk of change?*

Why interfere with tradition and the certainties of established custom?…There must always be change.…If we do not accept the need for change, for renewal and reform, we deny dynamism to our profession.

(Widdowson, 1984: 86).

(a)   (b)   (c)   Why?

5 *I feel a need for change …*

I think I feel a need for change. I become very restless. I think I just get fed up with a certain type of exercise. I think I've seen everything concerning a certain type of work. (…) So after a while, I really feel I must do something else, or at least I must do it differently.

(teacher)

(a)   (b)   (c)   Why?

PART 2

In pairs, compare your responses to the above statements.

Which were similar and which were different?

Together, think of factors which will help you to change and/or innovate in your schools in the future. For example, 'being able to work together with other teachers'. Be ready to report to the group by making notes about your idea(s) on slips of paper your trainer will give you. Spend 20 minutes on Part 2.

Worksheet 15 Reflecting on the nature of change in education: factors which will help us to change and/or innovate

(see Tasks 1.8 and 1.9)

This worksheet will help you to record factors which will help you to change and/or innovate in your schools and classrooms.

Factors which will help us to change and/or innovate:

●

●

●

●

●

●

●

●

●

●

Date:

 © Cambridge University Press 2001 Photocopiable

Worksheet 16 Innovation in our schools: How can we help to promote it? Questionnaire
(see Task 1.9)

This worksheet will help you to (a) analyse an educational innovation you are familiar with, and (b) consider your future role in promoting innovation in education.

Think of an educational innovation that you are familiar with, and answer the following questions about it, making notes in the spaces provided. Do not worry if you cannot answer a particular question – leave it blank. Recommended time: 20–25 minutes. Be ready to show your completed worksheet to your trainer and/or your colleagues.

1 What was the innovation? In materials, technology, organisation, curriculum, etc.?

2 Why was the innovation introduced?

3 Who first suggested the innovation?

4 How was the innovation first introduced?

5 What factors promoted or inhibited the innovation?

6 What was the effect of the innovation on yourself or others involved?

7 If you could implement the innovation again, what improvements would you make to the way it was implemented?

8 What factors are important in the implementation of an innovation?

(adapted from White, 1988: 171)

Name: Date:

© Cambridge University Press 2001 Photocopiable

Worksheet 17 Examining critical incidents: questions
(see Task 2.1)

This worksheet will help you to reflect on, exchange information about, and analyse your own critical incidents.

Can you remember something that happened in your classrooms or schools that made you question the way you work?

PART 1

Consider the question above and think of a 'critical incident' from your own professional experience – your trainer will give you an example. Analyse your incident by answering the questions below. (If you cannot answer all of the questions, don't worry, leave them unanswered.) Make notes if you wish, and be ready to exchange information about your incident with a colleague. You will have at least 20 minutes to prepare this before sharing your information.

Questions:

 1 What happened?
 2 Who was involved?
 3 What/who made it happen?
 4 What did it feel like? For whom?
 5 What does it mean? To whom?
 6 Why did it happen?
 7 Did I like it?
 8 Was it a good thing?
 9 Why?
10 What is it an example of?
11 What do I do as a result / should I do as a result?
12 How?
13 When?
14 Where?

(adapted from Tripp, 1993: 27)

PART 2

In pairs use the above questions to interview each other about your incidents for about 20 minutes, making sure you both have time to talk about your own incident. As you do so, try to answer the following questions:

As a result of reflecting on and discussing critical incidents, have you learned / become aware of anything about your own work? What?

Compare your incidents, and be ready to summarise and share at least one important idea with the other teachers in the group. Maybe start like this: 'We now realise that…' .

  © Cambridge University Press 2001 Photocopiable

Worksheet 18 High-priority topics for the group to investigate

(see Task 2.1)

This worksheet will help you to record topics which are high priority for the group to investigate.

Priority 1

Priority 2

Priority 3

Date:

© Cambridge University Press 2001 Photocopiable

Worksheet 19 Effective educating, teaching and learning in the language classroom (1): What are our priorities?

(see Task 2.2)

This worksheet will help you to decide what your professional priorities are.

PART 1

On another piece of paper, individually write down ideas about what you think is important regarding the contributions made by (a) learners, or (b) the teacher, or (c) the curriculum / syllabus / teaching materials / tasks to effective educating, teaching and learning (your trainer will help you to decide which element to focus on). For example, 'I think that *learners* should...'. You will have 10 minutes for this activity.

PART 2

In groups of three or four, select and rank in order of importance 5–10 priorities from those that you have written down individually. Be as specific as possible. Make notes in the spaces provided below. Be ready to justify your selection to the rest of the group. You have about 30 minutes for this activity.

.... *should*:

-
-
-
-
-
-
-
-
-
-

EXTRA ACTIVITY

If your sub-group finishes before the others, consider which of these priorities you would like to focus on in your future practice? Why? How?

Names: Date:

     © Cambridge University Press 2001 Photocopiable

Worksheet 20 Effective educating, teaching and learning in the language classroom (2): my priorities
(see Task 2.3)

This worksheet will help you to record your personal priorities for your work, and provide a framework for you to write a 'pedagogic manifesto' afterwards.

I consider the following to be of high priority in terms of what I, my learners and the curriculum / syllabus / teaching materials / tasks should contribute, for educating, teaching and learning to be effective in my personal situation, in order of importance (spend a maximum of 30–40 minutes on this worksheet, and be prepared to show it to your trainer):

-

-

-

-

-

-

-

-

-

Name: Date:

Trainer comment:

Worksheet 21 Our current professional practice: strengths, weaknesses, opportunities and benefits

(see Task 2.4)

The worksheet will help you to identify topics for investigating on your training programme.

PART 1 REFLECTING: WHAT IS HAPPENING IN MY SCHOOL AND CLASSES?

Individually, reflect on the following questions or partially complete sentences about yourself as a teacher, as well as your school, classes and learners; make notes if you wish. Use only those questions and sentences which help you to express your views effectively. Spend about 15 minutes on Part 1. Be ready to share your ideas with the other teachers.

Strengths

1 An aspect(s) of my school or my classes I am *happy* with

.... Why? How I can further enhance

this aspect ....

Weaknesses and opportunities:

2 An aspect(s) of my school or my classes I am unhappy with

.... Why? What can I do, if anything, to

change the situation? ....

....

3 Some people in my school are unhappy about ....

Why? What can I do, if anything, to change this situation? ....

....

4 I would like to improve .... Why? ....

5 An idea I would like to try out in class is ....

Why? ....

(adapted from Hopkins, 1985: 47)

 © Cambridge University Press 2001 Photocopiable

(Worksheet 21 continued)

PART 2 IDENTIFYING PRIORITY TOPICS AND BENEFITS

In pairs, discuss your responses to Part 1. Select one example of
something you are happy with in your schools, and one priority topic –
from points 2–5 on the worksheet – to focus on in your programme,
making notes in the spaces below. Be as specific as possible. You will have
15 minutes before telling the others. When considering your priority,
think how it might *benefit* your learners / school / you as teachers.

A strength: something in our schools we are happy with: ....

....

Our priority topic: ....

....

Name: Date:

© Cambridge University Press 2001 Photocopiable

Worksheet 22 My best lesson / teaching idea

(see Task 2.5)

This worksheet will help you to describe your best lesson or teaching idea so that other teachers can read it, and then consider trying out your idea in class themselves.

When deciding what information to include about your lesson or teaching idea, select what is essential for other teachers to know, so that they can try out your idea without necessarily being able to talk to you. Spend about 20 minutes on this worksheet.

1 Name of teaching idea/activity	
2 How I found out about the idea; why I like it; it links up with…	
3 Age/level of learners	
4 Teaching aids	
5 Preparation, how I organise the learners (stages, timing, etc.)	1 2 3 4 5
6 Don't forget to…	
7 Other information	

Name: Date:

Comment from another teacher:

   © Cambridge University Press 2001 Photocopiable

Worksheet 23 Reading survey: review sheet
(see Tasks 2.6 and 3.8)

This worksheet will help you to review a book or article and to share your recommendations for reading with the other teachers.

Please read the book, journal, magazine or article that you have selected, and make notes about it on this review sheet, using the following points as a guide, by .... (date). You may leave a space blank below if you cannot think of anything to write. Spend about 20 minutes on this worksheet. Be ready to show your completed review sheet to the other teachers or the trainer.

Title of book/magazine/ article (volume, page number, etc.)	
Author/date/publisher	
Subject (main, useful ideas, key quotations or terms, etc. with page references)	
Your opinion (Would you recommend it to a colleague? Why? Why not?)	

What do you want to *know*, if anything, about the topic of the book now?

What do you want to *do*, if anything, about the topic of the book now?

Name(s) of reviewer(s):   Date:

Comment from teacher or trainer:

© Cambridge University Press 2001 Photocopiable

Worksheet 24 Reading survey: alternative review sheet

(see Task 2.6)

This worksheet will help you to review a book and to share your recommendations for reading with the other teachers.

Please read the text that you have selected or been given, and consider its relevance to your own teaching situation, by using the following points as a guide (you may leave a space blank if you can't think of anything to write). Spend about 20 minutes on this worksheet. Be ready to show your completed review sheet to the other teachers or the trainer.

Text (author, date of publication, title and publisher)	
1 An idea in the text that I (strongly) agree with, and why	
2 An idea in the text that I (strongly) disagree with, and why	
3 A question I would like to ask the author, other teachers in our group or our trainer, and why	
4 Something I don't understand in the text	
5 Other comments	

What do you want to *know*, if anything, about the topic of the book now?

What do you want to *do*, if anything, about the topic of the book now?

Name: Date:

 © Cambridge University Press 2001 Photocopiable

Worksheet 25 Keeping a diary

(see Tasks 2.7 and 2.8)

This worksheet will help you to describe and evaluate in a diary what happens in a class you teach or on your training programme.

1 Discuss these questions briefly with your group:
   Have you ever kept a diary in your personal or professional life before? When? Why? Did you enjoy it? Was it valuable? Why? Why not?

2 There are two types of diary (in this book):
   (a) A classroom diary: Select one particular class of learners that you would like to focus on. Over the next .... days, after each lesson with the selected class, or at the end of the school day, spend 10–15 minutes writing about it.
   (b) A diary based on the training programme: You will be given a regular opportunity in the sessions to write for 10–15 minutes about your experience of the training programme.

   Note: for both types of diary, record and try to evaluate what happens in the class/session in English or your own language. Use a particular section of a file or use a separate notebook to write your diary.

3 Benefits of keeping a diary:
   There are many. For example, it provides a little time for teachers to consolidate and reflect quietly on their learning. Other benefits include:

   ....

   ....

4 Organising the diaries:
   Before starting your diary, discuss and decide with the other teachers and your trainer what exactly you wish to do with your diary, once it is finished. Do you wish to show all or parts of it to others? Do you wish to keep it completely confidential? Your trainer can help you to decide.

5 What you can write about:
   There is no fixed agenda, but the following points may help you to get started. Write about:
   (a) something that happened or something that worked well / did not work well in class or in a training session
   (b) something you read about / discussed with reference to a class or training session
   (c) your priorities, beliefs, principles, generalisations, understandings, insights, assumptions, feelings, critical incidents, questions, problems related to your experience of the class / training session

   The following phrases might also help you to get started:
   Today in class I noticed that...
   I now realise that...

   Your trainer will give you other phrases if you need them.

At first, you might find writing a diary difficult, but persevere. Good luck!

© Cambridge University Press 2001 Photocopiable

Worksheet 26 'We can do it!' Self-esteem, us and our learners

(see Task 2.9)

This worksheet will help you to identify practical recommendations for enhancing learners' self-esteem.

PART 1

Before reading the rest of this worksheet, spend ten minutes on your own reflecting on and completing one or two of the following sentences. Make notes if you wish.

1 I have a good day at work when…
2 One of my greatest strengths as an educator is…
3 As a teacher I am good at…
4 As a teacher I am not good at…
5 What I would most like one of my colleagues to say to me is…

PART 2

Read the following three quotations related to the topic of self-esteem.

What is self-esteem?

> If you have self-esteem, you feel that you are a good, worthwhile person, and for that reason you behave confidently.
>
> (*Collins Cobuild English Language Dictionary*)

Few would argue that self-esteem is not central to the issue of the education of young people…

> education means more than the learning of academic rules. If we can help children to understand themselves better and to feel more confident about themselves then they are going to be in a stronger position to be able to cope with the inevitable stresses of life and to be better citizens. Teachers are in an ideal role to be able to influence this development. Self-esteem enhancement contributes positively towards both academic achievement and towards personal and social development.
>
> (Lawrence, 1987: xi)

 © Cambridge University Press 2001 Photocopiable

(Worksheet 26 continued)

Yet the challenge of developing learners' self-esteem is not without its difficulty...

> 'We seem to spend so much time moaning about problems and difficulties – and they are very real difficulties – that it can be hard to keep spirits up. ....If one person says something negative, then it can lead to negativity all round, but if one person is positive...'. Teachers are under great stress. ...And they put themselves under pressure from their own self-critical voices and perfectionism. In the current climate, it takes a bold teacher and a bold school to find time to devote to enhancing self-esteem.
>
> (Kahn, 1993)

PART 3

You will have 20–30 minutes for this part of the task.

1 Five minutes: in pairs, exchange information about your completed sentences from Part 1 above.

   What do you have in common with each other? What differences are there?

2 Five minutes: discuss the following questions related to the second and third quotations:

   Do you both agree with the quotations? Why? Do you both disagree with the quotations? Why?

3 'It takes a bold teacher and a bold school to find time to devote to enhancing self-esteem'. (Kahn)

   In what practical ways can we enhance our learners' self-esteem?

   Ten minutes: try to think of at least *one practical recommendation* for enhancing your learners' self-esteem, and be ready to share your idea with the others.

Worksheet 27 'We can do it!' Practical recommendations for...

(see Task 2.9)

This worksheet will help you to record different practical recommendations related to a particular topic you are interested in investigating.

Practical recommendations for ....

1

2

3

4

5

Date:

© Cambridge University Press 2001 Photocopiable

Worksheet 28 What do I understand by the topic 'x'? (What? Why? Who? etc.)

(see Task 3.2)

This worksheet will help you to: (a) focus on a particular topic by defining it, and (b) identify difficulties you experience concerning the topic.

Topic: ....

Please consider individually the topic selected. Complete the nine related points below. Leave a space blank if you do not have anything to write about it. You can work through the points in any order. Be ready to show your completed worksheet to your colleagues and/or your trainer. Spend about 15 minutes on this worksheet.

1 *What* I think it means or is	
2 *What* I think it does not mean	
3 *Why* is this topic important?	
4 *Who* is involved?	
5 *Where* and *when* does this take place?	
6 *What* I do in school or class	
7 *What* I like about this topic in school or class	
8 *What* I find difficult about this topic	
9 Other comments	

Name: Date:

© Cambridge University Press 2001 Photocopiable

Worksheet 29 What do we already do in school or class regarding the topic 'x'? Find someone who...

(see Task 3.3)

This worksheet will help you to focus on a particular topic by sharing your professional experience related to it, and to identify practical recommendations concerning this topic.

Topic: ....

1 With a pen or pencil and your worksheet, join the other teachers in a group. Then mingle or mix, as if you were at a party, and talk to the other teachers about the points below. Ask questions based on the partially complete sentences (your trainer will give you examples of the types of questions required).

2 When you find someone who answers a question affirmatively, write that person's name in the space provided; in addition, try to find out a little more information about this teacher's experience by asking a few more related questions.

3 Speak to as many different teachers as possible in the 10–15 minutes that you have for this activity. Be ready afterwards to tell the whole group something that you have learnt about another teacher or other teachers.

Find someone who...

(Teacher's name)   (Partially completed sentences)

1 ....

2 ....

3 ....

4 ....

5 ....

EXTRA ACTIVITY

If you have time, consider the following questions: *Was anyone able to give you a practical recommendation for implementing the topic with learners? Who? What was the advice?*

Be ready to share this information with the others.

Name: Date:

   © Cambridge University Press 2001 Photocopiable

Worksheet 30 Do we agree that...?

(see Task 3.4)

This worksheet will help you to (a) establish what you already know about a particular topic, (b) discuss related key aspects, and (c) identify practical recommendations related to it for school and the classroom.

Topic: ....

PART 1

Fill in the name of the topic you are investigating in the space above. Read each of the statements that your trainer has selected and decide individually if you agree strongly (✓✓), agree (✓), disagree (✗), disagree strongly (✗✗), or don't know (?). Put the appropriate response in the boxes provided below. You may also make notes in the spaces provided if you wish, explaining your choices. Spend a maximum of 10 minutes on this. Be ready to share your views with another teacher.

Statement 1
(Write ✓✓, ✓, ✗✗, ✗ or ? here:) ☐
Notes:

Statement 2
☐
Notes:

Statement 3
☐
Notes:

PART 2

In pairs, compare your responses to Part 1 with those of your partner; do you agree or disagree with each other? Try to identify at least one practical recommendation for your learners to achieve something relevant to your topic, as follows:

When .... *we teachers / our learners / the teaching materials should...*

You will have at least 10 minutes for Part 2. Be ready to share your recommendation(s) with the others.

Name: Date:

© Cambridge University Press 2001 Photocopiable   259

Worksheet 31 Understanding key terms related to a specific topic

(see Task 3.7)

This worksheet will help you to understand and use specialist terms related to the topic identified.

Topic: ....

PART 1

Individually, consider the list of terms you have been given for the topic. How well do you understand them? Classify and write the terms (in pen if you are sure, and in pencil if you are less sure) in the appropriate section of the grid below according to whether you (1) understand them; (2) are not sure, or (3) have no idea. You have 5–10 minutes to complete Part 1.

1 I understand these terms, and feel confident using them	2 I am not sure about these terms	3 I have no idea about these terms

PART 2

Compare your response to Part 1 with that of another teacher. Can you help each other with any difficulties? You have 5–10 minutes for this; be ready to report to the other teachers.

EXTRA ACTIVITY

If you finish before the others, try to use some of the above terms to describe (a) yourself as a teacher/learner, (b) your learners, or (c) another aspect of language teaching and learning.

Name: Date:

 © Cambridge University Press 2001 Photocopiable

Worksheet 32 Preparing a debate: instructions
(see Task 3.9)

This worksheet will help you to explore a topic by formally debating an issue related to it.

For the debate you choose *one* of three possible roles (your trainer will give you further information about each role):

- a member of the team *for* the motion, i.e. the topic to be debated (with a maximum of four members); this team agrees with the motion

- a member of the team *against* the motion (with a maximum of four members; this team does not agree with, or opposes, the motion

- a member of the audience

Now read the *rules for the debate* carefully:

1 The two debating teams prepare their arguments (either for or against), while the other teachers representing members of the audience prepare questions to put to the teams. A maximum of 30 minutes is allowed for all participants' preparation. The trainer will help when needed during the preparation phase.

2 The trainer or a teacher will moderate the debate. At the beginning of the debate, each debating team in turn has a maximum of five minutes to present its arguments to the others. After both teams have spoken, each team has one minute to comment on the other team's arguments and/or to sum up their own arguments.

3 The members of the audience then have an opportunity to ask members of the debating teams their questions. They first identify themselves, and then ask their question. Questions can be addressed to both teams, or to one in particular.

4 After the debate has finished, there is a formal vote by members of the audience, who choose the team which has best convinced them with their arguments.

Worksheet 33 The benefits of investigating in class: teachers' perspectives

(see Task 4.1)

This worksheet will help to (a) familiarise you with the potential benefits to you of investigating in class, and (b) enhance your confidence to investigate in class.

Below is a list of potential benefits of investigating (A–F). Read the statements (1–6) made by teachers who have been investigating in their classes. Match each benefit to one of the teacher statements by writing the corresponding number in the space provided (the first one has already been done for you). You will have 5 minutes for this. Be ready to discuss your response with your colleagues.

Potential benefits

Investigating helps:

A ...6.... teachers to develop practical investigating skills
B .... teachers to value their learners' opinions about what happens in class
C .... teachers to perceive their work differently (raising new questions)
D .... other teachers to learn
E .... teachers feel more confident in their own ability to change things successfully
F .... teachers to learn not only about the topic they are focusing on but also about other topics

Teachers' statements/perspectives

1 Doing this work has made me realise that not only was I learning about how to teach writing but about how a second language is learned (or acquired) as well.
2 It is evident from the learners' feedback and from comments I made that progress was made…. This feeling of success is going to be my starting point for future investigating…. I'm conscious of the fact that there is a lot to do, but at least the first step has been taken.
3 Investigating has helped me to value my learners' judgement and to make up my mind to ask for their opinion about our classroom practice more often and formally than before.
4 I hope my colleagues will take advantage of my work. I'm aware of the fact that anything can be improved, and so I hereby invite all of you to risk story-telling in your classrooms.

  © Cambridge University Press 2001 Photocopiable

(Worksheet 33 continued)

5 I have learnt a lot through this period, questions that I had not considered before.

6 I have spent three weeks experimenting with different things related to this work. I gave children a questionnaire to find out about their feelings about English and writing; I gave them adapted activities to improve this skill; I read a lot about general teaching and about writing in particular.... From now on, I will try to do something similar when I have any difficult skill or topic to improve.

EXTRA ACTIVITY

If you have time, think of any other benefits of investigating in class. What difficulties do you think you might face when investigating in class yourself?

Worksheet 34 Which data collection method?

(see Task 4.2)

This worksheet will help you to (a) consider the appropriateness of different data collection methods, (b) select relevant ones, and (c) evaluate them afterwards.

Data collection method	Description: for the period of investigating, the teacher...	Who wishes to experiment with which method, when	Comment after experimenting with method
1 Photographs	...takes photos of learners in action in class or school (see Task 4.3)		
2 Lesson plans	...collects lesson plans (see Task 4.8)		
3 Classroom diary	...keeps a diary about what happens in class (see Task 2.7)		
4 Learner questionnaire	...writes a simple questionnaire for learners to respond to, focusing on topic in question (see Task 4.4)		
5 What did you learn today?	... asks this question at the end of lessons, and learners respond on slips of paper (see Task 4.5)		
6 Audio or video recording	...records part of lesson and listens to or watches it afterwards (see Option 26 on p. 115)		
7 Learner-produced materials	...selects written work produced by a learner related to topic (see Option 28 on p. 119)		

© Cambridge University Press 2001 Photocopiable

(Worksheet 34 continued)

Data collection method	Description: for the period of investigating, the teacher...	Who wishes to experiment with which method, when	Comment after experimenting with method
8 *Mini-case study*	...records in writing how an individual learner responds to topic (see Task 4.6)		
9 *Interview*	...informally interviews an individual learner regarding topic (see Task 4.7)		

© Cambridge University Press 2001 Photocopiable

Worksheet 35 Consulting learners (1): planning, administering and evaluating a simple questionnaire

(see Task 4.4)

This worksheet will help to you plan, conduct and evaluate a learner questionnaire related to the topic your group is investigating.

Session 1. Planning

Form small sub-groups of three or four teachers, preferably so that you are working with colleagues who are teaching learners of the same age group. Consider the following question:

What are the advantages and disadvantages of using a questionnaire to find out about learners' views?

Together, write a brief, simple questionnaire to conduct with your learners in order to investigate an aspect of the topic chosen by the whole group. It is strongly recommended that each of you conduct the questionnaire with only one class of learners, otherwise you will end up with too much data to collate and interpret. (For practical reasons, it may not be possible for everyone in your sub-group to conduct a questionnaire with a class, but there should be at least one teacher in each sub-group who can do so.)

While planning, bear in mind the characteristics of an effective questionnaire. For example, you need clear aims, as well as a clear idea of how to report your data (bar graphs, pie charts, etc.). Your trainer will help you with this and other aspects of the task. You will have at least one hour to plan and write your questionnaire. Make sure you take away a copy of the questionnaire with you at the end of the training session!

Conducting the questionnaire

Give your learners your questionnaire to fill in, and collect in the completed questionnaires in time to bring them to the training session on the agreed date. If possible, begin analysing and interpreting your data before the second session. Good luck!

 © Cambridge University Press 2001 Photocopiable

(Worksheet 35 continued)

Session 2: Evaluating the results

In the same sub-groups as for Session 1, collate the results of the questionnaires that have been conducted. Together, analyse and interpret the results, preparing to report to the rest of the group, in the format you agreed on in your plan. Consider the following questions:

What, if anything, have you learnt about the topic you are investigating?

Was there anything surprising in the results? What? Why?

What practical recommendations are there, if any, for the topic in your future teaching?

You will have 5–10 minutes to present your results and answer any questions from your colleagues. Ask your trainer for the materials you need to present your results (paper, pens, overhead transparencies, etc.). You will have at least an hour to prepare for your presentation.

Reporting the results: sub-groups present their results, or everyone views the posters.

Further action

Is there another (related) topic you would like to write a questionnaire on?

© Cambridge University Press 2001 Photocopiable

Worksheet 36 Ten characteristics of an effective questionnaire

(see Task 4.4)

This worksheet will help you to write an effective questionnaire.

Consider the following points before writing your questionnaire:

1	*Aim*	The aim of the questionnaire should be as clear as possible; for example, ask yourself/yourselves which precise question(s) you wish to answer with it. Plan carefully; ask your trainer for advice. Remember, small is beautiful.
2	*Ethics*	Explain the purpose of the questionnaire – you can also do this briefly at the top of the questionnaire – and what you will do with the results. Ask the learners to respond frankly; if you think they will not respond in this way, make the questionnaire anonymous. At the end of the questionnaire, thank the respondents for co-operating, and tell them that feedback concerning the results of the questionnaire will be available, if they are interested.
3	*Length*	The questionnaire should be short and easy to answer (one or two pages?).
4	*Layout*	The layout – how the text is arranged on the page – should be as neat, professional and clear as possible (word-process the text if possible; leave plenty of spaces).
5	*Language*	Consider carefully which language to use for the instructions and/or questions: the respondents' mother tongue, or English if you think they will read and comprehend it satisfactorily. The words you use should also be clear and unambiguous.
6	*Response*	The response method – how the learners show their opinion – e.g. by a non-linguistic response such as a tick, or circling an answer – should be very clear; give an example of the appropriate response. Such non-linguistic responses are easier. Or use so-called 'structured questions' with statements requiring a *yes/no* response. Especially recommended for young children are 'happy faces', (☺ ☻). Or use 'open questions'. For example, 'Which song did you like best?', 'Why?' Vary the question types in order to avoid tedium, but not too much, as this might cause the respondents too much difficulty.
7	*Order*	Give the respondents an easy start to the questionnaire, arousing their interest with questions eliciting personal information (date, class, age, etc.); use open questions after structured ones.

© Cambridge University Press 2001 Photocopiable

(Worksheet 36 continued)

8	*Pilot*	Try out the questionnaire on somebody else before you use it. Perhaps a colleague could help in this respect, as he or she may be able to identify difficulties you were unaware of; modify the questionnaire accordingly. Maybe pilot the questionnaire with learners who are not in the class you wish to investigate.
9	*Reporting*	The results should be easy to analyse, collate and report (e.g. visually, with bar graphs, etc.). Will you present the results orally or use a poster? Plan this carefully.
10	*Other*	Can you think of any other characteristics of an effective questionnaire?

(adapted from Youngman, 1984)

© Cambridge University Press 2001 Photocopiable

Worksheet 37 Consulting our learners (2): What did you learn today? Sample data
(see Task 4.5)

This worksheet will encourage you to consult your learners by asking them 'What did you learn today?' at the end of a lesson(s).

INTRODUCTION

While teaching English to a group of French learners aged 12 to 13, I regularly asked them 'What did you learn today?' at the end of lessons. Individually the learners then wrote down their ideas in French on a separate slip of paper. Below you will find all the learners' statements that I collected in at the end of one lesson.

PART 1

Individually, read the statements and consider the questions below; you will have 10–15 minutes to do this.

Learner statements

My translations of the statments are presented below in random order.

1 I learnt to say: history, coursebook, travelling.
2 I learnt to ask questions in English about a person's identity.
3 I learnt to say: I was born, I was born in…, work, coursebook, coursebook work, travelling.
4 We learnt how to write a summary in English; I learnt the words: born, gym, physics.
5 We learnt how to fill in a form in English and to spell our first name in English letters.
6 I learnt more English.
7 We learnt how to fill in a form in English.
8 I learnt lots of words in English.
9 We learnt the names of school subjects in English, for example: mathematics, English, French, gym, music, physics, history.
10 I learnt to say: biology.
11 I learnt to say: I don't like.
12 We learnt to repeat the questions on the photocopy, to ask questions in English, to say what we liked.
13 We learnt to ask questions about people (what they liked), and to fill in forms in English.
14 We learnt school subjects in English, for example, history, French, physics.

 © Cambridge University Press 2001 Photocopiable

(Worksheet 37 continued)

15 Today I learnt new words in English, and to say what we liked and also things we didn't want to do any more.
16 I learnt to express what I like and dislike; I learnt how to write school subjects in English.

Questions

1 What do the statements have in common and how are they different?
2 In your opinion, how typical are the statements for 12- to 13-year-olds, in terms of how they reflect the learners' cognitive development?
3 Would you consider asking your learners the same question at the end of a lesson? Why? Why not? If you do this, what might the long-term benefits be to you as teachers and to your learners?

PART 2

In pairs, compare your answers to the above questions; you will have 10 minutes to do this. Be ready to share your ideas with the rest of the group.

© Cambridge University Press 2001 Photocopiable

Worksheet 38 Writing a learner profile
(see Task 4.6)

This worksheet will help you to write about an individual learner of your choice, and discuss him or her with a colleague.

PART 1

Choose a learner that you wish to write about (your trainer will help you to do this). Then complete the first column below for this learner. There are six categories with suggestions as to what to write about for each one, but don't feel that you have to write about everything; only choose those topics that are appropriate, or that interest you. You will have 20 minutes for this activity.

	Learner 1	Learner 2
1 *Personal information* (age, sex, personality, family background, interests outside class, etc.)		
2 *Relationships* (with you, with other learners)		
3 *Attitudes* (e.g. to school, other school subjects, English)		
4 *Learning* (behaviour in class, likes/dislikes, strengths/weaknesses, etc.)		
5 *Development* (progress achieved, future progress, etc.)		
6 *Other comments*		

PART 2

In a training session, in pairs exchange information with a colleague about the learner you chose, and fill in the second column with notes about your colleague's learner. As you do so, identify at least one similarity and at least one difference between your learners. You will have 20 minutes for this activity. Be ready to report to the whole group.

Name: Date:

     © Cambridge University Press 2001 Photocopiable

Worksheet 39 An informal interview with a learner

(see Task 4.7)

This worksheet will help you to prepare and evaluate an interview with a learner.

	Learner 1	Learner 2
Part 1, before interview 1 Topic and aims of interview		
2 Name of interviewee (where appropriate); why have you chosen this learner?		
3 Date of interview. How long will it take?		
4 Are you going to record the interview?		
5 Is it a structured or semi-structured interview?		
Part 2, after interview 6 What did you learn about the topic as a result of the interview?		
7 What did you learn about giving interviews?		
8 Advice for teachers wishing to give interviews		

Name: Date:

© Cambridge University Press 2001 Photocopiable

Worksheet 40 Experimenting in class
(see Task 4.8)

This worksheet will help you to evaluate the effectiveness of a teaching idea that you have tried out in class.

After trying out a new idea in class, complete this worksheet by making notes in the spaces provided, spending a maximum of 15 minutes on it. Your trainer will check with you that you understand what is required for each of the seven questions. If you cannot think of anything to write for a particular item, don't worry, leave it blank.

1 Which teaching idea did you try out? (Give it a name, and describe it briefly.)

2 Where did you get the idea from? Why did you select it? What attracted you? What were your teaching aims?

3 What did the learners do? (See your lesson plan where appropriate.)

4 What do you think the learners learnt? What evidence do you have (where appropriate, photographs, questionnaire, learner profile, interview data, etc.)?

5 What did you do? (See your lesson plan where appropriate.)

6 What did you learn?

7 How worthwhile is/was the teaching idea? Will you use it again? If so, why? If not, why not?

(adapted from Ebbutt, cited in Hopkins, 1985: 49)

Comment from trainer or colleague:

Name: Date:

  © Cambridge University Press 2001 Photocopiable

Worksheet 41 Lesson plan sheet

(see Task 4.8)

This worksheet will help you to plan a lesson and to record what happened in it.

Class/group:

Date:

Remember to:

Stages	What I plan to do	What happened/comments
1		
2		
3		
4		
5		

New vocabulary/grammar to review in next lesson:

Homework:

© Cambridge University Press 2001 Photocopiable

Worksheet 42 Has this task helped me/us to learn?
(see Task 5.1)

This worksheet will help you to reflect on whether, how, or what a task or activity has helped you to learn.

Individually, consider the task or activity in question, and try to answer some of the following questions about it *from your personal perspective*, making notes if you wish. Please read all the questions before you start writing. Don't worry if you can't answer all of the questions – you can leave some blank. Spend about 10 minutes on the worksheet. Be ready to share your ideas with the other teachers and/or your trainer.

1 How successful was the task or activity in terms of the aims which were specified for it?

2 What have you learnt about the topic selected (increasing your knowledge, developing skills and attitudes, or something else)?

3 Is there anything you have learnt from this task or activity that is very important for your school, learners and/or yourself as a teacher? If so, what?

4 Is there anything you have learnt which is not directly connected with the topic selected? If so, what?

5 As a result of doing this task or activity, do you wish to modify your personal theory of educating, teaching and learning? If so, in what way?

6 What do you want to know or to do about the topic now, if anything? What help do you require to do this, if any?

7 Is there another topic(s) that you wish to investigate now? Which topic(s)? Why?

Name: Date:

Comment from trainer:

    © Cambridge University Press 2001 Photocopiable

Worksheet 43 Which learning strategies are helping us?

(see Task 5.2)

This worksheet will help you to (a) reflect on the ways in which you are learning and developing as a teacher, and (b) select relevant, effective learning strategies for the rest of the training programme.

PART 1

Read the descriptions of 15 strategies which may promote teachers' professional learning in Part 3 of this worksheet (see Worksheet 43 continued). Individually, reflect on one or more of the questions below with regard to these strategies. Ignore any items that are not relevant in your context. You may make notes in the spaces after each question, if you wish. You will have 20 minutes for Part 1. Be ready to share your ideas with other teachers.

1 Which strategies are most significant for your learning on the

   programme? Why? Please select five. ....

   ....

2 Can you give specific examples of some of the strategies from your

   own learning experience on the programme? ....

   ....

3 Are there any strategies missing in the light of your own learning

   experience on the programme? Which? ....

   ....

4 Further comments? ....

   ....

PART 2

In sub-groups of three or four teachers, discuss those questions above which you find most interesting with regard to the strategies. As you do so, try to consider the following questions:

What are the implications for our future professional learning?

Is there anything that we need to change in the way that we work together?

You will have 20 minutes for Part 2. Be ready to share your sub-group's ideas with the others.

Name: Date:

© Cambridge University Press 2001 Photocopiable

(Worksheet 43 continued)

PART 3

Examples of strategies which may help teachers to learn on training programmes (adapted from Lennon and James, 1995):

Agreeing on priorities (in teaching and for the training programme)	Developing a conceptual framework for teaching	Questioning assumptions about teaching
Articulating a personal theory of teaching	Discussing and sharing experiences and ideas	Reading about teaching
Clarifying ideas, questions, doubts	Evaluating teaching ideas, methods and materials	Reflecting on teaching
Consulting learners	Experiencing being a learner: observing and noticing	Self-evaluating
Considering alternative teaching practices	Experimenting in class	Supporting each other

 © Cambridge University Press 2001 Photocopiable

Worksheet 44 What I most like about our training programme is...

(see Task 5.3)

This worksheet will help you to reflect on aspects of your training programme to date, and to share these views, opinions and feelings with other teachers and your trainer.

What I most like about our programme is...

What I least like about our programme is...

I'm not quite sure about...

I found the following very useful...

I think our programme will...

So far one of the things I've learnt is...

I found the following surprising...

I've been reading about...

I'd like to ask if...

© Cambridge University Press 2001 Photocopiable

Worksheet 45 Making sense: reviewing and finding connections

(see Task 5.4)

This worksheet will help you to (a) review the different components (topics, tasks and activities) which you have covered on your training programme to date, (b) look for connections among these, and (c) consider any implications for your own teaching.

Work in sub-groups of three or four teachers. Your trainer will give each sub-group a set of cards, each card showing the name of a different component of your programme. (Please note that each sub-group has a different set of cards.)

PART 1 REVIEWING

In your sub-group, use the following questions to review each component/card together:

1 What was the aim of the topic/task/activity?
2 What did the trainer do?
3 What did you do?
4 What did you learn? What have you learnt since then?

You may make notes if you wish. You will have 15 minutes for Part 1.

PART 2 LOOKING FOR CONNECTIONS

Once you have reviewed all the individual components/cards, look for any connections or links among them. For example:

Topic 'x' is linked to topic 'y' because...

You will have 10 minutes to complete Part 2. Be ready to share your response to Parts 1 and 2 with the others.

 © Cambridge University Press 2001 Photocopiable

Worksheet 46 Applying our learning: looking back and looking ahead

(see Task 5.5)

This worksheet will help you to reflect on and discuss the relationship between what you have learnt on your training programme and your future teaching and professional development.

PART 1 INDIVIDUAL REVIEW AND REFLECTION: WHAT HAVE I LEARNT?

Individually, look back over the notes and materials that you have collected on the programme from the perspective of a learner and/or teacher, and consider the following question:

What learning points/principles are there which are significant in terms of your own future teaching practice and professional development (realistic strategies, techniques, activities, ideas, etc.)?

Make notes if you wish. Spend about 30 minutes on this activity, and be ready to share your ideas with the other teachers.

PART 2 SUB-GROUP ACTIVITY: COMPARING LEARNING POINTS WITH OTHERS

1 Discuss: in sub-groups of three or four teachers, compare your answers to the question in Part 1. Allow everyone in your sub-group to express their opinions, feelings or insights. What, if anything, do your opinions have in common? While not wanting you to ignore any constraints that you work under, emphasise what you feel you will be able to do realistically when teaching in the future, rather than emphasising what you cannot do!

2 Record your ideas: on the 5–10 slips of paper your trainer will give you, write down statements or questions summarising the key points from your sub-group's discussion that you all agree are important. For example, 'We now feel confident to use warm-up activities.' Please note that the slips you produce are to be shared with the rest of the group and the trainer. Choose someone in your sub-group to report to the whole group. You will have 30 minutes for Part 2.

PART 3 APPLYING OUR LEARNING TO OUR FUTURE TEACHING AND DEVELOPMENT

Whole-group comparison: in whole-group mode and time allowing, read out the statements on your sub-group's slips of paper, and compare and discuss with the rest of the group the points that emerge. Try to produce a written summary of these points to take away with you; your trainer will suggest how.

© Cambridge University Press 2001 Photocopiable

Worksheet 47 Applying our learning: a checklist
(see Task 5.5)

This worksheet will help you to record what you have learnt on the training programme in terms of (a) what you can apply in your teaching (teaching ideas, techniques and activities), and (b) realistic strategies for your future professional development.

1

2

3

4

5

6

7

8

9

10

Name: Date:

  © Cambridge University Press 2001 Photocopiable

Worksheet 48 Teacher portfolios

(see Task 5.6)

This worksheet will help you to (a) evaluate your learning, development and progress by means of a portfolio, and (b) identify opportunities for further investigation and development.

WHAT IS A PORTFOLIO, AND WHY KEEP ONE?

It is a way of collecting and organising evidence of your learning, development and progress throughout your training programme. If appropriate, you may put the items for your portfolio in a special file. Discuss with your trainer the possible benefits of keeping a portfolio.

WHAT EXACTLY IS INVOLVED IN KEEPING A PORTFOLIO?

Stage 1: Collect

Collect completed worksheets and other related documents you have produced during the programme. Write your name and date on these items; this will help you and others to identify them and locate them in a time sequence.

Stage 2: Review

From time to time, look back over the different materials that you have collected, and select important items, separating these for your portfolio. It should not include everything that you have produced; instead, try to reflect the highlights of your learning, development and progress. The following questions may help you to select items:

1 *Reviewing:* What are the highlights in the materials to date? What is significant, meaningful or surprising? Why? Do you now feel differently about a particular task or activity since you originally completed it ('Now I realise that...')? Which one(s)? Why?
2 *Changing:* Have there been any significant changes in your knowledge, skills or attitudes? What? How did this happen?
3 *Action:* What are your strengths, weaknesses and opportunities? What would you now like to know or do related to an item(s) you have collected?
4 *Questions:* Do you have any questions for the other teachers or a trainer? Is there something you do not understand and need help with?

Stage 3: Report

What will we do with our portfolios once we have collected the material? One possibility is to discuss your portfolio with another teacher, and in the process try to identify opportunities for further professional investigation/investigating. Where appropriate, agree on a date for such a discussion in a training session.

© Cambridge University Press 2001 Photocopiable 283

Worksheet 49 Planning an informal presentation
(see Task 5.7)

This worksheet will help you to plan your informal presentation systematically.

In sub-groups, complete this form about your presentation, and give it to your trainer. You will have at least 30 minutes to complete it.

1 What are our aims for the presentation? How will we communicate them? What do we hope that the audience will learn?

2 What resources do we need (paper, glue, card for posters, coloured pens, photocopier, overhead projector, etc.)?

3 How much time do we have for the presentation? Who will keep time?

4 Who will do what during the presentation? (Will one of us present, or more than one?)

5 What will the audience do during the presentation (listen, participate actively in some other way, ask questions, etc.)?

6 What will we give the audience (handouts, worksheets, bibliographies, etc.)?

7 Questions for the trainer:

Names: Date:

Comment from trainer:

© Cambridge University Press 2001 Photocopiable

Worksheet 50 Evaluating informal presentations
(see Task 5.7)

This worksheet will help you to describe and evaluate other teachers' informal presentations.

Work individually. While you are watching, or after you have watched, your colleagues' presentation, evaluate their presentation by considering the points listed below. Make notes in the spaces provided, if you wish. Be ready to share your ideas with the others.

1 *Describing:* What did the presenter(s) do?

2 *Describing:* What did I/we do during the presentation?

3 *Evaluation:* What did I/we learn about the focus of the presentation?

4 *Evaluation:* Something I/we really liked about the presentation:

5 *Evaluation:* Something I/we think the presenter(s) can improve next time they present:

6 *Evaluation:* Something I/we learnt about giving an effective presentation:

Name(s):   Date:

© Cambridge University Press 2001 Photocopiable   285

Worksheet 51 Some ways of sharing our learning in the wider educational community
(see Task 5.8)

This worksheet will help you to evaluate the appropriateness and relevance of different ways of sharing your learning with other people in the wider educational community.

Read about the four ways of sharing below, and then discuss the following questions in sub-groups of three or four.

Which ways do you feel are possible or useful? What are the advantages and disadvantages of each way? Are there other ways in which you can share your learning?

Be ready to tell the whole group what you think. Make notes if you wish in the spaces provided. You will have 15 minutes for the worksheet.

Giving a public talk

Give a public talk at a local teachers' centre or a teachers' conference on an aspect of your work. Are there such centres or events in your region or country? Do you attend them? If so, how useful are they? If not, why not?

Advantages   **Disadvantages**

Producing a poster

Produce a poster summary of your work and present it at a teachers' centre or conference, such as the IATEFL annual conference, where, instead of addressing an audience in a lecture hall, you exhibit and stand by your own poster in a special area and talk to interested teachers and delegates as they pass by.

Advantages   **Disadvantages**

 © Cambridge University Press 2001 Photocopiable

(Worksheet 51 continued)

Publishing an article

Publish an article in a local, national or international professional journal, magazine, newsletter or publishers' newsletter. Which publications do you know of this type? Which do you prefer? Why? Is there one that is suitable for publishing an article that you could write?

Advantages   **Disadvantages**

Writing a report

Write a brief report for other interested teachers in your group or at your school to read. This could take the form of an academic report with a formal structure, or a more informal text.

Advantages   **Disadvantages**

Other

Advantages   **Disadvantages**

Worksheet 52 Our English teacher will explain: role-play

(see Task 5.8)

This worksheet will help you to organise a role-play in which you discuss with parents the teaching of English at your school.

Choose one of the roles.

Role 1: Teacher

You are an English teacher addressing a group of parents at a parents' meeting at the beginning of the school year (you have been asked by the school director to talk for a few minutes). Explain the aims and methodology of English teaching in your school or classroom. Before you start, consider the following questions:

Which points will you emphasise? What changes have there been recently in the teaching of English? How does the teaching of English fit in with the general school curriculum? How can parents help both teachers and their children?

Role 2: Parent(s)

You are a learner's parent(s). After listening to your child's English teacher talking about English in the school at a parents' meeting at the beginning of the school year, you are able to ask questions. Before the role-play, prepare some questions to ask the teacher. For example: *Will there be a lot of homework? How are learners assessed? Will the learners speak English in class? Will your child need a dictionary? If so, which one?*

Role 3: Observer

You do not take an active part in the role-play discussion. Rather, you will provide feedback afterwards. To do this, you observe, listen to, and take note of, the following aspects of the role-play: *Which strategies used by the teacher to communicate with the parents were successful? Please give examples. Were there any problems in the discussion, and how were they were dealt with? Please give examples. Which questions were asked by the parents?*

 © Cambridge University Press 2001 Photocopiable

Bibliography

Allwright, R. (1988). Autonomy and Individualisation in Whole-Class Instruction. In A. Brookes and P. Grundy (eds.), *Individualisation and Autonomy in Language Learning, ELT Documents* 131. London: Modern English Publications in association with The British Council.

Bampfield, A. (producer) (1997). *Looking at Language Classrooms* (four video cassettes). Cambridge: Cambridge University Press. Trainer's Guide by D. Lubelska and M. Matthews.

Bell, J., Bush, T., Fox, A., Goodey, J. and Goulding, S. (eds.) (1984). *Conducting Small-Scale Investigations in Educational Management.* London: Paul Chapman Publishing in association with The Open University.

Bolam, R. (1981). Conceptualising Inservice. In Hopkins (1986).

Bolitho, R. and Tomlinson, B. (1995). *Discover English.* Oxford: Heinemann.

Bowers, R. and Brumfit, C. (eds.) (1991). *Applied Linguistics and English Language Teaching. Review of ELT,* 2, 1. London: Modern English Publications in association with The British Council.

Calderhead, J. (1990). Conceptualising and Evaluating Teachers' Professional Learning. *European Journal of Teacher Education,* 13, 3.

Calderhead, J. and Gates, P. (eds.) (1993). *Conceptualizing Reflection in Teacher Development.* London: Falmer Press.

Carr, W. and Kemmis, S. (1983). *Becoming Critical: Knowing through Action Research.* Victoria: Deakin University Press.

Cockburn, A. (1996). Strategies to Help You Fight Stress. *Times Educational Supplement,* 9 February.

Dam, L. (1991). Mimeo extract from paper given at a teachers' conference held in Zaragoza, Spain.

Department for Education and Employment (1995). *The School Curriculum: A Brief Guide.* United Kingdom: Crown Copyright.

Dickinson, L. (1993). Talking Shop: Aspects of Autonomous Learning. *ELT Journal,* 47, 4.

Dickinson, L. and Carver, D. (1980). Learning How to Learn: Steps towards Self-Direction in Foreign Language Learning in Schools. *ELT Journal,* 35, 1.

Edge, J. (1989). *Mistakes and Correction*. Harlow: Longman.

Edge, J. and Richards, K. (eds.) (1993). *Teachers Develop Teachers Research: Papers on Classroom Research and Teacher Development*. Oxford: Heinemann.

Elliot J. and Ebbutt, D. (1985). *Facilitating Educational Action Research in Schools*. York: Longman.

Ellis, G. and Sinclair, B. (1989). *Learning to Learn English*. Cambridge: Cambridge University Press.

Ellis, R. (1990). Activities and Procedures for Teacher Training. *ELT Journal*, **40**, 2.

Eraut, M. (1994). The Acquisition and Use of Educational Theory by Beginning Teachers. In Harvard and Hodkinson (1994).

Freire, P. (1972). *Pedagogy of the Oppressed*. London: Penguin.

Fullan, M. (1993). *Change Forces: Probing the Depths of Educational Reform*. London: Falmer Press.

Gobierno Vasco. (1992). *Diseño Curricular Base de la Comunidad Autónoma Vasca*, Spain.

Griffiths, M. and Tann, S. (1992). Using Reflective Practice to Link Personal and Public Theories. *Journal of Education for Teaching*, **18**, 1.

Guardian (1994). Comment. A Big Idea that Takes its Time. 25 July.

Gutierrez, M. (1996). Students Committed to Equality Project. *Comunidad Escolar*. Spain, 20 March (Translated by the author from the original article 'Estudiantes compremetidos en un proyecto de igualdad'.)

Halliwell, S. (1992). *Teaching English in the Primary Classroom*. Harlow: Longman.

Harvard, G. and Hodkinson, P. (eds.) (1994). *Action and Reflection in Teacher Education*. Norwood, NJ: Ablex.

Head, K. and Taylor, P. (1997) *Readings in Teacher Development*. Oxford: Heinemann.

Holt, J. (1982). *How Children Fail*. London: Penguin.

Hopkins, D. (1985). *A Teacher's Guide to Classroom Research*. Milton Keynes: Open University Press.

Hopkins, D. (ed.) (1986). *In-service Training and Educational Development: An International Survey*. London: Croom Helm.

Kahn, T. (1993). It's Time We All Stood up for Teacher. *Observer,* 28 November.

Klein, R. and Neumark, V. (1997). In Her Element. *Times Educational Supplement*, 3 January.

Kolb, D. (1984). *Experiential Learning*. Englewood Cliffs, NJ: Prentice Hall.

Lamb, M. (1995). The Consequences of INSET. *ELT Journal*, **49**, 1.

Lawrence, D. (1987). *Enhancing Self-Esteem in the Classroom*. London: Paul Chapman Publishing.

Lennon, A. and James, P. (1995). What Do Successful Trainees Do to Promote their Professional Development? Unpublished paper presented at the second IATEFL Teachers Develop Teachers Research Conference, Cambridge.

Lightbown, P. M. and Spada, N. (1999). *How Languages are Learned*. New Edition. Oxford: Oxford University Press.

Littlewood, W. (1981). *Communicative Language Teaching: An Introduction*. Cambridge: Cambridge University Press.

Maley, A. (1991). Classroom Practice: An Overview. In Bowers and Brumfit (1991).

Ministry of Education and Science, Madrid, Spain *(1995)*. *Core Curriculum, Foreign Languages, Primary and Secondary Education*.

Nisbet, J. and Watt, J. (1984). Case Study. In Bell *et al.* (1984).

Nunan, D. (1989). *Designing Tasks for the Communicative Classroom*. Cambridge: Cambridge University Press.

Parrott, M. (1991). Teacher Education: Factors Relating to Programme Design. In Bowers and Brumfit (1991).

Parrott, M. (1993). *Tasks for Language Teachers*. Cambridge: Cambridge University Press.

Pinker, S. (1996). *The Language Instinct*. London: Penguin.

Pollard, A. and Tann, S. (second edition, 1993). *Reflective Teaching in the Primary School*. London: Cassell.

Richards, J. C. and Lockhart, C. (1994). *Reflective Teaching in Second Language Classrooms*. Cambridge: Cambridge University Press.

Richards, J. C., Platt, J. and Weber, H. (1985). *Longman Dictionary of Applied Linguistics*. Harlow: Longman.

Richards, J. C. and Rodgers, T. (1982). Method: Approach, Design and Procedure. *TESOL Quarterly,* **16**, 2.

Roberts, J. (1998). *Language Teacher Education*. London: Arnold.

Sallabank, J. and Brussaards, I. (1995). Effective Presentations. *IATEFL Newsletter*, **128**.

Sancho, J. M. and Hernández, F. M. (1994). Interview with Donald Schön. La práctica reflexiva: aceptar y aprender de la discrepancia. *Cuadernos de Pedagogía*, February, **222**. Spain.

Scott, W. A. and Ytreberg, L H. (1990). *Teaching English to Children*. Harlow: Longman.

Seaton, B. (1982). *A Handbook of English Language Teaching Terms and Practice*. London: Macmillan.

Simons, G. F., Vasques C. and Harris, P. R. (1993). *Transcultural Leadership: Empowering the Diverse Workforce*. Houston: Gulf.

Spratt, M. (1994). *English for the Teacher.* Cambridge: Cambridge University Press.

Stenhouse, L. (1975). *An Introduction to Curriculum Research and Development.* Oxford: Heinemann.

Tann, S. (1993). Eliciting Student Teachers' Personal Theories. In Calderhead and Gates (1993).

Thornbury, S. (1991). Metaphors We Work by: EFL and its Metaphors. *ELT Journal,* **45**, 3.

Thornbury, S. (1997). *About Language.* Cambridge: Cambridge University Press.

Tripp, D. (1993). *Critical Incidents in Teaching. Developing Professional Judgement.* London: Routledge.

Ur, P. and Wright, A. (1992). *Five-Minute Activities: A Resource Book of Short Activities.* Cambridge: Cambridge University Press.

Wajnryb, R. (1992). *Classroom Observation Tasks.* Cambridge: Cambridge University Press.

Wallace, M. J. (1991). *Training Foreign Language Teachers: A Reflective Approach.* Cambridge: Cambridge University Press.

Wallace M. J. (1998). *Action Research for Language Teachers.* Cambridge: Cambridge University Press.

Ward, C. (1996). Encouraged to Tell Tales. *Times Educational Supplement,* 15 November.

Weir, C. and Roberts, J. (1994). *Evaluation in ELT.* Oxford: Basil Blackwell.

Wenden, A. and Rubin, J. (eds.) (1987). *Learner Strategies in Language Learning.* Hemel Hempstead: Prentice Hall International.

White, R. V. (1988). *The ELT Curriculum: Design, Innovation and Management.* Oxford: Basil Blackwell.

White, R. V. and Arndt, V. (1991). *Process Writing.* Harlow: Longman.

Widdowson, H. G. (1984). The incentive value of theory in teacher education. *ELT Journal,* 38, 2.

Williams, M. and Burden, R. L. (1997). *Psychology for Language Teachers: A Social Constructivist Approach.* Cambridge: Cambridge University Press.

Woodward, T. (1992). *Ways of Training.* Harlow: Longman.

Wragg, E. C. (1997). *The Cubic Curriculum.* London: Routledge.

Wright, T. (1994). *Investigating English.* London: Edward Arnold.

Youngman, M. B. (1984). Designing Questionnaires. In Bell *et al.* (1984).

Index

NOTE: Tasks are in **bold** print. Worksheets are in *italics*.

action research 14–15
  aims and nature of 15
  see also investigating
advantages and disadvantages of a topic
  81, 196
agreeing, or disagreeing 41, 83–5, 237
Applying our learning: a checklist (47)
  282
  looking back and looking ahead **(5.5)**
  135–8, 210–14, *(46)* 281
Are we speaking the same language? **(1.7)**
  43–5, 170, *(12)* 238
articles
  advantages and disadvantages (6.39.1)
  218
  publishing **(5.8)** 146, 287
assumptions, examining 53, 68, 76–9,
  192–3
attitude 7
  see also teachers' attitudes
audio-diaries 115
audio-recordings 115
autonomy, of teachers 12

beliefs, examining 76–9, 192–3
Benefits of investigating in class: teachers'
  perspectives **(4.1)** 101–2, 200–1, *(33)*
  262–3
bibliographies 63–6, 158–9, 182–4
  sample for teachers (6.20.2) 182–3
  suggestions for trainers (6.20.1) 182
blackboard/whiteboard 26
books
  recommending and sharing 63–6
  reviews **(2.6, 3.8)** 16, 66, 97
bottom-up approach 141, 152
  defined 46
brainstorming 81

case studies
  extract from a formal (6.32.1) 203–4
  framework for mini 117 Fig. 4.2
  ineffective in-service training (6.3)
  153–4

teacher classroom research project (6.4)
  154–6
cassette recorder 26
change
  defined 46
  extracts from a conversation about
  professional (6.36) 210–13
  and teacher learning 9–10
change agents, defined 46
change in education 45–7
  promoting 45–7
classroom research *see* investigating
collaborative learning 161
community of learning 17
comprehensible input, defined 92
concepts
  mapping 38–40, 235
  sample list (6.10.1) 164
  use of teaching 43–5
  using key 39
conceptual frameworks **(6.10)** 38–40,
  164–5, 235
confidence 12, 72–4, 101
connections, making 133–5
consciousness raising 11, 54–5
Consulting our learners (1): planning
  administering and evaluating a simple
  questionnaire **(4.4)** 110–13, 201–2,
  (35) 266–7
Consulting our learners (2): What did you
  learn today? **(4.5)** 113–16, 202–3,
  (37) 270–1
cooperation 11
correction
  as inhibiting learning **(2.1)** 16, 18
  techniques for oral mistakes **(3.6)**
  16–17
  see also errors
coursebooks, examining 97
critical awareness 11, 68
critical incidents
  defining 52
  examining 52–4, (6.15) 174–6,
  244

curriculum
  example of a school curriculum
    information leaflet (6.11.2) 166–9
  extract from an official Spanish
    curriculum document for secondary
    education (6.11.3) 169–70
  official 41, 42–3
  whole school 9

data collection
  classroom 100, 201–2
  informal interviews as 119–21
  methods 102–5, 264–5
  selecting and evaluating methods 102–5,
    201–2
  see also recording
debate
  implications in wider social context
    97–9, 198–200
  motion in 98, 198, 199–200
  preparing for a formal 97–9
Debate: understanding the wider
  implications of a topic (3.9) 97–9,
  198–200
decision-making
  evaluating learning to inform 126
  skills 6, 10
decisions
  evaluative 6
  interactive 6
  planning 6
developmental error, defined 92
dialogue, between trainers and teachers
  25
diaries (2.7) 16, 18, 67–9, 115, 184–5
  discussion based on 70–2
  prompts (6.21) 184–5
  sample of classified extracts (6.22)
    185–6
disagreeing, or agreeing 41, 83–5, 237
discourse, academic 43–5, 91–2
discussing 20, 135
Do we agree that...? (3.4) 83–5, 197–8,
  (30) 259
drawing 109

education, purpose of 8–9
educational change *see* change in
  education
Effective educating, teaching and learning
  in the language classroom
  What are my priorities? (2.3) 57–8, (20)
  247

What are our priorities? (2.2) 54–6,
  176–7, (19) 246
effectiveness, of teaching 10, 12
enabling skills 7, 64
English
  use in teaching 40–3, 166–70, 236
  use in training programme 25
English language teacher education, action
  research in 14
environment
  creating a suitable 25
  wider educational 144–7
errors (3.7) 16–17
  and correction (2.4) 16–17, 192
    pupil's attitudes to, questionnaire
    (4.4) 16
    teacher's attitudes and assumptions
    (3.1, 3.9) 16
  developmental error 92
  overgeneralization error 93
evaluating 6, 10, 12
  defined 125
  see also formative evaluation
Evaluating informal presentations (50)
  285
evaluating learning 17, 125–47
Examining critical incidents (2.1) 52–4,
  174–6, (17) 244
examples, using 116
experience
  sharing 122–4
  teachers' own previous 30
experiential learning 20, 126
  Kolb's cycle 12, 89
experimenting 12, 20
experimenting in class 122–4
  moral dimension 122
  motivation 122
Experimenting in class (4.8) 122–4,
  205–7, (40) 274
exploring
  teachers' professional knowledge
    28–49
  a topic 16, 75–99

'fastwriting' 86
feedback
  summary feedback letter 87–9
  trainer's 86–9
files/ring-binders 26
Find someone who (3.3) 32, 82–3, (29)
  258
fluency (3.7) 16

foreign language teaching, curriculum
    document (6.11.3) 169–70
formative evaluation, self-directed as
    teacher development 126
formulaic patterns, defined 92
fossilization, defined 92

Getting to know each other (1.1) 29–32,
    225–8
    focus on me as a teacher (3) 160, 228
    questionnaire (1) 225–6
    something about us (2) 227
glossaries 44, 239
    of specific terms 92–4
goals
    clarifying 41
    of teaching 41–2
group, professional development as a 32
group discussion, mindmap summary
    137–8
groups, and sub-groups 17, 43
groupthink 41

Has this task helped me/us to learn? (5.1)
    127–8, (42) 276
*High-priority topics for the group to
    investigate* (2.1) 52–4, (18) 245
How do I learn? (1.2) 32–3, (4) 229

ice-breaking 29–32, 82–3
ideal self 73
ideas 12
    organising, clarifying and developing
        85–9
    sharing 60–3
identifying topics 16, 50–74, 127–8
identities *see* teachers' identities
images, exploring teachers' 35–8, 234
imperative form 21
'In her element' (6.19) 180–1
in-service, defined 151
in-service teacher education, effective 2–10
in-service training, case studies of
    ineffective (6.3) 153–4
individual learners
    informal interviews with 119–21
    profiles of 116–19
Informal interview with a learner (4.7)
    119–21, (39) 273
innovation
    analysing 47–9, 171
    defined 46, 48
    promoting 47–9, 171–4

*Innovation in our schools: How can we
    help to promote it?* (1.9) 47–9,
    171–4, (16) 243
input 20
    defined 93
instructions, giving in class 81
interaction in the classroom 3 Fig. 1
interactive skills 6
interlanguage (3.7) 16
    defined 93
International Association of Teachers of
    English as a Foreign Language
    (IATEFL) 145
interviewing skills 119–21
interviews
    informal (4.7) 119–21, 273
    semi-structured, defined 120
    structured, defined 120
intuitions, verifying 101
investigating 7, 14–19
    an overview (1.3) 33–5
    benefits of 101–2
    defining 33
    guidelines for writing a formal report
        about (6.39.3) 221–2
    key features and benefits of 15–19
    learner autonomy, sample (6.5) 157–60
    Possible stages of investigating (6, 7)
        162, 231–2, 233
    practical example of 15, 16–17 Fig. 5
    stages of (6.8) 162
investigating in class 14, 16, 34, 100–24
    teachers' perspectives 101–2
investigating cycle 13 Fig. 4; 28 Fig. 1.1;
        50 Fig. 2.1; 75 Fig. 3.1; 100 Fig. 4.1;
        125 Fig. 5.1; 148 Fig. 6.1
*It's quite obvious the teacher's a gardener:
    exploring teachers' metaphors* (1.4)
    35–8, (8) 234

jigsaw reading activity 95
journals, classroom 67–9

Keeping a classroom diary (2.7) 67–9, (25)
    253
knowledge *see* teachers' professional
    knowledge

language acquisition, defined 93
language learning
    compared with language acquisition 93
    defined 93
    strategies 128–30

language teaching
  task-based materials 19–20
  use of English in 40–3, 236
learner autonomy
  reading extracts for 95–6
  sample sequence of tasks, activities and
    options for investigating (6.5) 157–60
learner profiles (4.6) 116–19, 272
  example of a baseline (6.32.2) 205
learners
  consulting 110–13, 113–16
  passive 152
learning
  active 20, 57
  evaluating 17, 125–47
  list of ways of professional learning for
    teachers (6.7) 161
  strategies 128–30, 177–8, 213–14
  transmission model of 152
  ways of 32–3
learning society 144
lecture, by trainers 26
lesson, recording information about a
  60–3, 122–4
lesson plan 41, 123–4, 275
  example (6.33.2) 206–7
Lesson plan sheet (4.8) 123–4, 206–7,
  (41) 275
libraries, class 63–6
life-long learning 9, 11
listening, reflective 85, 197–8
listening skills 55, 85, 197–8
logs, classroom 67–9

Making sense: reviewing and finding
  connections (5.4) 133–5, (45) 280
mapping, concepts 38–40, 235
Mapping the whole (1.5) 38–40, (6.10)
  164–5
materials 12
  learner-produced 119
  workshop 90
Meister, Sandra 154–6
mental maps 38–40, 235
metalanguage 43
metaphors, exploring teachers' (6.9) 35–8,
  162–4, 234
methodological skills 6
methods, shortlists of priorities 6
mindmap summary, of group discussion
  137–8, 214
mini case studies 117
mistakes see errors

mother tongue
  informal interviews in learner's 121
  status of teacher's 25
motion, debating 98, 198, 199, 200
motivation
  and correction techniques 16, 18
  experimenting in class 122
  teachers' 135
My best lesson/teaching ideas (2.5) 60–3,
  180–1, (22) 250

National Curriculum 168–9

open forum, on reading 63–6
oral mistakes, and correction techniques
  16–17, 192
Our current professional practice (2.4)
  59–60, (21) 248–9
Our English teacher will explain: role-play
  (5.8) 146–7, (52) 288
Our experience of the training programme
  (2.8) 70–2
Our learners in action: using photographs
  of learners (4.3) 105–9
outcomes 20, 22n
output 20
overgeneralization error, defined 93
overhead projector 26

parents
  communicating and cooperating with 6
  explaining work to 146–7, 288
pedagogic manifesto 57–8
  example of (6.17) 177–9
performance gap 101, 116
Personal glossary of key terms related to
  educating teaching and learning (1.7)
  43–4, (13) 239
personal theories 4–5, 10–11, 28, 37, 53,
  57–8
  defined 54
  relating to public theory 5, 52
  writing about 85–9
photographs, using (4.3) 16, 18, 105–9
  from local context 108
  to introduce a topic 109
plagiarism 77
plain English 22
Planning an informal presentation (49)
  284
planning decisions 6
portfolio
  defined 138

stages of a 138 Fig. 5.2
  see also teacher portfolios
Possible stages of investigating 162, (6, 7)
  231–2, 233
poster
  advantages and disadvantages (6.39.1)
    217–18
  producing a (5.8) 145–6, 286
Preparing a debate: instructions (3.9)
  97–9, (32) 261
presentation skills 7, 140–3
  framework for developing teachers' 141
    Fig. 5.3
  general strategies for developing
    (6.38.1) 215–16
presentations
  characteristics of effective (6.38.2)
    216
  effective (6.39.2) 219–20
  informal 140–3, 284–5
    evaluating 140–3, 285
    planning 140–3, 284
presenting results 24
primary teachers, task-based materials 20
principles 54–8
  practice contrary to 101, 116
priorities
  establishing shared 54–6
  examining 52–4
  listing 51
  personal 57–8
procedures 20
*Producing maps of key concepts related to
  our training programme* (9) 235
professional development 11–12
  as a group 32
  strategies for 137
  of trainers 26
professional literature, using 63–6
professional practice
  current 59–60
  future 135–8
  sharing 82–3
public talk
  advantages and disadvantages (6.39.1)
    217
  giving a (5.8) 145, 286
public theory 5, 12
  academic discourse of 91–2
pupil profiles 138
pyramid discussion 43

questioning 41

questionnaires
  characteristics of an effective 111–12,
    268–9
  on pupils' attitudes to mistakes and
    correction (4.4) 16
  summary of advantages and
    disadvantages of classroom (6.30)
    201–2
  using 110–13

ramification 97n
reading 7, 20
  example of completed review sheet
    (6.20.3) 183
  jigsaw reading activity 95
  targeted 94–7
  as a way of learning 63–6
Reading survey: review sheets (2.6) 63–6,
  182–4, (23, 24) 251–2
real people 116–19
recording
  classroom data, methods 115
  information about a lesson 60–3, 122–4
  results 19
records of achievement 138
reference skills, developing 44, 239
reflecting 8n, 10, 20, 32, 45–7, 53, 67–8,
  70, 113, 127, 135, 166–70
*Reflecting on the nature of change in
  education: factors which will help us
  to change and/or innovate* (1.8) 45–7,
  171, (15) 242
  What helps us to change? (1.8) 45–7,
    171, (14) 240–1
reflective listening 85
report writing (5.8) 146, 287
  advantages and disadvantages (6.39.1)
    218
  guidelines for formal about investigating
    (6.39.3) 221–2
resources 12, 148–222
  list for the trainer 149–51
  necessary 25–6
results, sharing 19, 24
review of book (2.6, 3.8) 16, 66, 97
ring-binders 26
role-play (5.8) 146–7, 288
routines, formulaic 92
rules, establishing ground 25

scheme of work 41
school curriculum, information leaflet
  example (6.11.2) 166–9

selecting 20, 51
self-disclosure 67
self-esteem 8, 12, 72–4, 186–91
   practical recommendations for
      enhancing learners' (6.23.2) 187
self-image 73
sentence completion (6.34) 208–9,
      (44) 279
sequences of tasks 21
sharing learning 140–7
   wider educational environment 144–7
*Sharing our learning (1): giving informal
   presentations* (5.7) 140–3, 215–16
*Sharing our learning (2): joining forces in
   the wider educational community*
   (5.8) 144–7, 217–22, (51) 286–7
skills 5–7 Fig. 3
   see also teachers' professional skills
social constructivism 4, 6, 17
   personal interpretation of (6.2) 152–3
social context 4 Fig. 2
social skills 6
Spanish, extract from secondary education
   curriculum document (6.11.3) 169–70
specialist terms 91–4
   sample 92–3
strategies
   analysing, evaluating and selecting
      129–30, 131–3
   defined 128n
stress, strategies for fighting 74, 188–91
sub-groups 17, 43
subject matter skills 5–6
suggestions 25–6
summarising key points (40) 16
summary feedback letter 87–9
supervisors *see* trainers
support 17
syllabus 41
systematicity 18

*Talking about real people: writing a
   learner profile* (4.6) 116–19, 203–5
Targeted reading: key extracts (3.8) 94–7
task format 21–2
   background information 21
   pedagogic procedures for 21
   preparation for 21
   task aims 21
tasks 19–22, 75
   adapting 20
   combining 22
   further reading 22

more options 22
   selecting 20
   sequences of 21
   using the 20–1
teacher classroom research project, case
   study (6.4) 154–6
teacher development, defined 152
teacher education
   defined 152
   method: 'approach, design and
      procedure' model (6.10.2) 165
   reflective model for (6.10.3) 165
   social constructivist model 152–3
teacher educators *see* trainers
teacher learning, and change 9–10
teacher portfolios 138–40
   benefits of 139
Teacher portfolios (5.6) 138–40, 215, (48)
   283
teacher training
   defined 151–2
   learning needs 151
teachers
   autonomy 12
   collaborating with trainers and other
      colleagues 17
   improving practice 17–18
   as individuals 2
   as learners 89–91
   as protagonists 15
   as reformers 19
   as social beings 3–4
   use of tasks by 21n
teachers' attitudes 7–8, 12
   to change in education 45–7
teachers' expectations, of the training
   programme 30
teachers' feelings about their work
   7–8
teachers' identities 2–4
teachers' perspectives, on investigating in
   class 101–2, 200–1
teachers' professional knowledge 4–5
   exploring 28–49
teachers' professional skills 5–7, 10
teamwork 140
*Ten characteristics of an effective
   questionnaire* (4.4) 111–12, 119, (36)
   268–9
terms
   collecting key (3.7) 92–4
   key (6.1) 151–2
   related to language acquisition (31) 20

related to a specific topic 91–4
use of teaching 43–5
theorising 7, 20, 39, 54–6
thinking, ways of 35–8, 234
tides of change, defined 46
time, lack of 18
top-down approach 151–2
    defined 46
topics
    advantages and disadvantages of 81,
        196
    breaking down into manageable units 51
    exploring 16, 75–99
    high-priority 16, 52–4, (18) 245
    identifying 16, 50–74, 59, 127–8
    sample list to investigate (6.18) 179
    small-scale and realistic 18
    suggestions for 51
    trainer's shortlist 60
trainers
    danger of imposing topics 51
    investigating model for 26
    participation in worksheet responses 24
    professional development of 26
    sharing 26
    use of tasks by 21n
training programme
    discussion based on diaries 70–2
    favourite aspects 130–3, 208–9
    sample list of components (6.35) 133,
        210
transfer 92
    defined 93
tutorials, general recommendations
    concerning (6.37) 215
tutors see trainers

understanding 11, 79–81
Understanding key terms related to a
    specific topic (3.7) 91–4, (31) 260

video materials
    published 109
    teacher-produced 109
visual data 109

Ways in which we can learn together (1.2)
    32–3, (5) 230
We can do it!
    Practical recommendations for ... (2.9)
        72–4, (27) 256

Self-esteem, us and our learners (2.9)
    72–4, 186–91, (26) 254–5
wh-questions 79–83
What do I understand by the topic 'x'?
    (What? Why? Who? etc.) (3.2) 79–81,
        193–6, (28) 257
What do we already do in school or class
    regarding the topic 'x'? Find someone
    who... (3.3) 82–3, 196, (29) 258
What I most like about our training
    programme is... (5.3) 130–3, 208–9,
        (44) 279
What we agree about and what we
    disagree about (1.6) 40–3, (11) 237
Which data collection method? (4.2)
    102–5, (34) 264–5
Which learning strategies are helping us?
    (5.2) 128–30, (43) 177–8
whole-learner development 8
Why, why, why? Examining our
    assumptions and beliefs about a topic
    (3.1) 76–9, 192–3
Why teach English? (1.6) 40–3, (6.11),
    166–70, (10) 236
'Why? Challenge' 76
worksheets 22–5
    access to 23
    comparing responses to 23–4
    example of completed (6.6) 160
    explaining intended use of 23
    list of 223–4
    practical uses of 24–5
    purpose of 22–3
    recording results on 19
    signing and dating 24
    time needed for 23
    understanding 23
    using the 23–5
Workshop: experiencing teaching ideas as
    learners (3.6) 89–91
workshops 89–91
    teaching materials 90
writing 85–9
Writing about a topic: organising,
    developing and clarifying my ideas
    (3.5) 85–9
Writing a learner profile (4.6) 116–19,
    (38) 272